HOW THE
PARANOID
STYLE
FLOURISHES
AND WHERE IT
COMES FROM

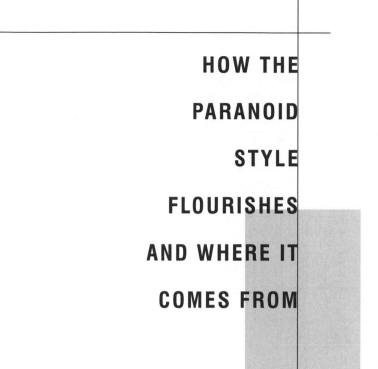

CONSPIRACY

Daniel Pipes

The Free Press
New York London Toronto Sydney Singapore

*f*P

THE FREE PRESS
A Division of SImon & Schuster Inc.
1230 Avenue of the Americas
New York, NY 10020

THE FREE PRESS and colophon are trademarks
of Simon & Schuster Inc.

Manufactured in the United States of America

10 9 8 7 6 5 4 3 2 1

Library of Congress Cataloging-in-Publication Data

Pipes, Daniel, 1949–
    Conspiracy : how the paranoid style flourishes and where it
comes from / Daniel Pipes.
      p. cm.
    Includes bibliographical references and index.
    1. World politics. 2. Conspiracies. I. Title.
    D21.3.P55 1997
    909.8—dc21   97-20949
                                                  CIP

    ISBN 0-684-83131-7

To Sarah Pipes, an Avid Reader

... trifles, light as air,

are to the suspicious,

Strong as proofs of holy writ.

—*American Mercury*, 1799

What may have been his motive?

—Prince Metternich, on hearing of

the death of the Russian ambassador

I trust no one,

not even myself.

— Joseph Stalin

CONTENTS

A new kind of explanation for political events came into existence almost exactly two centuries ago, when some opponents of the French Revolution ascribed to their enemies an inhuman capacity for planning and a hideous intention to rule the world. This set of fears, which began as the midnight thoughts of malcontents, took shape in the course of the nineteenth century as a body of political ideas that I call conspiracism. Conspiracism took on two main forms, one focused on the dangers posed by secret societies, and the other preoccupied with Jews. With time, these fears grew to include governments as well—specifically the British, American, and Israeli. Conspiracism gained a steadily larger constituency through the nineteenth century; by its end, ruthless political operatives had adopted this approach and promoted its ideas, imbuing it with a hardness of tone and using it as the basis of ambitious, radical movements. In the period of the two world wars, leaders rode conspiracism to power in Russia and Germany, then used it to justify aggressive campaigns of territorial expansion. For about two years, from 1939 to 1941, they were within striking distance of seizing control of the entire world. Monumental errors on their part prevented this from happening, and the subsequent decades have seen a diminishment of conspiracism, though by no means its elimination.

In this book, I develop a unified interpretation of conspiracism. The following pages trace the history of conspiracy theories from their earliest beginnings in the Crusades (when the two main enemies emerged) to the present (when their appeal has moved to the political and geographical margins). Along the way, we encounter some of the most disturbing of people, the strangest of ideas, and the greatest of tragedies in the modern era. The cast features intellectuals obscure (Augustin de Barruel, Sergei Nilus) and famous (J. A. Hobson, Oswald Spengler), rabble-rousing politicians (Wilhelm Marr, Louis Farrakhan), and world-historical figures (Adolf Hitler, Joseph Stalin). Even some unexpected names turn up endorsing conspiracism (Benjamin Disraeli, Winston Churchill).

Two topics have particular relevance for understanding the role of conspiracy theories today: the manner in which, since World War I, the antisemitic and anti–secret society traditions have somewhat fused together, and the way these ideas began on the Right, were embraced by the Left, and still continue to ricochet from one end of the political spectrum to the other.

This is an interpretive essay, not a research study. To hold down its size, I concentrate on the most original or most important aspects of conspiracism. The emphasis here is on ideas, not information; I apologize in advance for what may seem like arbitrary decisions in coverage—for example, ignoring actual conspiracies (e.g., the Bolshevik seizure of power), the factors that explain why conspiracism gains in appeal (such as in Weimar Germany) or declines (in the recent West), and the personality traits conducive to conspiracism (such as in the Montana militiamen). I skip over whole centuries in the early period and decades more recently. The Soviet Union is far more present here than the other totalitarian states (such as Nazi Germany or Mao's China), which perhaps calls for explanation. The Soviet exemplar came first, lasted longest, and had by far the most influence. Stalin was "deeper and more complex than Hitler,"[1] he stood at the center of the greatest number and most elaborate versions of conspiracy than anyone else in history, he killed by far the largest number of people for reasons connected to political paranoia,[2] and he spawned a great many other, almost equally murderous, regimes.

I happened on this topic in the course of writing *The Hidden Hand*, a study of conspiracy theories in the Middle East, my area of specialty. In tracking down the origins of the paranoid ideas expressed by such figures as Gamal Abdel Nasser, Ayatollah Khomeini, and Saddam Husayn, I discovered that their fear of plots was not original to them but derived in great part from European and American sources. As a result, my research wandered from current Arab and Iranian politics to Western intellectual history. This subject did not, however, fit the confines of a study on the Middle East, so my sketch on the subject settled into quiet obscurity on the hard drive, only to revive when Bruce Nichols of The Free Press urged me to turn that scrap into something publishable. I thank him for that impetus; this book is the result.

I also thank the board, supporters, and staff of the Middle East Forum, my home institution, for providing the right ambience to write this book. Roger Donway, Paul Hollander, Richard Pipes, Gerald Posner, and Arthur Waldron kindly replied to sometimes repeated questions about their areas of special knowledge. My research assistants—Leora Aster, Seyit Ali Avcu, J. Michael Barrett, Nick Beckwith, Randy Figatner, Seth Lasser, Tamala T. Montgomery, Jacqueline Portugese, Erika Triscari, and Zena Yoslov—put in stellar performances in their library work and reading, cheerfully moving from one completely unrelated subject to the next.

Commentary, The New Republic, and *The Wall Street Journal* kindly permitted me to draw on the small portions of this book that first appeared in their publications.

So as not to weigh down the text with innumerable qualifiers to distance myself from the text ("alleged," "supposed," "reported"), I ask the reader to supply these mentally where they belong.

Philadelphia   *D.P.*
February 1997

ONE

CONSPIRACY

THEORIES

EVERYWHERE

Conspiracy theories—fears of nonexistent conspiracies—are flourishing in the United States. Republican, Democratic, and independent presidential candidates espouse them. Growing political institutions (the Nation of Islam, the militias) are premised on them. A majority of Americans say they believe John F. Kennedy was killed not by a lone gunman but by a conspiracy, and a majority of black Americans hold the U.S. government responsible for the spread of drugs. O. J. Simpson famously beat his criminal rap by convincing a jury of a conspiracy theory: that the Los Angeles police framed him. Two young men, their heads spinning with conspiracy theories about Washington's taking freedoms away from Americans, blew up a government building in Oklahoma City, killing 168 (including 19 children) and wounding 550.

This suspicious approach even affects the actions of government. Legislation in New York State requires schools to teach about the Irish potato famine with the intent to show, as New York's Governor George E. Pataki commented while signing the bill, that the famine was "the result of a deliberate campaign by the British to deny the Irish people the food they needed to survive."[1] A Conference of the States, planned for October 1995 in Philadelphia, was to have asserted state power at the expense of the Federal Government. But when the extreme Right got wind of this meeting, it floated conspiracy theories about its being a sneaky effort to subvert the Constitution and submit the United States to a one-world government—proved by the fact that the conference had been scheduled to coincide exactly with the United Nations' fiftieth anniversary. So effective was this campaign that one state after another backed out, the conference had to be canceled, and the debate over federalism was ruptured.

A survey of conspiracy theories in American public life shows that these tend to come disproportionately from two broad groups of people: the politically disaffected and the culturally suspicious.

THE DISAFFECTED

Conspiracy theory is the sophistication of the ignorant.
RICHARD GRENIER[2]

Among the politically disaffected, the black community and the hard Right are most overtly conspiracy theory-minded. Both dislike the existing order and offer radical ideas about changing it; both resort to an outlook that depends heavily on the existence of powerful forces engaged in plots.

Conspiracy theories may well be most prevalent in black America. A columnist calls these "the life blood of the African-American community,"[3] and a clinical psychologist notes that there is "probably no conspiracy involving African-Americans that was too far-fetched, too fantastic, or too convoluted." She finds four recurring themes, all centered on the U.S. government: it uses blacks as guinea pigs, imposes bad habits on them, targets their leaders, and decimates their population.[4]

But the sense of being surrounded by evildoers shows up in many ways, ranging from the petty to the cosmic, and does not always focus on the government. In a minor but indicative example, a new and inexpensive drink named Tropical Fantasy appeared throughout the northeastern United States in September 1990 and sold extremely well in low-income neighborhoods during the next half year. The fact that most of its Brooklyn, New York, employees were black made the beverage the more appealing. But anonymous leaflets turned up in black areas in early 1991, warning that the soft drink was manufactured by the Ku Klux Klan and contained "stimulants to sterilize the black man." Although journalistic and police investigations found this accusation to be completely fraudulent, it struck a chord among consumers, and sales plummeted by 70 percent. Other products, including Kool and Uptown cigarettes, Troop Sport clothing, Church's Fried Chicken, and Snapple soft drinks, suffered from similar slanders about the KKK and causing impotence, and they too went into a commercial tailspin.[5]

On a larger scale, the assassinations of Malcolm X and Martin Luther King, Jr., continue to arouse suspicions among blacks. Nation of Islam leaders point to the FBI's not protecting Malcolm X; in King's case, they claim the U.S. government "set up his death."[6] Joseph Lowery, another black leader, agrees: "We have never stopped believing for a moment that there was not some government complicity in the assassination of Martin Luther King Jr."[7] The activist Dick Gregory, a comedian who long ago gave up laughs for conspiracy theories, also blames King's death on a government plot, as he does the mysterious murder of twenty-eight blacks in Atlanta in 1979–81 (which he ascribes to government scientists' taking the tips of their penises to use in a serum for countering cancer).

But the two main conspiracy theories concern fears that the U.S. government takes steps to sabotage blacks, and the cluster of accusations promoted by Louis Farrakhan and the Nation of Islam.

AIDS AND DRUGS. The disproportionate incidence of AIDS and drug use among blacks prompts prominent figures to endorse a conspiracy theory that the U.S. government is behind these epidemics. The comedian Bill Cosby asserts that AIDS was "started by human beings to get after certain people they don't like."[8] The movie director Spike Lee announced (in an advertisement for the Benetton clothing shops, of all places) that "AIDS is a government-engineered disease."[9] On late-night television, rap singer Kool Moe Dee portrayed AIDS as a genocidal plot against blacks, with no dissent from host Arsenio Hall. A mass-circulation magazine for blacks ran as its cover story, "AIDS: Is It Genocide?"[10] Steven Cokely, a well-known former Chicago municipal official, gave the plot an antisemitic twist, telling of Jewish doctors who injected black babies with AIDS as part of a plot to take over the world. Drugs and crime inspire similar fears. In the acclaimed 1991 movie about black life, Boyz 'N' the Hood, a character proffers a full-blown conspiracy theory about crack and guns being available to blacks because "they want us to kill each other off. What they couldn't do to us in slavery, they are making us do to ourselves."

With a black leadership falling over itself to endorse such ideas, it comes as little surprise that a 1990 poll showed 29 percent of black New Yorkers stating their belief in AIDS' being "deliberately created in a laboratory in order to infect black people," and 60 percent thinking the government was "deliberately" making drugs available to poor blacks.[11]

These views set the stage for the sensational reception given "Dark Alliance," a three-part series published in *The San Jose Mercury News* in August 1996. The author, Gary Webb, strongly implied that the Central Intelligence Agency knew about drug dealing in Los Angeles by anticommunist Nicaraguans but did not stop them because it welcomed the funds they sent to the *contras* fighting in Nicaragua. Cocaine, Webb states in the first article, "was virtually unobtainable in black neighborhoods before members of the Central Intelligence Agency's army started bringing it into South-Central in the 1980s at bargain-basement prices"; this drug network "opened the first pipeline between Colombia's cocaine cartels and the black neighborhoods of Los Angeles." The Nicaraguan traffickers, he also maintains, "met with CIA agents both before and during the time they were selling the drugs in L.A."[12] This, the series suggested, made the government complicit in the spread of crack, a cocaine derivative.

The *Mercury News* drew this connection even more directly on the Internet. Its World Wide Web site showed the CIA insignia superimposed over a man smoking crack. In a talk-radio interview available on the *Mercury News*'s state-of-the-art Web site, Gary Webb asserted that "the cocaine that was used to make the crack that flooded into L.A. in the early '80s came from the CIA's army."

In addition to reviews by the CIA, the Senate Intelligence Committee, and the Los Angeles sheriff that found no evidence to support Webb's conspiracy theory, several investigative articles found his evidence lacking. *The Washington Post* determined that "available information does not support the conclusion that the CIA-backed contras—or Nicaraguans in general—played a major role in the emergence of crack as a narcotic in widespread use across the United States."[13] *The Los Angeles Times* stated flatly, "The crack epidemic in Los Angeles followed no blueprint or master plan. It was not orchestrated by the Contras or the CIA or any single drug ring."[14] *The New York Times* found "scant proof" to support the allegations.[15] These and other debunkings[16] did force the *Mercury News* to backtrack somewhat; the editor insisted that "Dark Alliance" had only stated that individuals associated with the CIA sold cocaine that ended up on the streets of Los Angeles, not that the CIA approved of the sales. In addition, the CIA insignia disappeared from the World Wide Web site.

This reversal had little impact on black opinion, however, which widely accepted "Dark Alliance" as truth. Leaders immediately endorsed it. Jesse Jackson accused the government, through the CIA, of being "involved in subsidizing drugs."[17] Dick Gregory got himself arrested at the CIA headquarters and proclaimed, "There is evidence inside those buildings that confirms that the CIA helped to destroy black folks. That's called genocide."[18] Maxine Waters, South-Central Los Angeles's member of Congress, told a rally, "People in high places, knowing about it, winking, blinking, and in South Central Los Angeles, our children were dying."[19]

Black journalists picked up the topic and ran with it. Derrick Z. Jackson wrote in his *Boston Globe* column: "the only conclusion is that Ronald Reagan said yes to crack and the destruction of black lives at home to fund the killing of commies abroad."[20] Wilbert Tatum, editor of *The Amsterdam News*, found the thesis "entirely plausible."[21] An editorial cartoon showed a car full of CIA agents driving in a black part of town, throwing packets of crack out of windows. The conspiracy theory even developed its own form of commerce, as Los Angeles vendors sold baseball caps reading "C.I.A. Crack Inforcement Agency."

The CIA allegations then provided the basis for yet more sweeping accusations. Kobie Kwasi Harris, chairman of the department of Afro-American studies at San Jose State University, discerned a larger pattern: "If America had a choice they would choose a disorganized, criminal black community over an organized, radical one."[22] Barbara Boudreaux of the Los Angeles school board announced the existence of "a master plan to have mass genocide for every child born in the world, especially in Los Angeles and Compton."[23]

LOUIS FARRAKHAN AND THE NATION OF ISLAM. Louis Farrakhan deserves close attention, having become not just the leading black conspiracy theorist but also America's most prominent antisemite. In part, Farrakhan reflects Nation of Islam theology, which understands the white race's very existence as a conspiracy directed at the elimination of blacks. Along these lines, Farrakhan's associates at the Black Holocaust Nationhood Conference that took place just before the Million Man March of October 1995 held whites responsible for 600 million black deaths over the past six thousand years.[24] Farrakhan's newspaper accuses whites of pursuing this goal through many avenues, foremost of which is AIDS, "a man-made disease designed to kill us all."[25] (By "us,"

Farrakhan means also Africans: the U.S. government shipped a billion units of AIDS to Africa, he said, to annihilate that continent's entire population.) Other mechanisms include propaganda about black inferiority, substandard education, long prison terms, and making guns, drugs, and junk food available. Getting rid of black men through addiction, incarceration, or death also has the advantage of making black women conveniently available to white men, who then control them through a deadly combination of birth control, abortion, and welfare.

Farrakhan goes beyond the theology he inherited from his mentor, Elijah Muhammad, and displays an inclusive conspiracism of his own making. It began with the very death of Elijah Muhammad in 1975; Farrakhan rejected the official causes (heart failure and arteriosclerotic disease) and insisted that a conspiracy of family members, the U.S. government, and Sunni Arabs did him in. Farrakhan also focuses on Jews, a people the Nation of Islam had previously ignored, adopting many classic antisemitic themes. Jews, he says, are responsible for capitalism and communism, the two world wars, financing Hitler, controlling the Federal Reserve Board and Hollywood, and causing the U.S government to go into debt. They dominate U.S. politics ("all presidents since 1932 are controlled by the Jews") and media ("any newspaper that refused to acquiesce to controlled news was brought to its knees by withdrawing advertising. Failing this, the Jews stop the supply of news print and ink").[26] In all, "85 percent of the masses of the people of earth are victimized" by Jews.[27] The Nation of Islam purveys the *Protocols of the Elders of Zion*, a notorious antisemitic forgery, at its meetings and publishes its own literature of conspiratorial antisemitism.[28]

Farrakhan also makes novel assertions about Jews. They carried out the transatlantic slave trade that he claims killed 100 million Africans. Jews owned three-quarters of all slaves, and they kept the slave system functioning. They inject the AIDS virus into black newborns and puncture a hole in the ozone layer. In a particularly clever bit of revisionism, Farrakhan turns around the active and lasting Jewish participation in black civil rights efforts, claiming that it was self-interested. By helping integrate blacks, he says, Jews managed to destroy the autonomous black economic institutions and took over the businesses for themselves. By encouraging blacks to work within the system rather than confront it, Jews kept them from escaping the strictures of white supremacy. In all, Jewish "bloodsuckers" have successfully blocked black advancement.

*   *   *

The Right constitutes the other organized group of malcontents. During the cold war, it feared that a conspiratorial body of Americans, known variously as the Money Power, the Insiders, the Secret Team, or the High Cabal, were ready to sell out their country to the Soviet Union, which would then establish a one-world government. Contrary to expectations, the Soviet bloc's collapse did not end this fear. A few Rightists still worry about the Kremlin, eyeing the Soviet collapse suspiciously as a charade intended to get Americans to put down their guard. Many more continue to worry about a one-world authority, but changing the object of their worry from the (powerful) Soviet Union's imposing communism to the (toothless) United Nations' imposing a New World Order. The parallel between these two is quite precise; like Moscow, the U.N. disposes of mechanisms of subversion and an army of occupation.[29]

Rightist groups expect an invasion of the United States by forces under United Nations command, sometimes called the Multi Jurisdictional Task Force. Some imagine the invasion yet to come and interpret the backs of highway signs as embedded with codes for invading troops (for example, in Michigan, blue indicates the presence of water nearby, green a resting place, and brown petrol). Others think it already underway, with some 300,000 Russian, Hong Kong, and Gurkha troops secreted away in locations around the United States. Reports are sometimes highly specific, mentioning 40,000 U.N. troops in San Diego, 14,000 in Anchorage, and a battalion of Gurkhas in Montana.

The Federal Emergency Management Agency (FEMA), ostensibly established to coordinate government actions in time of disaster, will first oversee the U.N. takeover, then become the "secret government" that runs the United States. As befits a planning agency, FEMA has already tested the waters; for example, it scripted the 1992 riots in Los Angeles following the Rodney King trial to test reactions to a gang uprising. Black gangs such as the Crips and the Bloods will also have a major role in enforcing the new order. Other important institutions include the Environmental Protection Agency (which will keep track of vehicles) and the National Education Association (to ensure that children get badly educated).

And where will the U.S. military be during all this? Off in distant lands, creating a New World Order under United Nations auspices. The placement of U.S. troops under U.N. command in Somalia established the precedent, which was then followed in Bosnia.

The new order will not be pleasant. Immigrants will take over the country, and Americans will lose all their constitutional rights, especially the right to bear arms. Controls will be unprecedented: "it will only be a matter of time before humans are tattooed with a similar mark" to the codes in the supermarket.[30] Or tiny microchips will be inserted into Americans' buttocks to keep track of each person's whereabouts and activities. (Timothy McVeigh, the Oklahoma City bomber, believes the government performed this operation on him during his army service.) Those who step out of line will meet with severe consequences. Dissidents will be removed by unmarked black helicopters to detention camps located at government installations such as air force bases. Some of these have already been prepared; ominously, barbed wire around an unused airfield in California faces inward. As a last resort, four crematoria have been built around the country, each capable of disposing of three thousand corpses a day, or over four million per year.

To forestall this scenario, the Right has taken a variety of steps. In 1994, it spurred the Oklahoma legislature to pass a resolution calling on the U.S. Congress "to cease any support for the establishment of 'a new world order' or any form of global government."[31] It also takes active measures, with some ten to forty thousand individuals organized into militias that train with guns during weekends in the backwoods of Michigan, Montana, and other states, preparing for the showdown. They engage in "bluehat spotting," or watching for U.N. troops in the United States, as well as keeping a sharp eye out for black helicopters ("When I see a helicopter without markings, I refer to it as an enemy helicopter").[32] They also paint over highway signs—and thereby confuse highway crews, which lose their maintenance records. To get around this problem, the Indiana Transportation Department changed its methods of keeping codes, hoping this would "reassure those in the motoring public who had these suspicions."[33]

The militias worry not just about defending the homeland; in addition, they increasingly challenge the government of the United States. To many on the Right, Washington has been irretrievably lost to "real" Americans, and they believe it necessary to destroy the U.S. government. William Pierce, the leading exponent of insurrection, avoids charges of seditious conspiracy by presenting his ideas in the form of novels. In *The Turner Diaries*, called "the bible of the extremist Right," he recounts with chilling enthusiasm the story of the Organization, an underground racist white group financed through counterfeiting and robbing Jewish stores. The action culminates in a racial uprising and the "Day of the Rope," when whites who have "betrayed their race" hang from tens of thousands of lampposts. Then follow massacres of Jews and blacks. Ultimately the Organization takes over the government. In a second novel, *Hunter,* an admiring Pierce tells the story of a single individual who kills miscegenists, Jews, and others unsuited to live in his vision of America.[34] Pierce does not hide his operational ambitions in writing these novels: "I don't write just for entertainment. It's to explain things to people. I'd like to see North America become a white continent."[35]

THE SUSPICIOUS

Humpty Dumpty Was Pushed!
—U.S. BUMPER STICKER, 1970S

Paranoids have the facts.
—OLIVER STONE[36]

One doesn't have to live in the inner city or in Montana to worry about plots; conspiracy theories also flourish among society's favored. Plenty of centrist, rich, and educated people share this disposition, including presidential candidates and important figures in popular culture.

That several recent candidates for the presidency of the United States espouse conspiracism displays the prevalence of this mentality; that none of them came close to victory points to its limits. Their numbers include three Republicans, one Democrat, and two independents.

PATRICK BUCHANAN. Republican Patrick Buchanan ran for election in 1992 and 1996 and, the second time especially, spoke in the hoary tradition of American populism. "Real power in America belongs to the Manhattan Money Power," he stated,[37] recalling an archaic term referring to bank and financial interests. He raised the bogey of a New World Order, by which he meant a situation in which Americans no longer retained full sovereignty; instead, the United Nations, International Monetary Fund, World Bank, World Court, and World Trade Organization would make the key decisions. He deemed American taxpayers the "designated fall guys of the New World Order."[38]

PAT ROBERTSON. The American evangelist and politician Pat Robertson, a 1988 candidate, was the presidential aspirant with the most elaborate ideas about a plot against the United States; he may also be the single most influential conspiracy theorist in the contemporary United States. But, it bears noting, few of the following ideas are original to Robertson himself, and he kept them almost completely under wraps during the 1988 campaign (though he did occasionally refer to the Council on Foreign Relations, the New York-based think tank and a great bogeyman of American conspiracy theorists). Only in 1991 did he fully reveal his views, in a book titled *The New World Order*.

Robertson offers two very different scenarios for the New World Order, one financial, the other moral. In the first, he foresees a European seizure of American wealth via a world currency and a single global bank. The conspirator's identity is Money Power; its motivation is a mixture of greed and a preference for the simplicity of dictatorship over the messiness of democracy. As early as 1865, European bankers arranged for Abraham Lincoln's murder to prevent him from issuing interest-free currency, which would have broken their hold over the U.S. money supply. In 1912, to maintain that hold, the banking interests engineered a three-way race for the presidency, permitting Woodrow Wilson to win. A year later Wilson and his aide Colonel Edward House institutionalized the Money Power by getting the Sixteenth Amendment passed, permitting Congress to collect an income tax, and establishing the Federal Reserve Board.[39] These two developments are closely connected, for the central bank relies on the income tax to advance an "international financial assault on the freedom and integrity of America."[40]

Robertson's second and far uglier scenario concerns the Illuminati, the Freemasons, and extreme New Age religionists who aspire not to money but to undermine the Christian social order. To achieve this they seek "a one-world government, a one-world army, a one-world economy under an Anglo-Saxon financial oligarchy, and a world dictator served by a council of twelve faithful men." This tyranny will attempt to "destroy the Christian faith" and "replace it with an occult-inspired world socialist dictatorship." In another place, he foresees nothing less than a world under "the domination of Lucifer and his followers" in which spiritual forces will be set into motion "which no human being will be strong enough to contain." Robertson offers Hitler's attempts at world hegemony as the closest historical parallel to the "giant prison" of the New World Order.[41]

Robertson is also strangely contradictory about the course of American history. Sometimes he implies that the country has been on the wrong track from the very start. Perhaps some founding fathers, he muses, had intended "to bring forth, not the nation that our founders and champions of liberty desired, but a totally different world order under a mystery religion."[42] In this context, the Masonic imagery on the Great Seal of the United States has great significance. Alternatively, he dates the rot to the time of Cecil Rhodes (1853–1902); since then, American policy has moved steadily closer to the New World Order, regardless of whether Democrats or Republicans are in charge. He portrays some U.S. presidents, including Jimmy Carter and George Bush, as "men of goodwill," but that did not prevent them from doing their part to bring on this wretched future.[43] Robertson sees the Council on Foreign Relations (as well as the Trilateral Commission) as the New World Order's main agent in the United States. The conspirators have not yet brought down the United States, but they did cause the Great Depression and several recessions; in addition, they "helped destroy" the Soviet bloc, China, Cuba, Nicaragua, and many countries in Southeast Asia and Africa.[44]

Writing in 1991, Robertson finds that recent events point to "a giant plan" in which everything is "perfectly on cue." Note the particulars: "Europe sets the date for its union. Communism collapses. A hugely popular war [against Iraq] is fought in the Middle East. The United Nations is rescued from scorn by an easily swayed public. A new world order is announced [by George Bush]." Looking ahead, Robertson sees a financial collapse that prompts the U.S. government to turn over its defense and its sovereignty to the United Nations. The U.N. then imposes socialist and anti-Christian rules. The leaders "elect a world president with plenary powers who is totally given to the religion of humanity."[45] The New World Order is in place.

LYNDON LaROUCHE. If Robertson regurgitates long-standing fears of secret societies, Lyndon LaRouche offers highly original formulations. His many references to ancient philosophers and world history give his theories a seemingly profound quality that in fact masks extreme incoherence. Indeed, so mixed up are his ideas that they almost defy characterization along the Left-Right spectrum; but he does run for office as a Democrat, he comes out of a radical leftist background, and many of his policies have a left-wing cast. Confusing matters further, LaRouche constantly redefines terms, so that a word has both its normal meaning and something like its opposite. Drug fighters become drug traffickers, Jews become Nazis, and so on. "LaRouche's followers thus ended up with a topsy-turvy view in which the real Nazis were seen as anti-Nazis, and anti-Semitism was perceived as a moral necessity—to 'save' the Jews from themselves."[46] Conspiracism does not get much more convoluted than this.

A world conspiracy theory has served as the main platform for LaRouche's many organizations, publications, and repeated presidential campaigns (starting in 1976). He argues that a single oligarchic conspiracy has been bedeviling mankind since the dawn of history. Its headquarters were first in Babylon, then in Rome, Venice, and (now) London. The British aristocracy aspires to achieve world hegemony through conspiratorial means; the queen of England is the number one danger to humanity. In his view, the British gain power in large part by reducing the status of other populations through war, starvation, and contraception, and in part by drugging them with popular culture and hallucinogens. Once the British have achieved a "new Dark Ages" of unrestrained capitalism, London-based conspirators will reign supreme and will use their power to kill off large parts of the human race through nuclear weapons, AIDS, and other methods. To prevent this catastrophe, LaRouche advocates preparation for total war against Great Britain.

Alone, the British might not pose much of a threat; their strength lies in the many and varied allies and agents they employ, starting with Zionists and also including Orthodox Christians, Jesuits, Freemasons, the Rockefeller family, environmentalists, drug traffickers, and fundamentalist Muslims. Insisting that these many unrelated, even mutually hostile, elements are all working together takes LaRouche to spin bizarre hypotheses. Freemasons established the Jewish organization B'nai B'rith as a proslavery spy ring providing intelligence to the South before the Civil War. The Rothschilds assassinated Abraham Lincoln. British and German aristocrats financed the Bolsheviks, who were really nothing but the old Okhrana (tsarist secret police). The Anti-Defamation League imports drugs into the United States. A bomb in Saudi Arabia that killed nineteen American soldiers in their barracks is "a new flank" in Britain's "war on the Clinton administration."[47]

LaRouche also personalizes these accusations, associating all his adversaries with the forces of darkness. The Rockefeller clan, the CIA, and their many agents are always poised to strike at him.

ROSS PEROT. Ross Perot, the candidate who won 19 percent of the presidential vote in 1992 and 8 percent in 1996, raised many conspiracy theories the first time he ran, but learned to keep quiet about them the second. He met at least twice with the head of the Christic Institute, a fringe outfit claiming that a conspiratorial group (the "Secret Team") runs the U.S. government even as it engages in drug trafficking and arms running. He associated with such conspiracy theorists as James "Bo" Gritz and Roy Cohn. He took seriously some woolly charges (dubbed the "October Surprise") that George Bush in 1980 had gone to Europe to try to stop the release of American hostages in Tehran, and thereby to hurt Jimmy Carter's electoral chances. Perot went so far as to dispatch a team to the Missouri state prison to investigate a jailbird's claim about flying Bush home in a supersonic plane from a phantom meeting in Madrid with Iranians. Perot sees a conspiracy of neglect on the part of the U.S. government, and Bush specifically, toward captured American military men in Southeast Asia; officials shy away from this issue to hide their long-established and deeply corrupt relations with drug traffickers. Perot's rage against these conspirators, an in-depth analysis concluded, was "at the heart, if not the very soul, of his bid for the presidency" in 1992.[48]

Perot also has a streak of personal paranoia that especially colored his first campaign. He has frequently engaged private investigators to look into the backgrounds of employees and adversaries. Worried about attacks from his enemies among Vietnamese, Iranians, Black Panthers, drug traffickers, and their allies in the U.S. government, he routinely monitors the movements and friendships of his family members. His wife did not join him at a political rally in Florida, he announced, because "I love her too much to put her at risk."[49] He explained having pulled out of the presidential campaign in 1992 for six weeks due to political rivals' engaging in "dirty tricks" to disrupt his daughter Carolyn's wedding: "I had three reports that the Republican Party intended to publish a fake photograph of my daughter," putting her head on another body.[50] Of course, Perot also worries about himself. His Dallas mansion is surrounded by walls, cameras, movement sensors, alarms, and security guards; on occasion, armed with an automatic rifle, he roams the grounds. During the third debate of the 1992 presidential campaign, he announced that "the Vietnamese had sent people into Canada to make arrangement [sic] to have me and my family killed. The most significant effort they had one night is five people coming across my front yard."[51]

Besides these major aspirants to the presidency, several minor ones fit in the paranoid style. Fred Newman, a one-time acolyte of Lyndon LaRouche who heads the New Alliance party, a group with its own variant Marxist approach to life ("social therapy," which blames all personal problems on racism and sexism), bears special note. Though antisemitic, the leadership (including Newman himself) is mostly Jewish. It forwards an elaborate and confusing conspiracy theory and has several times run Lenora Fulani as its candidate for president. In his 1996 presidential race, Perot joined forces with New Alliance, which also has a secret inner organization, the International Workers party.

Spiro Agnew is a special case; he did not run for the presidency but very nearly ascended to that position. Had he managed to hang on as vice president a few months longer, Agnew would have succeeded Richard Nixon in August 1974. Instead, he resigned in October 1973 because of evidence that came out about his corrupt practices when governor of Maryland. Looking back on this sequence of events, Agnew years later wrote in a private letter to Paul Findley, a prominent adversary of the Israel lobby: "I trace the advent of my difficulties to a confrontation with this same lobby."[52] It was not his taking kickbacks but his refusal to visit Israel, he claimed, that led to his ouster as vice president.

Much conspiracism in the United States is modish, reflecting a taste for puzzles and puzzlement. While polite society derides the rude notions of true believers, it also stylishly accepts some of their premises, as though adopting a declassé pose proves one's sophistication. Those who know better are lured by the very outlandishness and disrepute of conspiracy theories. The notion of clandestine elements' aspiring to universal power intrigues at one level and horrifies at another; it is almost akin to the Halloween celebrations that American adults have so taken to in recent years. One analyst correctly sees this sort of thinking as a form of "distracting thrills" and discerns "habits of mind" that "positively revel in mystification."[53]

The modish conspiracy theory with the greatest allure remains the assassination of John F. Kennedy in November 1963. This most elaborated and widely believed-in conspiracy theory of recent American history stands as a monument to titillation. Yes, the event shocked Americans and left many incapable of coming to terms with its senselessness, and especially with the notion that so puny an individual as Lee Harvey Oswald could singlehandedly rupture the polity. "If you put the murdered President of the United States on one side of a scale and that wretched waif Oswald on the other side, it doesn't balance. You want to add something weightier to Oswald. . . . A conspiracy would, of course, do the job nicely."[54]

But disproportion and disbelief hardly account for the enormous and enduring popularity of conspiracy theories about the Kennedy killing, all of which share the common assumption that Oswald was a patsy who got framed. So successful have the Kennedy "assassinologists" been that, according to opinion polls, some two-thirds of Americans in 1963 suspected a conspiracy and 56 percent of the population still did so in 1991.[55] Almost thirty years after the 1963 assassination, polls showed three-quarters of the American population believing Oswald was part of a conspiracy and an equal number suspecting an official cover-up of the case.[56]

Another favorite topic of modish conspiracy theorists concerns a malign group's taking over the government of the United States. Unlike the Right, which fears the Council on Foreign Relations or the Insiders, sophisticates play with imaginative notions about a clandestine takeover of the White House, the military, or (most commonly) the Central Intelligence Agency. These institutions get turned into conspiratorial outfits that exist within outwardly normal institutions. As the lead character in the movie *Three Days of the Condor* (1975) put it, "Maybe there's another CIA inside the CIA." In other versions, a secret group of CIA officials controls the American government and, through it, the rest of the world too.

Should a decent American citizen verge toward discovering the existence of the inner sanctum, he pays dearly. According to Joe Trento of the influential National Security News Service, a Washington-based organization, "You can't be anybody in this town successfully in terms of official position without their approval. . . . [I]f you do something they don't like, you're going to end up in trouble."[57] In one case concerning a top-secret military program, the conspirators supposedly bombard the wretch with disinformation about evil aliens and brain implants, eventually driving him crazy. Dozens of individuals connected to the Kennedy assassination are said to have died unnatural deaths.

A common theme concerns the U.S. government's suppressing information about its own mischief. Prominent examples of cover-ups include the Kennedy asssassination, Vietnam-era soldiers missing in action, and a cure for cancer. Immediately after the Federal building in Oklahoma City was bombed in April 1995, the Right theorized about a first explosion's having gone off just milliseconds before the truck bomb (i.e., it was an inside job). Similarly, when TWA Flight 800 went down off New York City in July 1996, killing all 230 on board, conspiracy theorists insisted that the cause was a missile sent up by the U.S. Navy. Perhaps the most colorful suspicions concern unidentified flying objects (UFOs) from space, and specifically the supposed crash of a UFO near Roswell, New Mexico, in July 1947.[58] The air force is said to have conducted a high-level inquiry into the incident in the early 1950s, named Operation Majestic 12, which it then covered up.[59] Some conspiracy theorists even see the aliens establishing a "Secret Government" in the United States and filling positions in the existing Federal government; indeed, the Trilateral Commission came into existence to negotiate with these outer-space beings because they had broken their promises.[60]

The enduring popularity of such conspiracy theories makes them highly commercial. The estimated six million people each year who visit the site of the Kennedy assassination are a significant source of revenue to Dallas. Dealey Plaza itself has become "a conspiracy theme park, with self-anointed 'researchers' on hand every day peddling autopsy pictures."[61] Those wishing to experience the assassination more vividly can ride in an open Lincoln Continental convertible limousine from Love Field through Dealey Plaza, hear rifle sounds when they reach the spot where Kennedy was killed, then speed off to Parkland Memorial Hospital. Then they can visit a museum devoted to conspiracy theories about the assassination and featuring a 108-foot-long mural connecting it to many of the other famous deaths in recent American history. True devotés attend annual three-day conventions in Dallas, where seminars delve into details, and self-proclaimed witnesses sign their autographs.

Beyond Dallas, the Kennedy puzzle has become a mainstay of popular culture, acquiring an iconic quality. For those who want a piece of history, artifacts are for sale, but pricey. The gun Jack Ruby used to kill Oswald has sold for $200,000. Board games, t-shirts, and bumper stickers deal with the subject. Oliver Stone's *JFK*, a conspiracy-saturated $50 million film about the president's assassination, appeared in late 1991 and caused a huge surge in conspiracism. The film was nominated for eight Academy Awards and Warner Brothers distributed a "*JFK* Study Guide" for use in high school and college history courses. It then inspired a host of other productions on the same theme, such as *In the Line of Fire* (1993), a thriller, and a November 1996 episode of *The X-Files* in which an army captain killed Kennedy on behalf of his military superiors. Two thousand books have been published on this subject in thirty years; in February 1992, no fewer than four books about the Kennedy assassination filled the American best-seller lists (listed under "nonfiction," though that may be a misnomer). A growing number of CD-ROMs and Internet sites deal with the issue. (For a listing of World Wide Web resources on this and other topics, see appendix C.) Such signs of unabated fascination point to the murder's becoming abstracted. It is hard to argue with Gerald Posner, the leading student of the Kennedy assassination, that "the JFK murder has, regrettably, become an entertainment business."[62] What began as an ugly reflection of the cold war ended as murder-mystery story and cult.

At a time when it takes fewer than 100,000 in sales to make the U.S. best-seller lists, books flogging conspiracy theories claim far greater sales. Over one million sold for Pat Robertson's *New World Order*; two million copies in two months for Phyllis Schlafly's *Gravediggers*; five million copies in print for *None Dare Call It Conspiracy*; six million copies of the similarly named *None Dare Call It Treason* in just eight months after publication in 1964, and then another million. (The author claims this represents "an all-time [American] record for the sale of so many books in so short a period.")[63]

More than a few novels dwell on the secret society tradition. *Foucault's Pendulum* playfully presents several centuries of secret society conspiracism ("If the Plan exists, it must involve everything").[64] Thomas Pynchon's works take place in a fantasy of conspiratorial networks. *The Illuminatus! Trilogy* is a three-volume science-fiction novel based on the Illuminati phobia by two former *Playboy* magazine editors, Robert Shea and Robert Anton Wilson.[65] Relying on what the authors call "guerilla ontology," the novel attempts to create doubts in the reader's mind about the nature of reality. It tells of two competing conspiracies, between order and chaos, and includes virtually every known conspiracy theory plus a few the authors made up for good measure (for example, that Adam Weishaupt quietly murdered George Washington and then replaced him). *Illuminatus!* became a cult best-seller, spawning a board game and spurring Wilson on to mine the same rich vein by writing many more imaginative books about conspiracies.

Feature films on conspiratorial themes abound and do well commercially. In addition to the Kennedy theme, prominent examples include *The Manchurian Candidate* (1962), *Seven Days in May* (1964), *The President's Analyst* (1967), *The Package* (1989), *Total Recall* (1990), *Point of No Return* (1993), and *The Conspiracy Theory* (1997). Television series with a conspiratorial content include *Dark Skies*, *The Fugitive*, *The Lazarus Man*, *Millennium*, *The Pretender*, *Profiler*, *Twin Peaks*, and *The X-Files*. Some of these stories toy with petty conspiracies; *Capricorn One* (1978) exposes the first manned flight to Mars as a hoax filmed on a stage set (and may have the distinction of portraying black helicopters for the first time as the enemy of righteous Americans). But world conspiracy theories make a more tempting subject. "People are funny," announces a character in the television series *Nowhere Man*. "They tend to fancy notions like democracy, freedom of speech, free elections. It's an illusion, of course." A computer game called *Interstate '76* simulates a conspiracy by the oil-exporting states to destroy energy supplies in the United States, and so cripple the country.

Reviewing the prodigious output of conspiracist materials from the vantage point of 1997, one analyst notes that what was once specific to politics has had a "domino effect" in the realm of culture. "In the last year or so, conspiracy thinking has been used as a narrative model by everyone from novelists to the makers of blockbuster movies."[66]

Consistent with this thrill-seeking approach, some American conspiracy theorists reach for anarchic hyperbole. To them, all the world is a staged reality. Though not a believer himself, Charles Paul Freund of the *Washington Post* captures this fear:

> Let's say that everything you know is not only wrong, it is a carefully wrought lie. Let's say that your mind is filled with falsehoods—about yourself, about history, about the world around you—planted there by powerful forces so as to lull you into complacency. Your freedom is thus an illusion. You are in fact a pawn in a plot, and your role is that of a compliant dupe—if you're lucky. If and when it serves the interests of others, your role will change: Your life will be disrupted, you could go penniless and hungry; you might have to die.
>
> Nor is there anything you can do about this. Oh, if you happen to get a whiff of the truth you can try to warn people, to undermine the plotters by exposing them. But in fact you're up against too much. They're too powerful, too far-flung, too invisible, too clever. Like others before you, you will fail.[67]

Unconstrained, conspiracism leads to doubts about everything, bringing life itself under suspicion. In this spirit, Jonathan Vankin writes that "civilization is a conspiracy against reality."[68] Oliver Stone, one of Hollywood's most renowned movie producers, asks the conspiracy theorist's ultimate questions: "Who owns reality? Who owns your mind?"[69] His answers allow little room for debate: "I've come to have severe doubts about Columbus, about Washington, about the Civil War being fought over slavery, about World War I, about World War II and the supposed fight against Nazism and Japanese control of resources . . . I don't even know if I was born or who my parents were."[70] Thus does thrill-seeking twist itself into absolute nihilism.

What is the importance of conspiracy theories and their potential to do damage? To reply requires an understanding of their background, for paranoid ideas current in the United States today are anything but new; nearly all their basic themes originated in other places and times. While a Farrakhan or Robertson may seem to respond to current issues and personalities, he is actually following an almost prewritten scenario, fitting his concerns into a text written decades or centuries earlier. Knowledge of the established literary traditions of conspiracism provides the context for the here and now and explains their likely consequences. Accordingly, this study focuses on the origins and evolution of conspiracy theories with a look over to Europe and back two and a half centuries.

Before taking up these historical subjects, however, we pause to consider the subject at hand and the peculiar challenges that it poses to research.

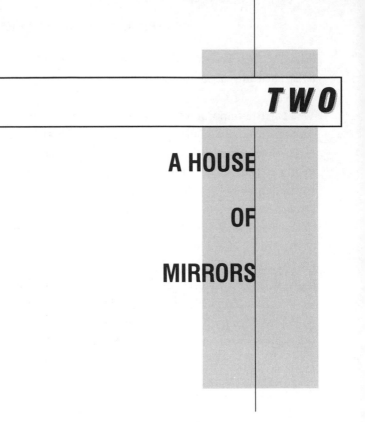

TWO

A HOUSE

OF

MIRRORS

Conspiracism is an introspective, self-conscious, and mirrored subject that can be maddeningly difficult to keep in focus. We therefore start with a discussion of key words and ideas, then look at the difficulty in distinguishing the real from the imaginary.

TERMS AND CONCEPTS

The vagueness and illogicality of conspiracism make exact words and precise concepts all the more important. I make two basic distinctions in this book: between conspiracies, which are real, and conspiracy theories, which exist only in the imagination; and between the anti-Jewish and anti-secret society traditions.

As defined in law, a *conspiracy* consists of a "combination or confederacy between two or more persons formed for the purpose of committing, by their joint efforts, some unlawful or criminal act."[1] Conspiracies do exist. Court dockets are replete with indictments for various sorts of criminal conspiracy such as bribery, racketeering, price fixing, and drug trafficking. Coconspirators, indicted and unindicted, are commonplace. The political record also contains major conspiracies. Perhaps the most spectacular and consequential of them involve the murder of leaders (Julius Caesar, Tsar Alexander II, Archduke Ferdinand, Anwar as-Sadat) or the seizure of power (by Napoleon III, Mussolini, Franco, Gamal Abdel Nasser). As a conspiracy theorist defensively puts it, "a belief in widespread conspiracies is not always to be regarded as a sign of loss of mental balance."[2]

Conspiracies divide into two sorts, the *petty* and the *world*. Petty conspiracies are limited in ambition, however dangerous their consequence. In the Iran/*Contra* affair of 1985–86, a small group clandestinely broke the law, but it did so only to improve relations with one state and fund opposition forces to another. It did not challenge the existing order or humanity at large. In contrast, world conspiracies aspire to global power and to disrupt the very premises of human life. Radical utopian ideologies—the Leninist, fascist, and fundamentalist Islamic—all involve a world conspiracy. All three of these movements, for example, had American affiliates (the Communist party, the German-American Bund, the World Trade Center gang, respectively) which aimed to reshape the United States in its image.

This distinction is not always intuitive, for it lies in the scope of the conspiracy's ambition, not its scale. World War I resulted from petty conspiracies (its initiators did not aspire to world power); World War II in Europe (precipitated by a Nazi effort to take over the globe) did result from a world conspiracy. The Soviet coup attempt of August 1991, an attempted seizure of power by apparatchiks, was a petty conspiracy, while Vladimir Ilyich Lenin's seemingly minor intrigues within the Russian Social-Democratic Labor party at the turn of the century took place within the context of a world conspiracy.

A *conspiracy theory* is the fear of a nonexistent conspiracy. *Conspiracy* refers to an act, *conspiracy theory* to a perception. While the first is an old term, dating to Middle English, the latter goes back only some decades.[3] The two terms can overlap. The Russian Revolution was a real conspiracy carried out by Lenin and others; it was also subject to conspiracy theories involving everyone from the eighteenth-century Illuminati to contemporary German socialists and the Elders of Zion.

Conspiracy theories divide into the same two variants as conspiracies: the *petty* and the *world*. The first fear concerns conspiracies with limited aims, the second those with unlimited aims. The unwarranted belief that rivals at work are ganging up on you is a petty conspiracy theory; fear of Jews' or Freemasons' trying for global power is a world conspiracy theory. The petty conspiracy theory is ageless, going back to the earliest forms of social life, existing in all places. The world conspiracy theory, in contrast, has a history, emerging from the distinctive history of Europe and dating back two and a half centuries, to the Enlightenment. The notion of an individual's or institution's trying to take over the world through clandestine means, in other words, is neither an eternal feature of the human mind nor a product of this century.[4]

World conspiracy theories—how they came to be, how they have changed over time, what impact they have had—are the main focus of this book. The theories usually contain three basic elements: a powerful, evil, and clandestine group that aspires to global hegemony; dupes and agents who extend the group's influence around the world so that it is on the verge of succeeding; and a valiant but embattled group that urgently needs help to stave off catastrophe.

Conspiracy theories have a way of growing on a person, to the point that they become a way of seeing life itself. This is *conspiracism*, the *paranoid style*, or the *hidden-hand mentality*. Conspiracism resembles other "isms" in defining an outlook that can become an all-encompassing concern. It begins with belief in an occasional conspiracy theory—Illuminati organized the French Revolution, Jews the Russian Revolution—and ends with a view of history that dwells largely or exclusively on plots to gain world power or even destroy the human race. In complete form, it takes over the lives of the faithful and becomes a prism through which they see all existence. Antisemitism fits this pattern especially well. Its novel and menacingly different quality lies in "its politicization and embodiment in permanent political parties, voluntary associations, and publishing ventures—in short, its institutionalization. . . . It rapidly developed into an alternative view of the world, with answers to all questions and prescriptions for salvation."[5] In its fullest expression, antisemitism becomes a kind of philosophy, a life-long cause, and a full-time commitment ("She talked nothing but anti-Semitism until we held a family conference and advised her to go up to the Wisconsin lakes for a long rest and forget all about the Jews").[6]

Conspiracism even claims priority over faith. In the words of one secret society theorist, those who have "probed the inner mysteries of this arcane tradition are the guardians of an Ancient Wisdom which is the secret teaching behind all established religions."[7] This ambition was especially clear in Nazism, which was intended to replace Christianity and which laid claim to truth in every sphere of life, even mathematics. Thus was Einstein's work deemed a Jewish effort to destroy German manhood. In like fashion, Lyndon LaRouche rides this outlook to the extreme, as one description of his worldview makes clear:

> It extends backwards in time tens of thousands of years, and also forward into man's future among the stars. It extends into every sphere of culture: music, art, poetry, philosophy, science—indeed into every aspect of human existence. It descends into sexuality and the unconscious mind and even deeper into the genes and chromosomes, the level of racial struggle. It also ascends *above* history into a neo-Platonic supersensible realm. It has its source in the geometric structure of reality. If one is a LaRouchian, one's belief system literally cannot be escaped, the struggle is everywhere.[8]

Conspiracism implies an outlook very different from conventional knowledge; accepting it requires a radical shift in perception. While some enthusiasts reach their new faith through a slow but steady corrosion of prior beliefs, most who made this change speak of it as an epiphany in which they realize how hopelessly naïve they had previously been. "You see things in a new way," says an American. "That leaflet changed my life," reports a former leftist upon reading an antisemitic tract, "it was a dizzy feeling."[9] "That night I didn't get much sleep," reports one adept after learning about the Council on Foreign Relations.[10]

In contrast, conspiracy theorists find disabusal a most unpleasant process: "I must painfully disassemble the evidence of a second gunman that I have both collected and uncovered over the years," confesses Dan Moldea about his investigation into the assassination of Robert Kennedy.[11] Not surprisingly, few individuals do as Moldea did: retrace his steps, let the evidence steer his thinking, and confess his error.

Conspiracy theorists, individuals attracted to conspiracy theories, range from full-fledged believers to social dilettantes.

Full-fledged conspiracy theorists devote themselves heart and soul to their faith, spending untold hours on learning about their chosen issue (Freemasonry, Jews, the assassination of John Kennedy). They see its symbols everywhere—in numerology (19 and 666 are favorites), shapes (triangles, circles), and animals (snakes, octopi). The truest believers devote their very lives to this cause. They engage in a compulsive and autodidactic inquiry ("The research was exhausting, but I felt driven to do it"),[12] then proselytize others. The amibitious among them publish the results (which helps explain the existence of so massive a conspiracist literature.) In some cases, this obsession pushes career and family to the side. A haunted existence results: antisemites and revolutionaries in late imperial Russia vowed themselves to their cause, cut themselves off from normal life, and inhabited the fringes of society. Occasionally, however, circumstances permit conspiracy theorists to enter the mainstream and even to gain power. Vladimir Lenin and Adolf Hitler are the outstanding examples of this transition, inspiring generations of would-be emulators.

Political paranoids need not suffer from personal paranoia, but often the two go together and mutually reinforce each other. Nesta Webster, an influential British conspiracy theorist, became so consumed by her own fearful ideas that she would not open the front door to her house unless she had a loaded revolver in hand. Grigorii Schwartz-Bostunich, a Nazi antisemitic theorist, relished his protection by the Gestapo—except that he sometimes saw his bodyguards as Masonic agents and even called on Himmler, their boss, for protection against them. A conspiracist witness in the proceedings against an alleged Kennedy assassin in New Orleans believed the police were impersonating his daughter, so he took her fingerprints each time she returned from school. Absolute power does not seem to assuage such anxieties. Years in Stalin's entourage left Nikita Khrushchev convinced that the dictator's "persecution mania reached unbelievable proportions." For example, Stalin waited for his aides to sample food before he would partake ("Look, here are the giblets, Nikita. Have you tried them yet?").[13] Stalin's fear that doctors were trying to kill him reached the point that he hardly let them near him, a factor that may well have sped up his death. Mao also refused medical care as he grew old, fearing that his enemies would use this as a means to kill him. "He never liked to hear bad news about his health and always suspected a plot."[14] This was part of a larger pattern, as Mao eventually found petty conspiracies nearly ubiquitous. If a guard entered his room without being called, he suspected the guard of spying for his rivals; or he thought his swimming pool poisoned.

Not all conspiracy theorists reach such pathological heights. Degrees of acceptance range from the obsessive and permanent to the aesthetic and temporary. On the right, a Louis Farrakhan sees nearly everything through their prism, while Patrick Buchanan merely touches on conspiracist ideas. On the left, if Stalin had an overwhelming case of conspiracism, Leon Trotsky had merely a mild one.

While aware of these degrees of conspiracism, I tend to consider anyone who believes in a single conspiracy theory to be a conspiracy theorist, presuming for two reasons that he subscribes to much more as well. First, acceptance of one conspiracy theory often indicates a susceptibility to others. The structure of belief, as well as the lack of logical constraints, makes it easy to follow the path from one phobia to another. Antisemites usually find antimasonry credible, and vice-versa. Militiamen who see the U.S. government as their enemy read up on the Kennedy assassination or sign on to the October Surprise thesis, though these have no direct bearing on their concerns. They accept allegations of U.S. government involvement in the drug trade and turn them into confirmation of United Nations power. Timothy McVeigh, the man who bombed the Federal Building in Oklahoma City, believed in UFOs. Gary Webb made a name for himself as the author of the series of articles connecting the CIA to the spread of cocaine in Los Angeles. In itself, that was not necessarily a sign of conspiracism, but then, hoping to take advantage of his sudden fame, he prepared a book proposal in which he told of plans to "explore a theory" that the seven-year-long civil war in Nicaragua "was not a real war at all. It was a charade, a smoke screen . . . to provide cover for a massive drug operation" by criminal elements in the CIA with others.[15] Further, other signs also pointed to Webb's readiness to find conspiracy.[16]

Second, aware of the disrepute that goes along with being labeled a conspiracy theorist, some believers take care not to express their views in full. Thus did Pat Robertson almost entirely tamp down his conspiracism while running for president in 1988. Others actually deny their conspiracy-mindedness. Just after writing about Soviet Russia's being a project of "the Anglo-American establishments," Lyndon LaRouche adds that "it would be a great error to attempt to explain all this in terms of merely some 'conspiracy theory.'"[17]

Even allowing for such discretion, it is often difficult to discern a person's real views, for some writers and politicians promote conspiracism even as they distance themselves from it. Take the puzzling case of Benjamin Disraeli (1804–81). Born a Jew and converted as a child to Anglicanism, he was on one level a famous conspiracy theorist who spun great speculative webs about Jews and secret societies. At the same time, Disraeli boasted of his Jewish origins, demanded the admission of Jews to the House of Commons, and berated Jews who concealed their religious identity. Disraeli's well-known sense of humor and his irrepressible whimsy probably best account for these claims. But his extraordinary achievements (which included six memorable years as the prime minister of Great Britain) give them great weight and permanent importance. The result is monumental confusion. Was Disraeli a conspiracy theorist, as some of his words would make him seem? Or was he a skeptic who merely amused himself with a conspiracist conceit? No one knows, as Léon Poliakov explains: "It would appear that the author of *Coningsby* and *Tancred* was an unavowable source of inspiration to generations of antisemitic hoaxers, falsifiers and illuminati, and that he was all the more easily believed and imitated, if not plagiarized, in that his spectacular career seemed to illustrate the validity of his theses."[18] The same uncertainty applies on a lesser scale to others too.

Some conspiracy theorists are among society's otherwise most idealistic, accomplished, sensible, and friendly individuals who suddenly say something like, "Of course, the media never tell you the truth" or "Israel was behind the Falklands War." At the same time, filled with loathing and fear, they can cause much terrible suffering to untold millions. The historian Walter Laqueur eloquently describes them as "fighters of chimeras and phantoms, a collective Don Quixote fighting with windmills, seeing everywhere outrageous giants, who nurse inveterate malice against our hero, who use pernicious wiles and stratagems. This Don Quixote is neither funny nor tragic; he is without any redeeming features, motivated only by hatred, a menace to himself and others."[19]

When it comes to adjectives, I use two in the pages ahead: *conspiratorial*, to refer to a real conspiracy, and *conspiracist*, to the fear of imaginary conspiracies. Though different, the two are organically connected. Bolsheviks reached power through conspiratorial actions; once in office, their conspiracist fears of encirclement by the imperialist powers led them to institute a reign of terror.

Operational conspiracism refers to circumstances in which conspiracy theories have an influence on the policy decisions of governments or other powerful institutions. In the West, Nazi Germany and the Soviet bloc offer paramount examples of conspiracism in power; current examples would include the regimes in Iraq and Iran.

But what of the targets of world conspiracy theories? They are chiefly two, Jews and secret societies, with other might-be world conspirators having a remarkably minor role.

Although anti-Jewish arguments and tropes have taken many forms between the third century B.C. and the present—intellectual disdain by sophisticated atheists from the Hellenists onward, resentment among fervent Christians or Muslims, jealousy among peasants, social snobbery among aristocrats, political anger among defeated Arab leaders—underlying emotions remain fairly constant. The case against Jews has varied with the complaint. Early pagans resented Jews for their aloofness; Christians charged them with deicide; Enlightenment thinkers (and Germans longing for a pagan past) blamed them for Christianity; populists held them accountable for modernity; racists turned them into a font of all evil; and fundamentalist Muslims portrayed them as the spearhead of Western values.

Antisemitism, a term coined in 1879 with the founding in Berlin of the *Antisemitenliga* (Antisemitic League), is a form of anti-Jewish hatred that differs in several ways from what came before: (1) it changes the emphasis from religion to race, (2) it transforms dislike into fear, (3) it turns a bias into an all-encompassing ideology, even a way of life, and (4) it replaces the episodic persecution of Jews with a permanent one. Antisemitism moved Jew hatred from the realm of emotions to that of political activism, from defensive to offensive, and from life's sidelines to its core. It also changed the depiction of Jews from heretics into malevolently powerful figures.

The word *antisemitism*, unfortunately, is triply inaccurate. It gets the victim wrong: Jews suffer this prejudice, not Semites in general (such as Arabs).[20] It is anachronistic: Jew-hatred turned into political ideology only in the 1880s but antisemitism has come to describe anti-Jewish bias in all ages. It is a misnomer: there is no Semitic race. If *Semite* means anything, it describes someone who speaks a Semitic language, and many, perhaps most, Jews do not speak Hebrew.

I use *antisemitism* here to describe not all anti-Jewish sentiments, only those that are institutionalized and turned into an ideology. I spell it in lower-case, without a hyphen (not *anti-Semitism*), to signal that it refers to an ideology and to imply that the phenomenon has almost nothing do with the actions of Jews.

Not all antisemitism involves the charge that Jews intend to gain power over the entire globe (some forms emphasize, for instance, that Jews are a source of evil or are racially inferior), but most does. *Conspiratorial antisemitism* is probably the most virulent form of Jew-hatred, for it turns Jews into everyone's foremost enemy. How else could it be when, in the words of one antisemite, "Jewry as a whole has a permanent policy which aims at establishing the individual Jew as a member of the 'chosen,' superior and dominant ruling class in every country and over the whole world."[21] While the origins of conspiratorial antisemitism go back to the Crusades and its legacy is felt even today, the fear flourished particularly for some eight decades up to the year 1953 (when the "Doctors' Plot," the accusation that Jewish physicians plotted against Soviet leaders, nearly devastated Soviet Jewry).

Anti-Zionism should have nothing in common with antisemitism: the former has no religious or racist content but condemns Jewish nationalists in the Middle East for ill behavior. Indeed, more than a few Jews renounce Israeli behavior and are anti-Zionist; conversely, some antisemites favor a Jewish state as a means of reducing the Jewish population in the their midst. Wilhelm Marr was just such a pro-Zionist antisemite: "The Jewish idea of colonizing Palestine could be wholesome for both sides [i.e., Jews and Germans]."[22] He even guaranteed that the antisemitic movement would win Palestine for the Jews. Most of the time, however, antisemites fear a Jewish state as a particularly worrisome ingathering of the most capable and dangerous people in the world. As a Soviet writer puts it, "Zionism and Judaism have as their common purpose world supremacy."[23] The more virulent an anti-Zionist's passion, the more certainly it amounts to antisemitism in disguise; condemning Israel's West Bank activities signals less going on below the surface than does seeing Zionism as the tip of a vast empire that menaces the whole world. Most anti-Zionism is functionally identical with antisemitism.

The term *secret society* also requires explanation. It arose in the eighteenth century, when "secret" meant *non-state* or *private* (rather than *clandestine* or *covert*).[24] In today's usage, it refers to an organization that makes confidentiality the very basis for its existence, such as fraternal groups at colleges and among adult men. A secret society can range from a social club with its own handshake to revolutionaries intent on overthrowing the established order. Nearly all secret societies involve rituals that stress the need for discretion; in a typical initiation procedure, the adept swears to keep the group's secrets in confidence, upon threat of dire consequence. Members tend to be overwhelmingly male (except in radical political groups); they often talk of intense communion with other members, a spiritual rebirth, and a profound religious-like experience.

The *anti-secret society conspiracy theory* is a non-Jewish equivalent of antisemitism; it targets members of conspiratorial groups as enemies intent on gaining world hegemony through the destruction of the existing order. It permits the concentration on just one group (the Jesuits, the Anglo-American governments) or their linking into one "endless conspiracy" going back to the very dawn of history; occultists, for example, trace the original secret society to ancient Egypt. In perhaps the first listing, Charles Louis Cadet de Gassicourt (1769–1821), a French pharmacist with radical views writing at the height of the French Revolution, drew up a chain that began with the Assassins, a Muslim group dating from the Crusader era, then included the Templars, Jesuits, Freemasons, and Illuminati, and ended with the Jacobins.[25] Other names often mentioned include the Knights of Malta, witches, the Prieuré de Sion, Rosicrucians, Philosophes, the Carbonari, the British and American governments, arms merchants, international bankers, the Council on Foreign Relations, and the Trilateral Commission. "One conspiracy theory overlaps with another, forming a giant web enclosing centuries and continents."[26] Each group is believed to pass on its views and secrets to the next organization. For example, the body of wisdom that started with the cult of Isis in ancient Egypt was passed through the centuries to the Pythagoreans, Gnostics, Cathars, Templars, Rosicrucians, and finally the Freemasons.

I also use some other terms that require definition. *Extremism* means taking an idea to an excessive point, usually by means that are also excessive. In contrast, *moderation* accepts limits and constraints. Extremism in politics virtually always involves conspiracism to the point that conspiracy theories are a key element of extremism.

Mainstream refers to socially sanctioned ideas and institutions, ones that enjoy the patronage of the government and leading private institutions; *fringe* to those elements that do not. In some cases, most notably Nazi Germany and the Leninist states, the mainstream can become extremist.

The terms *Right* and *Left* turn up often in this book, where they refer to the extremes of these outlooks—not moderate Republicans and Democrats in the United States or their counterparts in other countries (who are *conservatives* and *liberals*), but the hard political traditions at the further ends of the political spectrum. Rightists exalt their own race, religion, or nation over that of others; leftists pursue a vanguard socialist or anarchist program.

In the American political scene, Newt Gingrich is not a rightist, but Pat Buchanan is, for the latter has a whiff of the fascist to him. Ted Kennedy does not fit the leftist label, but Jesse Jackson does. To be sure, Buchanan and Jackson use much milder words than do the out-and-out extremists, but they touch on the same themes. Where the hard Right speaks of the "Zionist Occupied Government" in Washington, Buchanan softens it to Congress as Israel's "Amen corner."[27] If Soviet propagandists referred to the United States as a "Zionist colony,"[28] Jackson merely called Jews "Hymies" and New York City "Hymietown."[29]

Some political figures are clearly conspiracist but not clearly on the Right or the Left. For example, Louis Farrakhan and Lyndon LaRouche defy characterization along the usual axis. And, as the Nazi-Soviet non-aggression pact established and our tour of history confirms, extremists often find more in common with each other than with moderates.

HOW FANTASIES CONVINCE

The conspiracy theorist . . . is to the professional histo-rian what the treasure-hunter is to the archaeologist; only in the case of the conspiracy theorists, there is no means of convincing them that their quick dig among the documents has revealed only false gold.
MICHAEL BILLIG[30]

When the topic is conspiracy, it is often difficult to distinguish truth from falsehood. In part, this is because objective criteria—logic and evi-dence—do not clearly demarcate one from the other. Further muddying the waters, individuals in the know sometimes make untruthful claims, serious scholars endorse wild claims, and pseudoscholars pass off their work as genuine research.

Logic alone does not conclusively uncover a conspiracy theory, for the simple reason that almost any sequence of events is logically possible. Logic cannot belie that Jews plan to use the subway tunnels under Euro-pean capitals to blow those cities "into the air with all their organisations and archives," as claimed in the *Protocols of the Elders of Zion*.[31] Nor can it show false the Ku Klux Klan claim of the 1920s that six Roman Catholic churches near the United States Capitol, along with the Georgetown and Catholic universities, were covert military bases for seizing control of Washington and replacing the president with the pope. Nor can it dis-prove that most of the Soviet leadership was helping Trotsky in 1937–38, that the CIA plotted John Kennedy's death, or that Ronald Reagan con-nived with Ayatollah Khomeini to keep American hostages in Iran.

If anything, these imaginary plots tend to be more rigorously logical and have fewer loose ends than does real life. Like alchemy and astrology, conspiracism offers an intellectual inquiry that has many facts right but goes wrong by locating causal relationships where none exist; it is the "secret vice of the rational mind."[32] The rules of logic, ever neutral, cannot discern the mistakes that send all three disciplines spinning into falsehood and irrelevance.

A second challenge to discerning conspiracy theories results from their containing enough truth and reasonableness to make them plausible. An element of veracity gets mixed with a much larger proportion of fantasy. "There is a small grain of truth to even the most unimaginable things people come up with."[33] In the case of the alleged Jewish conspiracy, although Jews have never aspired to global control or anything remotely like it, biblical and Talmudic materials do tell of a messianic age when the God of Israel will establish His rule. It will be a spiritual rule, not a political dictatorship, Jewish scholars all stress. Maimonides (1135–1204), the great Jewish thinker, explains: "The sages and prophets longed for the days of the Messiah not in order to rule over the world and not to bring the heathens under their control, not to be exalted by the nations, or even to eat, drink, and rejoice. All they wanted was to have time for the Torah and its wisdom with no one to oppress or disturb them."[34] But the texts promise that whoever opposes the Messiah will suffer terribly: "God will cause all the kings of the earth to tremble," Maimonides writes. "Their kingdoms will fall. . . . He [the Messiah] will slay anyone who tries to kill him and none shall escape or be saved from him."[35]

This promise has inspired generations of Jews. At the same time, as it filtered down, the scholars' high-minded interpretation was vulgarized into a rather more mundane expectation of the Messiah's coming and releasing the Chosen People from their tribulations. Such hopes resonated widely among Jews, especially after the disasters of the First Crusade; victims of ignominy and repression, they could hardly resist dreaming of a time when the tables would be turned and the oppressor would be devastated on the occasion of the Messiah's appearance.

Secret societies have similarly provided evidence to their tormentors. Some continuity does exist: "It is very rare to find a secret association which starts absolutely from scratch, with no debt to any predecessor."[36] Further, to make an organization appear more historical and weighty, its leaders commonly made up long histories of connections to other groups. For example, the Freemasons claim a pedigree from Hiram and the builders of the Jewish Temple (thereby making a connection to Jews that their enemies found most useful) and from the Templars (thereby making them obnoxious to the French state). An interest in occult secrets then somewhat confirms the accusation that Freemasons dispose of great and malign power. Freemasons do use "illuminated" terminology; the corner-stone on a lodge in New York City reads not 1875 but 5875 A.L., where A.L. stands for *anno lucis*, "in the year of the light." And Freemasons did sometimes act in conspiratorial ways; according to a historian of this topic, "[c]ircumstantial evidence" points to their having murdered a way-ward brother, William Morgan, in September 1826 to prevent him from revealing his knowledge of the craft.[37]

Third, those in the know sometimes endorse conspiracy theories, thereby muddying the waters. Michael the Neophyte, an eighteenth-century Jewish convert to Christianity, not only swore that Judaism commands the ritual killing of Gentile children but provided gory details about his own participation in these murders. Benjamin Disraeli, the former Jew who became prime minister of Britain, made sensational statements about Jewish and secret society conspiracies' running Europe's public affairs. In *Coningsby*, a novel published in 1844, he had one character declare that "The first Jesuits were Jews. . . . that mighty revolution which is at this moment preparing in Germany, . . . and of which so little is yet known in England, is entirely developing under the auspices of Jews."[38] Two pages further, a character makes an even more ominous statement, one quoted time and again by conspiracy theorists: "So you see, my dear Coningsby, that the world is governed by very different personages from what is imagined by those who are not behind the scenes."[39] Nor did Disraeli confine himself to making such statements in fictional works. In a biographical work of 1852, he asserted that Jews "wish to destroy that ungrateful Christendom."[40] He even took his conspiracism to the floor of Parliament, announcing in 1856 that "a British Minister has boasted—and a very unwise boast it was—that he had only to hold up his hand and he could raise a revolution in Italy to-morrow. It was an indiscreet boast, but I believe it not impossible, with the means at his disposal, that he might succeed. What would happen? You would have a republic formed on extreme principles."[41] Who would know this better than Disraeli? Such statements add greatly to conspiracism's credibility.

Nor is Disraeli alone. An alleged renegade Freemason exposed the existence of Jewish-controlled Masonic orders that sought to dominate the globe. The *Times* of London gave an insight into British imperial thinking in an 1875 editorial when it declared, "To this country will belong the decision on every question, whether scientific, financial or political; administration and negotiation will be in our hands, and as we have the power, so we shall have the responsibility before the world."[42] A self-professed half-Jew from Hungary revealed in 1905 that England and France are "very nearly" dominated by Jews while the United States is "slowly but surely yielding to that international and insidious hegemony."[43] Perhaps most revealing was the confession by a member of the American elite, Carroll Quigley of Georgetown University:

> There does exist, and has existed for a generation, an international Anglophile network which operates, to some extent, the way the Radical Right believes the Communists act. In fact, this network, which we may identify as the Round Table Groups, has no aversion to cooperating with the Communists, or any other groups, and frequently does so. I know of the operations of this network because I have studied it for twenty years and was permitted for two years, in the early 1960s, to examine its papers and secret records. I have no aversion to it or to most of its aims and have, for much of my life, been close to it and to many of its instruments. . . . [i]n general, my chief difference of opinion is that it wishes to remain unknown, and I believe its role in history is significant enough to be known.[44]

In other words, Quigley wrote, there is a conspiracy by a small, well-placed group, and he agrees with its aims.

Fourth, there is the vexing matter of what Richard Hofstadter calls the "higher paranoid scholarship."[45] This is not the legitimate scholarship produced by academics with university training, membership in professional associations, and social esteem. It is, rather, the mirror world of conspiracism, with its amateur autodidacts who lack institutional affiliation and suffer exclusion from the established institutions. Stark differences between the two might suggest that the research of scholars and the speculations of conspiracy theorists cannot be confused, but the latter often mimic the former, making it quite possible to mix them up.

Conspiracy theorists parade academic titles ("Dr.," "Professor"), earned or not. No less than conventional historians, they steep themselves in the literature of their subject and become expert in it. The difference lies in their methods; rather than piece together the past through the slow accumulation of facts, they plunder legitimate historical studies to build huge edifices out of odd and unrelated elements.

Making the truth harder to discern, conspiracist subjects draw many more pseudoscholars than real ones. A vast body of spurious studies has emerged in nearly all the languages of Europe over the past two centuries. The connection between Jews and Freemasons is the subject of only two works by legitimate scholars but dozens, if not hundreds, of books by anti-Jewish and antimasonic writers. A 1923 bibliography contains no fewer than twenty-three thousand titles on the Freemasons,[46] very few of them by disinterested researchers. In the thousands of books written on the John Kennedy assassination, only a tiny proportion argue against a conspiracy. The size of this corpus impresses some readers; "there is so much written. . . , they figure some of it must be right."[47] The many books make it possible for conspiracy theorists to cite each others' works, thereby constructing an imposing edifice of self-referential pseudoscholarship. In the case of old topics such as the Templars, they republish centuries-old books and quote them as authorities. In the case of new ones, like the John Kennedy assassination, they learnedly discuss each other's conclusions.

Conspiracist texts often come packaged as solid-looking books with introductions, forewords, acknowledgments, quotations, footnotes, bibliographies, indexes, and the other conventional trappings of learnedness. Even forgeries come wrapped in a mock academic paraphernalia. By replicating these elements of academic authority, the pseudoexpert finds it easier to convince the gullible or inexperienced reader to accept his pet theories. In addition, a profusion of references serves as a shield against criticism. When defending his book *The New World Order* from charges of antisemitism, Pat Robertson raised the irrelevancy that it "was carefully researched and contains seven single-spaced pages of bibliography from original historical sources."[48]

Conspiracy theorists tend to choose sober and flat titles, as though to disguise their anything-but-sober ideas. The most influential conspiracist book of all time goes by the pedantic title of *Memoirs Illustrating the History of Jacobinism;* its forged counterpart bears an arch bureaucratic title (*Protocols of the Meetings of the Learned Elders of Zion*). *Jews in the Japanese Mind* is a serious study, while *The Japanese and the Jews*[49] is wholly fantastical; yet they sound similar and both have reputable publishers.

Conspiracy theorists also publish seemingly responsible academic journals. By its title and appearance, the *Revue internationale des sociétés secrètes* projects an appearance of sound scholarship by dignified truth seekers; in fact, it long served as the central clearinghouse for the anti-secret society crowd. The *Journal of Historical Review* sounds akin to the

American Historical Review; more than that, both quarterlies share a recognizably academic tone and list professorial boards of editors. But while the latter is a leading scholarly periodical, the former exists exclusively to disprove the reality of the Jewish Holocaust.

Nor can the reader rely on publishers to distinguish chaff from wheat; even some of the most reputable houses lend their names to conspiracist nonsense. The arch-respectable firm of Eyre and Spottiswoode published the first edition of the *Protocols* in England. Jonathan Cape in London (publisher of Samuel Butler, Len Deighton, Maksim Gorky, James Joyce, H. G. Wells, and William Carlos Williams) joined with Delacorte in New York to publish *Holy Blood, Holy Grail,* a study claiming that Jesus was a Jewish prince who had a son by Mary Magdalen who founded a monarchical dynasty, the Merovingian; and that a secret society named the Prieuré de Sion has since its founding in 1099 forwarded Merovingian interests.[50] A few years later, Jonathan Cape and Henry Holt combined forces to put out a second study on the same subject, this one sketching out the Prieuré de Sion's present activities "to bring about a monarchical or imperial United States of Europe" ruled by none other than the family of Jesus.[51]

Telling genuine scholarship apart from conspiracism becomes even more of a challenge in the topsy-turvy domain of the World Wide Web. Here, conspiracist materials have a disproportionate presence, the familiar signals of authority are harder to discern, and search engines indiscriminately turn up conspiracism and true scholarship. Texts that most individuals would disallow in their houses on paper turn up unheralded on their computer screens. The vilest hatemongers most insistently present themselves as stalwarts of free speech. In addition, the technology mesmerizes, and the slow pace of clicking and waiting can lull viewers into near-hypnosis.

Finally, genuine scholars occasionally get caught up in conspiracism, showing that the person alleging a conspiracy provides no sure guide to its truth or falsehood. The Austrian Joseph von Hammer-Purgstall (1774–1856), an immensely erudite scholar and one of the great orientalists of his age, wrote a number of monumental studies, some of which remain in print today; also, his translation of the Persian poet Hafiz inspired Goethe's *Westöstliche Diwan.* Yet he was an arch conspiracy theorist who did much to advance the notion of the Templars as a secret society.[52]

To make matters more confusing, some anti-conspiracy theorists turn into conspiracy theorists. Gary Sick offers a recent example of this evolution. His excellent 1985 book on the collapse of the shah of Iran and the

Tehran hostage crisis, *All Fall Down*, dwelled on the mistakes of conspir-acism. In it, Sick noted how Iranians "assume that a simple, forthright explanation of events is merely camouflage concealing the devious intri-cacies of 'reality,'" and he criticized Iranians for assuming that "[a]ny sig-nificant political, economic or social upheaval in Iran must be traceable to the manipulation of external powers."[53] These insights seemed to aban-don Sick soon after. Already in 1988, he was brewing the October Sur-prise conspiracy theory alleging that Ronald Reagan won the presidency in 1980 by colluding with Ayatollah Khomeini.[54] Sick's trustworthiness carried so much weight that his false notion of an October Surprise launched two congressional inquiries.

If the rules of logic do not signal "conspiracy theory ahead," if the alleged conspirators provide partial confirmation, and if those with insider knowledge indicate a conspiracy does exist, how does one unmask the conspiracy theory?

THREE

UNMASKING

THE CONSPIRACY

THEORY

Robert Welch, founder of the John Birch Society, once raised the possibility that the influential Senate Republican leader Robert Taft had contracted cancer and died due to "a radium tube planted in the upholstery of his Senate seat."[1] Why is this claim plainly absurd? Because Democrats do not kill their political opponents; Senate furniture cannot be rigged in such a way; killing someone with radium poisoning makes no sense; and the source is someone with a record of outlandish conspiracism. But then consider this example: in their history of the Soviet secret police, Christopher Andrew and Oleg Gordievsky write that, to get a suspected British spy out of his Moscow apartment without his realizing what was going on, "KGB toxicologists smeared a poisonous substance on [Oleg] Penkovsky's chair, which made him briefly but violently ill."[2] This is entirely plausible, for the KGB has an established history of dirty tricks, it could easily break into one of its employee's apartments, placing poison on a chair could work, and the authors are reputable, nonconspiracist writers.

In other words, telling the real conspiracy apart from the imaginary one—or, in the terminology used here, the conspiracy from the conspiracy theory—is a subjective process. Although some analysts think this differentiation is not crucial,[3] truth or falsity do matter. One cannot treat Winston Churchill's warnings of the Nazi conspiracy in the 1930s on a par with Hitler's contemporaneous ravings about a Jewish conspiracy. Reader and author alike need markers to distinguish the solid ground of fact from the swamp of fantasy, for it is this insiduousness that permits conspiracism to spread from the extremes to the mainstream.

Many questions arise: Do conspiracies actually exist? How does one distinguish between the justified and the imaginary fear of conspiracies? Which writings on this subject are reliable?

DISTINGUISHING REALITY FROM FANTASY

[T]here can be no generalizations, only one safe rule for the historian: that he should recognize in the development of human destinies the play of the contingent and the unforeseen.
HERBERT A. L. FISHER[4]

The crowning attainment of historical study is a historical sense—an intuitive understanding of how things do not happen.
LEWIS B. NAMIER[5]

Fortunately, tools do exist to identify conspiracy theories. They include common sense, a knowledge of history, and the ability to recognize the distinct patterns of conspiracism. But the most important may be an understanding of the assumptions that lie behind this way of thinking.

COMMON SENSE. Not everything logically possible is sensible. Not every enemy aspires to control the world; accidents do happen; churches, subway tunnels, and Senate chairs are not instruments of death; and Catholics, Jews, and Democrats do not use such methods. As a logician puts it, "when we introduce a hypothesis to explain something, we are not operating in a vacuum. We have a vast context of background knowledge—beliefs, principles, and theories for which we have accumulated a great deal of evidence."[6]

Common sense accepts simple explanations; in contrast, conspiracy theories add complicating elements. They require a chain of deception so complex, an intelligence so formidable, and a cast of accomplices so large (and silent) that the whole scheme collapses of its own implausibility. Take the case of John F. Kennedy's murder. Lee Harvey Oswald could not have been put up to the job by some unknown power because of the huge number of people who had to take part in the plot. Just placing Oswald at the Texas Book Depository where he could get a clear shot at Kennedy's motorcade would have required four conspirators working in concert; the whole assassination plot would have involved a cast of hundreds.[7] This is the principle of simplicity or parsimony: "other things being equal, one hypothesis is more plausible than another if it involves fewer number of new assumptions."[8]

Two conclusions follow: conspiracies take place only within a context (killings that make sense in Moscow do not in Washington), and the more elaborate an alleged plot is, the less likely it exists. Planning a coup d'état is reasonable; planning the French Revolution is not.

A KNOWLEDGE OF HISTORY. Familiarity with the past shows that most conspiracies fail. Random occurrences throw them off course, participants renege, furtive moves alert the opponent. In general, the more elaborate the plot is, the less likely it works. Niccolò Machiavelli, a witness to much intrigue, observes that conspiracy "always involves countless difficulties and dangers," and points to the usual disappointment: "There have been many conspiracies, but history has shown that few have succeeded."[9] The philosopher Karl Popper adds, "First, they are not very frequent, and do not change the character of social life. Assuming that conspiracies were to cease, we should still be faced with fundamentally the same problems which have always faced us. Secondly, I assert that conspiracies are very rarely successful. The results achieved differ widely, as a rule, from the results aimed at. (Consider the Nazi conspiracy.)"[10] In addition to the Nazi failure, the other great conspiracy of the twentieth century, communism, also failed in its every dimension. So too in the United States, where the historian David Brion Davis notes a gulf between the "pitiful weakness and incompetence of most [genuine American] conspirators and the willingness of many Americans to believe that a powerful, monolithic, and virtually infallible organization was about the overthrow the Republic."[11] The great conspiratorial efforts by European, Israeli, and American leaders in the Middle East had little success; quite the contrary, all came back to haunt their authors. The British and French governments secretly divided up the Middle East in the Sykes-Picot agreement but could not prevail for long; in the Lavon affair, Israeli agents tried to pin the blame for anti-American violence in Egypt on Gamal Abdel Nasser but got caught; in the Iran/*Contra* scandal, Americans clandestinely sold arms to Iran and got caught. The same pattern obtains worldwide.

DISTINCT PATTERNS. Conspiracist beliefs vary widely. The fascist and Leninist ideologies differ on most points, and a Kennedy assassination buff has little in common with Louis Farrakhan. But putting specifics aside and looking instead at underlying features, it becomes clear how much conspiracy theories have in common. Two main characteristics make it different from conventional thinking: its standards of evidence and its basic assumptions. Distinctive features of its evidence include these:

• Obscurity. On the assumption that appearances deceive, they reject conventional information and seek out exotic and little-known variants. A taste for the improbable and the occult gives their data a distinct and recognizable quality.

• Reluctance to divulge information. Usually this takes the form of passive verbs and vague pronouns ("they"), but sometimes it takes more overt forms: "To protect the names of those who might be implemented, I have chosen not to disclose my sources at this time."[12]

• Reliance on forgeries. These play an outsized role as evidence. The fear of Templars was built, brick by brick, with forgeries, culminating in 1877 with the publication of their allegedly six-hundred-year-old "Latin Rule" that has them engaged in clandestine (and obscene) rituals. A tract published by a renegade Jesuit in 1614 claimed to expose the tricks and ambitions of the Society of Jesus.[13] In 1811, Napoleon published a supposed "Testament" of Peter the Great dated 1709 in which the tsar laid out his plans for the Russian domination of Europe and predicted the events of the century after his own death with uncanny accuracy. The American Protective Association distributed many forged documents during the 1890s, the most important of which was a fraudulent encyclical of Pope Leo XIII to American Catholics calling on them to eliminate all heretics (i.e., non-Catholics). The entire case against Captain Alfred Dreyfus in 1894 was based on documents forged by his superior officers. But far and away the most important forged document was the so-called *Protocols of the Elders of Zion*, cobbled together in France and Russia out of several existing works, some of them overtly fictional.

• Inconsistencies. Conspiracy theorists recirculate the same basic assertions, with slight variations and revealing inconsistencies. For half a century, one American rightist group after another has raised the alarm about hostile troops massing at the U.S.-Mexican border. During World War II, one leader wrote: "There are 200,000 Communist Jews at the Mexican border waiting to get into this country. If they are admitted they will rape every woman and child that is left unprotected."[14] In 1962, the Minutemen raised the alarm about Communist Chinese troops at the Mexican border, posed to invade. A year later, the John Birch Society made the danger more specific: thirty-five thousand Chinese troops in Mexico were set to attack San Diego. In the 1980s, the antitax group Posse Comitatus turned this into thirty-five thousand Vietcong hiding in south Texas. More recently, stories have spread of Russian troops massing in Mexico. Jews, Chinese, Vietnamese, Russians: the exact identity hardly matters even as the fear lingers. Such factual insouciance points to the paranoid style.

• Overabundant learned factoids and pedantic references. Conspiracy theorists seem eager to overwhelm the skeptic with a barrage of names, dates, and facts. To prove that the CIA was involved in selling cocaine to Los Angeles street gangs, Gary Webb provides mind-numbing details about so many figures that the reader can hardly follow his argument.[15]

• Piling on conspiracy theories. The gap in one conspiracy theory (extra bullets not found in John F. Kennedy's body, for example), is explained by yet another conspiracy theory (doctors surreptitiously took them out).

• Dismissing contradictory evidence as a sign of a conspiracy. The conspiracy theorist begins with the conclusion and finds reasons to exclude whatever is inconvenient. As assistant to Jim Garrison, a leading JFK assassination theorist, explains his investigation into the Kennedy killing this way: "Most of the time you marshal the facts, then deduce your theories. But Garrison deduced a theory, then marshaled his facts. And if the facts didn't fit, he'd say they had been altered by the CIA."[16]

• Indiscriminately accepting any argument that points to conspiracy. On the one hand, the British antisemite C. H. Douglas declared Hitler an illegitimate descendant of the Rothschilds; on the other, Lyndon LaRouche claims Winston Churchill was a Rothschild stooge. A contradiction? Not at all. Louis Farrakhan exploits the loose logic of conspiracism and comes up with a synthesis: the Rothschilds "would loan money to both sides in the conflict, 'cause they really didn't care who won or who lost."[17] This is typical.

• Oblivious to the passage of time. Generations and centuries go by, but little changes. The Knights Templar, a militant Christian order that came into existence about 1119 and was eliminated by the king of France in 1314, offers an extreme case: no one has laid eyes on a Knight Templar for nearly seven centuries, but the mystique of this longest lived of all secret societies remains alive. The Bavarian Illuminati, defunct for over two centuries, also show impressive staying power in the minds of conspiracy theorists. The fascistic Mothers of the United States of America accused the Sanhedrin, a body of rabbis that went out of existence in 66 A.D., of encouraging Hitler to attack Poland (thereby discrediting him).

• Cavalier attitude toward facts. At times, conspiracy theorists make these up out of whole cloth. The Rosicrucians "were everywhere, aided by the fact that they didn't exist."[18] The idea of this organization originated in the publication of three fantastical books in 1614, 1615, and 1616 that announced its existence, prompting some readers, especially in Germany and England, to seek membership and to adopt its outlook of ancient secrets. In later centuries, charlatans and would-be conspirators such as Filippo Buonarroti, Eliphas Levi, Madame Blavatsky, and Annie Besant adopted the mysterious name of the rosy cross for their own purposes. In 1915, the Ancient Mystical Order Rosae Crucis was founded in San Jose, California, latterly transforming an apparition into stone structures and meeting lists. Also remarkable are those cases where specific evidence turns out to be wholly imaginary. To make the October Surprise vivid, Gary Sick offered startlingly precise details about events that never took place. For example, elaborating on a nonexistent meeting of conspirators in Madrid on 27 July 1980, he adds this flourish: "The conversation was interrupted twice, when hotel waiters arrived to serve coffee."[19]

Finally, conspiracy theories contain several recurring assumptions.

POWER IS THE GOAL. All else is illusory. In the conspiracy theorist's dreary view of mankind, the lust for power muscles lesser motives to the side. Piety is a fraud: Freemasons pretend to accept Christianity only "for the purpose of accomplishing its overthrow."[20] According to an antisemitic forgery, "Every man aims at power, everyone would become a dictator if only he could, and rare indeed are the men who would not be willing to sacrifice the welfare of all for the sake of securing their own welfare."[21] Wealth and sexual satisfaction usually rank as the first two perquisites of power. "They worship no other God than Mammon."[22]

Philanthropy is a disguised form of greed. When someone appears to do a favor, he is in fact subtly looking after his own interests. The imperial powers granted independence to their colonies after World War II, apparently to benefit the colonized peoples; in fact, "powerful international economic interests" gained from this premature autonomy and the rush into socialism. The consequent ruin of their economies protected the ex-colonial powers from competition and, better yet, ensured them cheap raw materials. Foreign aid is really a mechanism to foster dependence, and loans to poor countries are a way to "dominate and control" them.[23] Other forms of generosity are also a ploy: Jews helped blacks with their civil rights for their own commercial gain.

BENEFIT INDICATES CONTROL. Whoever gains from an event must have caused it. If you know who gained, you know who conspires. Ask *Cui bono?* (Italian for "Who benefits?"), and the answer will lead you to the conspirator. The French Revolution enfranchised Jews, so Jews must have caused it. Or was Napoleon a Jew? Business interests seeking new markets have the most to gain from imperialism, so they must have been the motor force behind the British Empire. Nearly thirty parties stand accused of organizing a conspiracy to kill President Kennedy, and the basis in every case is some alleged benefit from his demise. If the Soviets gained financially from Saddam Husayn's invasion of Kuwait, then Moscow must have encouraged him to take this step; others see the United States as the beneficiary and so also the instigator. Boris Yeltsin gained most from the 1991 coup attempt in the Soviet Union; he must have orchestrated it.

CONSPIRACIES DRIVE HISTORY. Other forces do not count. Whether the event is as minor as a failed crop or as massive as World War I, the cause lies in the hidden hand. The usual explanations of historical change go out the window. Ideological fervor, economic distress, victory at war—all these are symptoms, not causes. The real force is what Nesta Webster describes as "the superb organization and the immense financial resources" available to conspirators.[24] Giants of history such as Napoleon and Lenin become mere pawns, replaced by powerless or even nonexistent figures (the Masonic grand master in Charleston, South Carolina, is the antipope[25] while the fictitious "Rabbi Eichhorn" is a leader of the Jewish conspiracy). In this topsy-turvy world, the most powerful individuals turn out to be the weakest: "the Holy Father is little better than a prisoner within the Vatican *exactly* in the same way that the President of the United States is a prisoner within the White House, the Queen of England a prisoner in Buckingham Palace, and Khrushchev a prisoner within the Kremlin."[26]

Some see all history driven by the Jewish conspiracy: Jews are numerous, ubiquitous, and well organized. Others lay all the blame on secret societies. In the words of an American journalist, "The history of conspiracy theories, then, is the history of secret societies. The history of secret societies is the history of conspiracies. And that is the history of civilization itself."[27]

Important events take place only behind closed doors, where none but initiates can be found. The unwashed public may think it makes decisions, but it does not: "the real power to choose presidents and prime ministers is not in public view—it is behind the scenes."[28] Take the French Revolution. The standard account analyzes the circumstances leading up to 1789, and treats the revolution as a massive, loose-ended whole replete with clashing personalities and contradictory ideologies. The conspiracist version neatly traces the plans of secret societies and the meetings of obscure individuals. Elections and participatory politics are a sham; in the words of an American Nazi, democracy is nothing but "the rallying cry under which the American system of government is being prepared for despotism."[29]

The conspiracist vision of the past stands deeply at variance with conventional academic scholarship. The latter takes many factors into account to understand change; the former has found a unified theory or "a master monistic design"[30] to explain all. "The distinguishing thing about the paranoid style," Richard Hofstadter writes, "is not that its exponents see conspiracies or plots here and there in history, but that they regard a 'vast' or 'gigantic' conspiracy as *the motive force* in historical events. History *is* a conspiracy."[31]

NOTHING IS ACCIDENTAL OR FOOLISH. Chance has no role. For the conspiracy theorist, whatever happens in society, the philosopher Karl Popper explains, "is the result of direct design by some powerful individuals or groups."[32] For Pat Robertson "the events of public policy are not the accidents and coincidences we are generally led to believe. They are planned."[33] William Guy Carr is more specific: "The more we study the methods employed by the *Secret Powers* behind international affairs, the more obvious it is to see that they make private assassinations look like accidents or suicides; sabotage look like carelessness, errors of judgement, and unintentional blunders committed due to excusable circumstances."[34] Cause and effect substitute for coincidence: "wherever there is an effect, there's always a cause."[35] Mechanics take the place of human foible. Conspiracy theorists evince a startling faith in the capabilities of their enemies. A member of the American right-wing group E Pluribus Unum explains: "Nothing in Government occurs by accident. If it occurs know that it was planned that way."[36]

Stalin's show trials and the Great Terror assumed that mishaps in the Soviet economy (and there were many in a system aiming at rapid industrialization with scant regard for human life) had to be intentional: "there can be no talk of any accidental happenings."[37] From this he concluded that millions of saboteurs were helping the imperialist enemy, and he punished nearly all of them. AIDS could not have happened inadvertently but has to have been devised in a laboratory by malign forces intent on killing millions or even billions of people. Conspiracy theorists also look for a hidden hand behind such natural phenomena as earthquakes, storms, and abnormally warm weather.

APPEARANCES DECEIVE. Life is a staged reality. "To be effective, a conspiracy must camouflage itself and its true purpose and pretend to be the opposite of what it really is."[38] Seeming gains are losses; losses are in fact gains. Victims cause their own suffering, while perpetrators are innocent. "The ostensible is not the real; and the real is deliberately malign."[39] The good family man, honest businessman, and patriot turns out to be a two-timing, scheming traitor. To a reasonable person, the absence of evidence means no conspiracy exists, but to a conspiracy theorist, "the best evidence is no evidence at all."[40] Thus, when Lenin failed to locate a conspiracy against his new state, "his suspicions and anxieties intensified to the point where they became impervious to rational argument."[41] Innocuousness indicates sabotage: Stalin found that an "outwardly harmless" situation signified a "silent war against Soviet power."[42]

The assumption that appearances deceive leads to four main mistakes: finding enmity, collusion, hierarchies, and freedom where they do not exist.

• Apparent enemies are really friends. Jews created antisemitism and exploit it; in the words of the alleged Elders of Zion, "Anti-Semitism is indispensable to us for the management of our lesser brethren."[43] Antisemites also work for the Jewish conspiracy. The same premise—evil forces cooperate behind the scenes—applies to secret societies. Jesuits are not the enemies of the Illuminati but their quiet allies; alternatively, Jesuits constitute the core of Freemasonry (despite repeated papal censures of Freemasonry).

Many on the Right believe Marx was not the great enemy of capitalism but its agent. Nesta Webster, a prominent British fascist, writes that he "was not sincere in his denunciations of the Capitalistic system."[44] The renowned historian Oswald Spengler went further and argued that Western bankers founded and controlled the communist movement: "Every proletarian movement, even that of the Communists, operates—without the idealists amongst its leaders being at all aware of this fact—in the interests of Money [i.e., financial power], taking the direction that Money wishes for so long as it wishes."[45] Alfred Rosenberg, the Nazi ideologue, incorporated this notion in the Third Reich outlook. It continues to echo on the Right, especially in the John Birch Society. In 1966, the group's founder announced that "Communism is not at all the movement which it pretends to be, of downtrodden masses rising up against a ruling class which exploits them. It is exactly the opposite."[46] A quarter century later, Pat Robertson promoted an even more spectacular conspiracy theory, accusing Wall Street bankers of "enthusiastically financing" Bolshevism with an eye to "saddling the potentially rich Soviet Union with a totally wasteful and inefficient system" that rendered that country dependent on those very bankers.[47]

• Apparent friends are really enemies. Though less common than the reverse, this perception is also fairly widespread. The United States did not enter the world wars freewillingly, but only as a result of British conspiracies carried out by its agents, especially on Wall Street. The massive help Americans and Europeans have given the Jewish state counts for nothing in the eyes of two pro-Israel writers who argue that "the secret bias of Western governments against the Jews was and is the single largest obstacle to peace in the Middle East."[48]

These two illusions joined together to produce an almost surreal conversation between Hitler and Stalin's foreign commissar, Vyacheslav Molotov, in November 1940. American aid to Great Britain notwithstanding, the German dictator insisted that the Americans actually coveted the British Empire and were in the process of taking it over. Roosevelt, he told the Soviet, "is doing nothing but picking out of his bankrupt estate a few items particularly suitable to the United States."[49] Of course, whereas the Anglo-American bond stood firm, Hitler himself invaded his fine Soviet ally a half-year later. And Hitler's prediction that "England and America will some day have a war with one another, waged with the greatest hatred imaginable,"[50] instead applied precisely to his war with Russia.

• No discipline means discipline. There was no central Jewish authority in the nearly two millennia between A.D. 70 and 1948. But conspiracy theorists insist that the Elders of Zion through the centuries had controlled the Jews in an effort to gain world hegemony. The conspiracist ignores the Jews' famed fractiousness (as the joke puts it, two Jews means three synagogues) and turns them into docile foot-soldiers of an all-powerful politburo; he dismisses differences as a cunning mechanism to fool observers. Atheists and self-haters are no less part of the conspiracy than the pious. "Non-Jewish Jews" like Trotsky can deny their Jewishness in word and deed, but this just proves their true subservience to the Jewish authorities.

Freemasons claim voluntarily to join lodges for social and charitable purposes and can withdraw at any time. Hardly, replies the conspiracy theorist. Once in, they cannot leave. He cites the case of William Morgan, a lapsed Freemason abducted from Batavia, New York, on 11 September 1826, then allegedly murdered to prevent him from publishing a book spilling the Masonic secrets. So too with the Council on Foreign Relations. It may appear merely to sponsor events and publications for the foreign policy leadership, but the conspiracy theorist discerns a "very high" degree of influence over members,[51] especially the power to make or break careers. Conspiracy theorists look at the power of council members and wrongly assume that their prominence results from their membership; in fact, it is the other way around. In both cases, an innocent social activity is wrongly turned into a conspiracy.

Capitalism is not the competitive system it appears to be but is manipulated from the top; businessmen have no choice but to accept orders from politicians. Weak as it may appear, the United Nations closely controls elected American officials. The totally innocuous Federal Emergency Management Association, a government agency that springs into action when disasters occur, is really the future executor of martial law in the United States. In each of these cases, the conspiracy theorist imbues voluntary institutions with the coercive powers of a dictatorial state.

• Discipline means no discipline. When it comes to dictatorships, the conspiracy theorist makes the opposite mistake, failing to see true hierarchies such as those in the totalitarian regimes of Germany, Russia, China, Vietnam, and Iraq. In these cases he pooh-poohs the need for strict adherence to a party line, discerns conflicts ("moderates" versus "extremists") where none exist, minimizes the casualties of those evil states, and ignores their conspiratorial actions. Consider the Soviet case. Conspiracy theorists were inclined to believe that the Ukrainian peasantry or the British government were engaged in huge plots of sabotage against the Stalinist experiment. Thus did Beatrice and Sidney Webb, leaders of British socialism, report from on site that Soviet food shortages in 1932–33 resulted from "a population manifestly guilty of sabotage."[52] They were similarily taken in by the show trials, which they compared favorably to courts back in England.[53] One author of the 1950s goes so far as to deem Stalin "only the agent of the international bankers appointed to rule over Russia." Hitler he calls the advocate of "a moderate Fascist policy" who fell under the control of a group he calls "Nazi War Lords."[54]

More recently, some conspiracy theorists disbelieved that the Soviet state plotted either in its diurnal actions (such as anti-American disinformation campaigns) or in its ultimate goals (to rule the earth). Instead, they saw this worry as a construct of fevered American minds. Louis Halle, a political scientist and naturalist, scorns this fear as fantasy: "the West was governed by the myth of a single conspiracy for world conquest under the direction of a satanic band in the Kremlin to whom all who called themselves Communists, the world over, gave blind authority."[55] Referring to the Vietnam War, an author on popular culture claims that "if it were not for the widely accepted premises of the conspiracy theory, we [the U.S. government] never would have drifted into so ill advised a war in an area strategically so insignificant."[56] And in an extreme statement, the author of a history of anticommunism writes that "Million of innocents lie dead, whole societies have been laid to waste, a vigorous [American] domestic labor movement has been castrated, and the political culture of the United States has been frozen in a retrograde position—all for the sake of overcoming Communism."[57]

Curiously, conspiracy theorists tend to discount the power of governments, so much larger and more powerful than Jews or secret societies. The Right believed the Soviet Union a symptom of Jewish power or the Money Power, while both Right and Left see Washington dominated by hidden forces. This fits the pattern of "appearances deceive": insignificant players like Freemasons and minor players like Jewry are ascribed far more importance than powerful institutions like the U.S. and Soviet governments.

In short, "appearances deceive" is a passport to bad judgment. Conspiracism turns some of history's most powerless and abused peoples (Jews, Freemasons) into the most powerful; it turns the most benign governments in human experience (the British and American) into the most terrible. This fear of the harmless and benign also makes conspiracy theorists blind to totalitarians, so that they see despotism in a New York think tank but not in Stalinist Russia. In short, conspiracism leads to a monumental lack of judgment; it is hard to imagine getting the story more wrong.

In the aggregate, these distinctive patterns of evidence and of argument provide the mechanism by which we can tell the conspiracy from the conspiracy theory.

In the pages that follow, I have done my best to separate conspiracism from conspiracy, reality from fantasy. Yet no one can be sure in every case which is which, and I make no claim to certainty. Conspiracism manages to insinuate itself in the most alert and intelligent minds, so excluding it amounts to a perpetual struggle, one in which the reader is invited to join.

A HISTORY OF IDEAS

If other people come up with stuff, it's called history. If we come up with it, it's called conspiracy theory.
JOHN JUDGE, AN AMERICAN CONSPIRACY THEORIST[58]

In a way, this book is the opposite of a study in intellectual history. I deal not with the cultural elite but its rearguard, not with the finest mental creations but its dregs. Hume, Rousseau, Kant, and Weber barely appear, replaced by Robison, de Barruel, Starck, and Nilus. Familiar individuals enter this stage in eccentric ways: Richard Wagner appears not as a com-poser but as a thinker, Benjamin Disraeli not as politician but writer, Henry Ford not as industrialist but publisher, Noam Chomsky not as lin-guist but polemicist. So debased is the discourse ahead that even the Russian secret police and Hitler play important intellectual roles.

Indeed, conspiracist writings constitute a quite literal form of pornog-raphy (though political rather than sexual). The two genres became pop-ular about the same time, in the 1740s.[59] Both are backstairs literatures that often have to be semiclandestinely distributed, then read with the shades drawn. Elders seek to protect youth from their depredations. Librarians hold their noses, then limit access to the *Collection de l'Enfer* or "Private Case" to those with the maturity not to be influenced by them. Scholars studying them try to discuss them without propagating their contents: asterisks and dashes in the first case and short extracts in the second are preferred solutions.[60] Recreational conspiracism titillates sophisticates much as does recreational sex. Artists explore conspiracist fantasies in a spirit akin to sexual ones.

Conspiracism differs in another way from the usual study of ideas, in that it tries not to change. The fact that its rules of logic are loose, even nonexistent, does not liberate conspiracy theorists to let their imaginations roam. Quite the reverse is true: the absence of boundaries seems to make them the more likely to repeat old explanations and rely on the authority of predecessors. Originality, so prized by genuine researchers, is unwelcome in this strange world of pseudoscholars where the prestige of old sources overshadows anything recent. Conspiracy theorists bring to mind those medieval authors who gave the ancients pride of place, even ahead of their own experience. Thus, Augustin de Barruel (who wrote his main work in 1797–98) remains the outstanding authority on the Illuminati, as is Lenin on imperialism. Such innovations as do take place tend to be updates within a preexisting argument and disguised with archaic pedigrees.

In other ways, the study of world conspiracy theories is an ordinary inquiry into the history of thought: who first had an idea, who spread it, what influence it had, what legacy it left. Conspiracism is a fully formed body of ideas. As is usually the case in intellectual history, it is books— not newspaper or magazine articles, not the electronic media, and not live individuals—that have a primary role in the creation and transmission of conspiracism. Books alone have the gravitas to transform one's life by showing the world in a radically new way; also, books alone have the space to construct an alternate vision. Other media play a role—the Nazis used caricatures, Father Charles Coughlin leaned mainly on the radio, the Soviets tried television, the Nation of Islam depends on newspapers, William Pierce writes novels, and the Christian Identity movement relies on the Internet—but the conspiracist case ultimately relies on the published book. Even within organizations, books, not leaders, educate the cadres. In the National Front, a British neo-Nazi group, "there are not formal meetings held specifically to educate members into the intricacies of the conspiracy tradition. Instead members seem to be directed toward publications if they wish to discover more about the underlying ideology."[61]

Conspiracism fits into intellectual history in another way too: nearly all the ideas circulating today build on a written legacy. Antisemites do not appear in a void, but invariably get exposed to some part of the large body of writing that came into existence in the 1870s, then act under its influence. Baldur von Schirach, a Nazi politician who headed the Hitler Youth, explained at the Nuremberg trials that he read Henry Ford's *International Jew* "and I became an antisemite."[62] Alfred Rosenberg, the future Nazi ideologist, turned into a full-time antisemite on reading the *Protocols*. These experiences are common. "Without knowledge of the literary tradition of antisemitism—what the antisemites said, did and wanted to do—a sufficient explanation of the phenomenon will continue to elude us."[63]

Rosenberg, the Nazi "chief ideologue," referred in his writings to nearly the whole antisemitic tradition from de Barruel onward.

The study of conspiracism assumes (in Richard Weaver's memorable phrase) that ideas have consequences. While perhaps self-evident, this assumption is out of vogue in an era of materialistic emphasis, and so bears some explanation. Karl Marx's theory of historical materialism (the notion that economic conditions determine other facets of society) has many adherents even among those who do not call themselves Marxist. In keeping with his ideas, academic analyses tend to portray economic interests as paramount, and ideas appear in them as little more than rationalizations for those interests.

That, however, is simplistic. Of course, economic interests have vital importance, but not to the exclusion of other motives. Ideas count too, and they have a power that goes beyond simply reflecting interests. Passion, faith, fear, and idealism matter. Even the most ruthless and cynical rulers—a Heinrich Himmler or a Stalin—are swayed by ideas and know their power over others. Indeed, one can go further and describe the fascist and communist experience as efforts at living out intellectual dreams; in a sense, the totalitarian state makes the best case for the idealist argument, for it follows rules capriciously created in one man's mind and has no necessary connection whatsoever to sociopolitical conditions. To neglect the role of the mind is to neglect one of the richest and most important of human impulses.

This outlook has direct application to the understanding of conspiracy theories, implying that these are forces that can move history—and have done so repeatedly. Accordingly, serious people must take conspiracy theories seriously. It is a mistake to dismiss conspiracism as a minor phenomenon, even a laughable distraction. To do so ignores not just the vital role of conspiracism during the past two and a half centuries, but also their current role and future potential.

FOUR

THE ORIGINS,

TO 1815

I n 1306 King Philip IV of France expelled the Jews from his country on the grounds that they "dishonour Christian customs and behavior in innumerable ways."[1] The next year he suppressed the Knights Templar, a Christian order, accusing them in extravagant language of blasphemy, homosexuality, and a host of other misdeeds ("a detestable disgrace, a thing almost inhuman, indeed set apart from all humanity")[2] that proved they were the devil's helpers. In both cases, the king's motives included a fear of the suppressed group's power and a covetousness for their wealth, which he promptly confiscated. Philip's parallel and near-simultaneous strikes against Jews and members of a secret society neatly symbolize an early expression of the twofold conspiracist tradition that emerged in medieval Europe, and in recent times captured the political imagination first of Europeans, then of peoples around the world.

THE CRUSADES: GENESIS

Mundane and spiritual factors combined to make the Crusaders' march from France to the Holy Land in 1096–99 one of the most memorable events in world and Jewish history.
SALO WITTMAYER BARON[3]

In its very furthest reaches, the conspiracy mentality can be traced back to the dualist religions of Iran or the mystery religions that swept the Roman Empire.[4] For our purposes, however, the Crusades mark the earliest fears about a small band seeking power through conspiratorial means; they generated a recognizable form of the conspiracism about Jews and secret societies that reigns still today.

In the first millennium after Jesus, Christian attitudes toward Jews were largely defined by anger about the killing of Jesus. To the extent that conspiracy entered into the thinking of the Church Fathers, it concerned a plot against Jesus, not fears of a future Jewish effort to take power. The influential Hellenistic writer Origen (c. 185–c. 254), for example, blamed the Jews for committing "the most abominable of crimes, in forming this conspiracy against the Saviour of the human race."[5] Other early Christian writers, seeing themselves in rivalry with Judaism, painted Jews as murderers and agents of Satan. With time, however, as the Church gained in confidence, attacks on Jews faded. Although Jews continued to suffer many disabilities over subsequent centuries, they were not subjected to efforts at elimination; in this very restricted sense, a policy of toleration prevailed.

The launching of the Crusades in 1096–99 led to a new, and far more bellicose, attitude toward Jews. The Crusades, a military effort by West Europeans to wrest control of the Holy Land from Muslims that lasted until 1291 and in vestigial form as late as 1444, inspired a new, unsanctioned doctrine that Jews, nearer at hand and worse unbelievers than Muslims, should be the first target of holy war. This "radical reinterpretation of received tradition" about Jews[6] called on Christians to "wipe them out as a nation" and "let not a remnant nor a residue escape."[7] Such words did not necessarily mean physical annihilation, for conversion to Christianity was much preferred, but it did amount to a near-genocidal assault that ended the old tolerance of Jews and fundamentally transformed their position in Christendom.

The Church leadership sought to channel hostility away from Jews and against Muslims, but the crusading impulse aroused passions that quickly spun out of control. From 1096 on, marauding Christians engaged in unprecedented and terrible acts of violence against Jews, especially in the Rhineland. In a new and startling way, Jews came to be seen as an enemy people whose very existence was in question. For Jews and Christians alike, this attitude would have profound consequences over the next millennium.

As Jews suffered persecution, they responded with an intense hatred of Christianity; one historian goes so far as to characterize the Jews' active readiness for martyrdom as their "countercrusade."[8] Aware of this loathing, Christians looked for signs of Jewish vengeance. Their fears led to a blossoming of two variant conspiracy theories about Jewish plotting: either that Jews on their own sought world power or that they would do so in conjunction with the Muslims.

ON THEIR OWN.   The Jewish dream that the Messiah would come and destroy the existing powers became more prevalent after the First Crusade. Most Christians (including the Catholic church) derided it as vainglorious and delusional. How could Jews, perpetually damned for the death of Jesus, hope to win hegemony over Christendom? Others, however, responded with alarm, turning the Jews' distant dream into an operational program. Jews came to be seen as the devil's accomplices, carrying out his conspiracy to destroy Christendom. In what may have been the first such charges, rumors surged in Worms, Germany, in 1096 about a conspiracy of Jews to kill Christians by poisoning the sources of drinking water. Many of the other enduring calumnies against Jews also took hold about this time: the accusation of ritual murder of Christian children, the desecration of Christian cult objects, torturing the consecrated wafer, the blaspheming of Christian faith in the Talmud, and economic exploitation. As the dream of retaking Jerusalem receded into memory, "accusations of ritual murder or of profanation of the Host gradually replaced the Crusades as a pretext for mass exterminations."[9] Such fears had immense consequence. According to Norman Cohn, an authority on conspiracism, "the Jewish world-conspiracy grew straight out of these age-old superstitions."[10]

For our purpose, the suspicion with the most consequences concerned well-poisoning, for this eventually grew into a fear that Jews sought to kill all Christians and take power for themselves—the basis of conspiratorial antisemitism. The conspiracy theories included incriminating details about the nature of the poison and the means of administering it. Each incidence of plague seemed to confirm the truth of these accusations. With time, the fear of Jews became more widespread, for although the Church continued to reject it, some important political and Christian leaders adopted it, most notably the Protestant reformer Martin Luther (1483–1546). Luther explained that Jews entreat God "to return them to Jerusalem, to send them the Messiah, to kill all the Gentiles, and to present them with all the goods of the world. . . . the Jews will be the masters and will possess all the world's gold, goods, joys, and delights, while we Christians will be their servants."[11] From these fears, Luther drew an unsurprising conclusion: deploring the fact that Jews reside in and among Christians ("We are at fault in not slaying them. Rather we allow them to live freely in our midst"), he warned Christians:

> we make them lazy and secure and encourage them to fleece us boldly of our money and goods, as well as to mock and deride us, with a view to finally overcoming us, killing us all for such a great sin, and robbing us of all our property (as they daily pray and hope). Now tell me whether they do not have every reason to be the enemies of us accursed Goyim, to curse us and to strive for our final, complete, and eternal ruin!

Luther concluded ominously, "if they had the power to do to us [Christians] what we are able to do to them, not one of us would live for an hour. But since they lack the power to do this publicly, they remain our daily murderers and bloodthirsty foes in their hearts."[12]

Fears of Jewish vengeance resonated for centuries, amplified by current events. Nineteenth-century antisemites argued that the Jews' unhappy experience naturally turned them against their Christian tormentors and that Jews would use their power to exterminate the Christians. Hitler portrayed his assault on Jewry as a preemption. And then, in the bitter irony that so often accompanies conspiracism, antisemites presume that a Jewish intent to avenge the Holocaust inspires a conspiracy. Thus did Erich Priebke, perhaps the last Nazi to be brought to trial, assert in August 1996 that the Jews were after him.

ALLIED WITH MUSLIMS. The Crusades caused Christians to see Muslims and Jews in parallel, as the external and internal infidels. Several commonalities then confirmed this parallel, for Jews shared more with Muslims than Christians in the practice of their religion, their language, and many of their customs (such as circumcision and dietary regulations). Beyond these parallels, Jews preferred living under Islamic rule, from the dawn of Islam forward, for it caused them to suffer less: "The Jews of Islam, especially during the formative and classical centuries (up to the thirteenth century), experienced much less persecution than did the Jews of Christendom."[13] Living among Sunni Muslims brought a more regular legal status, more participation in the mainstream cultural life, and more social interaction. Christians had a horror of intermarriage, but Muslims allowed it on certain conditions. In all, Jews living among Muslims were less excluded, and thus less vulnerable to assault.

These differences meant that Jews tended to celebrate Muslim victories against the Christians (for example, the conquest of Jerusalem in 638) and on several occasions actually provided help to Muslim troops. Most famously, the Jews of Morocco and Spain conspired to assist the Arabian conquest of Spain in the 710s. After the massacre of Muslims and Jews that followed the Crusader seizure of Jerusalem in 1099, Jews not only wholeheartedly joined with Muslims to prevent further losses but in some cases (for example, Haifa) became the city's foremost defenders. In addition, Jews often held prominent positions in Muslim governments at war with the Christians.

These factors caused medieval Christians to see deep connections between Jew and Muslim. "A Jew is not a Jew, until after he turns Saracen [converts to Islam]," declares the Latin translation of a Christian Arab's polemic against Islam.[14] The two peoples were closely identified with each other. A woodcut published in 1508 pictures a Jewish and a Muslim figure: the Jew carries a banner with the name "Machometus" (Muhammad), the Muslim's banner depicts a Jew's hat. Soon after, Martin Luther wrote that Muhammad (i.e., the Muslims) "kills us Christians as the Jews would like to do, occupies the land, and takes over our property, our joys and pleasures. If he were a Jew and not an Ishmaelite, the Jews would have accepted him as the Messiah long ago."[15]

From this evidence Allan and Helen Cutler conclude:

> Since the rise of Islam, the *primary* (though by no means the only) factors in the history of antisemitism have been the following: the association of Jew with Muslim; the longstanding European tendency to equate the Jew, of Middle Eastern origin, with the Muslim, also of Middle Eastern origin; the intensely held Christian feeling that the Jew was an ally of, and in league with, his ethnoreligious cousin the Muslim against the West; the deep-seated Christian apprehension that the Jew, the internal Semitic alien, was working hand in hand with the Muslim, the external Semitic enemy, to bring about the eventual destruction of Indo-European Christendom.[16]

In the final analysis, the Cutlers argue, "[h]ad there been no great outburst of Christian hatred against the Muslims in the Crusades, there might well have been no great outburst of antisemitism in Western Europe during the High Middle Ages [the era A.D. 1000–1300]."[17]

With the Crusades, then, anti-Jewish bias took on a violent cast and acquired a conspiracist dimension. This built the anti-Jewish tradition that culminated in antisemitism.

The Crusades also spawned the other enduring target of conspiracism, the secret society. Early in 1119, a French nobleman named Hugues de Payns and nine of his companions dedicated themselves to protect Christian pilgrims on their way to and from Jerusalem, solemnizing this oath by adopting the monastic vows of poverty, chastity, and obedience. The group adhered to a rule not much different from that of other monastic orders, with the exception of provisions that permitted them to make war. Theirs was a new, remarkable, and confusing development that merged two utterly different callings: the clergy (absolutely forbidden to engage in conflict) and the soldiery (which did so incessantly). A group of soldiers, renowned for their anarchism and their devotion to plunder and women, had become soldiers for Christ. In effecting this combination, they "invented an absolutely novel figure, that of the monk-knight."[18] This radical notion turned out to be both powerful and threatening.

The king of Jerusalem welcomed the help provided by Payns and his companions; symbolic of this esteem, he installed them on the holiest spot in Jerusalem, the Temple Mount, where they lived in Al-Aqsa Mosque. The group came to be known as the Order of Poor Knights of the Temple of Solomon, or Templars for short. The Templars also won the fervent backing of Bernard of Clairvaux, an immensely influential cleric, and through him, the sponsorship of popes and noblemen as well as nearly universal acclaim in Catholic Europe. Their model inspired the founding of other Christian military orders, including the Knights Hospitallers of St. John and the Teutonic Knights.

As men engaged in fighting, always an expensive activity, the Templars had a constant need of funds that made them different from other monastic orders. Combined with their far-flung military power and their reputation for probity, this spurred the Templars to offer proto-banking practices at a time when deposit banking did not yet exist. Before long, they held vast sums in deposit; for example, they became bankers to most of the French royal family. Combined with their noble patronage, this occupation made the Templars very wealthy. But banking practices also made them morally suspect, for such financial activities transgressed deeply held feudal norms and were seen as contradicting their professed piety.

Another problem arose when Acre, the last Crusader stronghold, fell in 1291. The Templars had so active and prominent a role in the Crusaders' wars that their prestige, more than that of any other order, depended on the situation in the East, and the fall of Acre caused their reputation to suffer. The failure of these fighting monks to hold the Holy Land from the Muslims, when combined with their secrecy, great wealth, and arrogance, fueled resentment of their power as well as rumors about their having hidden goals.

In 1307, as the Templars were planning yet another Crusade to return to Palestine, this resentment boiled over. King Philip IV of France struck against the order, seizing its members and confiscating their wealth. After a seven-year legal process in which the prosecutors relied heavily on torture, humiliation, and other psychological inducements to get the answers they sought, the Templars were finally found guilty of apostasy. In a great show of power, Philip had their grand master, Jacques de Molay, burned at the stake. Rulers everywhere in Europe but Iberia followed Philip's example and succeeded in completely suppressing the order. Centuries later it is clear that, however powerful and perhaps even out of control the Templars were, they never engaged in heresy nor posed a threat to the existing order.

Several features about the Knights Templar make them enduringly enigmatic. They had a conspiratorial air about them; for example, at the initiation ceremony, a candidate was told that "of our Order you only see the surface which is the outside,"[19] implying that something very secret took place behind closed doors. At the end of the initiation, each knight kissed the adept on the mouth, an act with obvious homosexual overtones. Further, the brutal suppression by Philip had an air of mystery about it. To this day, "the accusations of heresy are unproven and the evidence for internal decline impossible to assess."[20]

Together, the spectacular rise, great power, and grisly end of the Templars turned them into a permanent feature of European conspiracy theories. The Knights Templar stand out as the original and most omnipresent of secret societies. Looking back, even those conspiratorial groups in the hoary mists of antiquity take definite shape only with the Knights Templar.[21] Looking ahead, virtually all secret societies in recent centuries are seen as deriving from them: "The Templars have something to do with everything."[22] Occultists imbued them with magical powers, and Enlightenment rationalists turned them into an anti-Christian conspiracy. In addition, many romantics fell under the spell of the Templars' sensational tale, wasting untold hours in search of their idols, secret rule, and hidden treasures, speculations that amount to nothing more than "a wild fantasy" of "mystagogy and obfuscation."[23]

There is something surprising about both of the conspiracist traditions that emerged from the Crusader era. Why Jews, when Muslims constituted a so much more substantial presence and threat? Why Knights Templars, who had served as Christ's most stalwart warriors? In retrospect, however, these odd choices fit a pattern: alleged conspirators are rarely those whom logic might point to; rather, they tend to be those most innocent of conspiracy.[24]

THE ENLIGHTENMENT: INSTITUTIONS

The organization of the Secret Societies was needed to transform the theorizings of the philosophers into a concrete and formidable system for the destruction of civilization.
NESTA WEBSTER[25]

The two conspiracy myths of medieval origins began their transformation into full-fledged conspiracist schemes in the decades before 1789 as real secret societies came into existence, most notably the Freemasons and the Illuminati, and the Jewish emancipation began. These events set the stage for the myth of secret societies to take its modern form in the 1790s and for conspiratorial antisemitism to follow in the 1870s.

Few organizations have inspired so much speculation and awe as does the Freemasons; one enthusiast calls it the "most successful secret society in the history of the world."[26] As its name implies, the organization originated in the medieval guild of freestone masons, the craftsmen who carved stone on such buildings as cathedrals and castles. Their work required them to travel from site to site; while on the road, they stayed in lodges. To enhance their reputation, the masons traced their craft back to ancient Israel, and to keep interlopers out, they both guarded trade secrets and (with time) devised confidential verbal and physical signs that enabled one accredited mason to recognize another.

Why noncraftsmen came to join Masonic lodges in seventeenth-century England remains obscure, but perhaps their secrecy and the implicit promise of hidden wisdom lured in these "gentlemen" or "speculative" Masons. By century's end, Masonic elements (unhewn stone, the compass, gradations of skill) had acquired moral symbolism. The Masonic organization acquired its mature form in 1717 with the founding of the Grand Lodge in London; six years later, it had a constitution. Meetings of Freemasons were innocuous enough, serving as nonpolitical social gatherings wherein men of different classes could meet in an egalitarian atmosphere of deism, tolerance, and self-improvement. These were middle-class liberals who sought to improve society through free speech, elections, and secularism. Their meetings echoed with tolerance, respect for all humans, and altruism. The attraction of Freemasonry lay in the possibility of mixing with like-minded members of other religious affiliations, classes, and political viewpoints. It offered an exhilarating way to escape the usual confines, and the distinctive symbols and elaborate rituals added to the pleasure.

In England, Freemasonry always remained an arch-respectable, somewhat snobbish institution; even so, it first attracted hostility in 1698, on the grounds of encouraging anti-Christian attitudes. This perception was not entirely wrong, despite clergy joining the lodges in considerable numbers: "As soon as men became Freemasons, they seemed to place themselves in opposition to both Church and State."[27] Formally, lodges were apolitical (a French oath dating from 1776 specifically promised "not to enter into any conspiracy against the state"),[28] but by the very fact that they demolished long-established boundaries, the lodges spurred reformist sentiments. They also proved important avenues for the spread of Enlightenment ideas, a heady and unsettling brew.

From today's perspective, it is strange to find that a secret society like the Freemasons represented reformist interests and moderate programs, for we are accustomed to secret societies having a radical orientation, attracting the disaffected, and seeking social upheaval. The closest modern analogy might be the reformers of Soviet Eastern Europe who met clandestinely in "flying universities," jazz appreciation groups, and religious gatherings. By 1848, moderates in all Europe except Russia—half Western, half not—had progressed far enough so that they no longer needed to hide in secret societies. They abandoned that format to revolutionaries, who, in the West at least, have ever since dominated it.

Lodges quickly spread from Great Britain to the Continent, where, entering countries with despotic governments, they took on a very different tone and role. Free-ranging conversations and open inquiry raised few hackles in England, but many almost everywhere else; reformist sentiments in England elsewhere had revolutionary implications. From the moment the first lodge opened in Paris in 1725, the organization aroused great controversy. In 1737, King Louis XV of France demanded that his subjects have nothing to do with Freemasonry. In 1738, the Vatican issued the first of fifteen papal bulls condemning the organization (the last came in 1902).[29] Jesuits blamed Freemasons for the abolition of their order in 1773 (an ironic accusation, given the many suspicions in the 1780s that Freemasonry had fallen under Jesuit influence).[30] To a lesser degree, in Protestant countries too the authorities persecuted Freemasonry. The Russian authorities banned it in 1822. Ironically, the fear of Freemasonry grew even as the membership came to be more prosperous, established, and conservative. The international fellowship that Freemasonry offered, including not just Europeans and Americans but even Muslims, also aroused suspicions.

Then came "Scottish" Freemasonry, an unruly growth almost without rules or organization. To inflate their social standing, continental lodges made spurious claims about their origins and acquired exotic traits. French lodges, for example, traced their descent to the builders of the Jewish Temple, tacked on secret ranks of membership, flaunted their secrecy, indulged in pretentious rituals, and divided into rival branches. Such chaos attracted confidence men and other disreputable characters to the order, who did much to compromise its reputation. Perhaps the outstanding of these individuals was Giuseppe Balsamo (1743–95, known as the Count di Cagliostro), an Italian imposter who founded the "Egyptian" branch of Freemasonry and had a small part in the French Revolution.

Trying to make sense of this madness, some Antimasons developed a new and powerful argument against their enemies: that the leaders keep the lower grades so ignorant and confused that they do not know their superiors' intentions, permitting the latter to effect their will. In *Freemasons Crushed,* a French abbot held that the leaders secretly conspired to create a golden age of radical egalitarianism.[31] By keeping secret this plan, as well as their own identities, they managed to win the patronage of the nobility, and even of royalty. This suspicion implied that whatever the innocence of specific members, the order as a whole might be guilty of insurgency or sabotage. There could always be a further, more hidden rank that manipulated all the others. Fears of this sort about higher ranks and inner secrets came to be a staple of conspiracism and had the liberating effect of eliminating the need to establish factual proofs.

Of particular importance for our purposes was the tendency to conjoin Freemasonry with other secret societies, a process that encrusted it with yet more occult and mystifying qualities. Starting in Germany in 1736, the Crusading orders were presented as precursors of Freemasonry (as well as the reverse). The Knights of St. John were first brought in, but as they were yet inconveniently extant, this proved difficult to sustain, and so, starting in 1752, a derivation from the Knights Templar was settled on instead. The Templars eventually came to be seen as a form of Freemasonry. From this developed the notion, as logical as it was fanciful, that the Freemasons had taken on the burden of avenging Jacques de Molay against the French monarchy, an idea that would have momentous consequences after 1789. In 1790, Freemasons were linked to the Philosophes. As we shall see later in some detail, Freemasons and Jews came to be seen as allies, if not twins. Less consequential, but indicative of Freemasonry's tarpaper-like quality, was the presumed association with Rosicrucians. Perhaps most amusing was the early nineteenth-century fear of a covert connection between the Freemasons and Phi Beta Kappa, the American honor society for college students. This deadly combination, one lecturer feared, could blow "up all our civil and religious *rights*."[32] Between its Scottish, Egyptian, Templar, Jewish, and Rosicrucian variants, Freemasonry came to be the most central and complex of all secret societies, to the point that no one person can comprehend its structures, much less fathom its secrets. Then, to complicate matters further, along came the Bavarian Illuminati.

Secret societies proliferated in the four decades after 1750, almost all patterned on the Freemasons or in opposition to them. The most consequential of these new organizations was the Order of the Illuminati, founded on 1 May 1776 by Adam Weishaupt (1748–1830), a professor of law at the University of Ingolstadt in Bavaria. Sometimes deemed history's greatest conspirator, Weishaupt was a complex and contradictory figure: an egalitarian who devised a severely hierarchical organization, a rationalist who reveled in obscurantism, a believer in Enlightenment ideals who sought their fulfillment through subterfuge. The Order of the Illuminati represented his effort to build a just community within a corrupt society and to modernize Germany through the discipline of a secret society.

It lasted only a few years, being repressed in June 1784 (along with other unlicensed societies) and completely shattered three years later.[33] In

1790, the Bavarian authorities imposed the death penalty for offences connected with Illuminati activities. Although a minor phenomenon in terms of its immediate impact and reach (at its height, the order counted about three thousand members, and it never did take the plunge into activism), the Illuminati quickly acquired both real and mythic importance.

On the real ledger, the Illuminati gained more influence after its demise than was ever the case during its existence. First, it replaced the aristocratic and self-indulgent incoherence of Freemasonry with serious and radical ideas. Freemasonry existed as an end in itself; Weishaupt created the Illuminati as a political tool. Through such figures as Count Mirabeau, Nicholas de Bonneville, and Filippo Buonarroti, its ideas had a subsequent impact on revolutionary thinking. For example, the Italian nationalist revolutionary Buonarroti (1761–1837) concluded that mass uprisings were useless and instead turned to clandestine alternatives; his Sublimes Maîtres Parfaits (founded about 1810 and reorganized as the Monde some time after 1818) drew extensively on the Illuminati for its initiation rites, hierarchical grades, specific terminology, and catechistic slogans.

Second, by demanding far more from the adept than had previous secret societies, the Illuminati developed a new kind of organization. By cutting members off from family and friends, then immersing them into a separate society marked by purpose and obedience, it created a model for the revolutionary society. In today's terms, if Freemasonry resembled the loose ways of New Age spirituality, the Illuminati had the strictness of a cult.

Third, the Illuminati challenge provoked strong and consequential responses. Of particular note was the *Wiener Zeitschrift*, a periodical dedicating to combating the Illuminati; one authority characterizes it as "the first avowedly Conservative journal in the history of Germany."[34]

Fourth, the Illuminati established the model of a secret society run by leaders who hide their purposes from the general membership; this is the "double doctrine." What had been falsely charged of the Freemasons, in other words, became a deliberate strategy of Weishaupt's Illuminati. The double doctrine implies that the rank and file learn of anodyne goals, while the *supérieurs inconnus* know the organization's true, and quite different, inner secrets. The double doctrine proved a powerful tool and had a central role in many subsequent secret societies. Buonarroti created a number of organizations whose ordinary members did not learn the organization's secrets, and the leadership disguised its purposes the better to serve the masses. In Buonarroti's organizations, it reached the point that he was suspected of manipulating conspiratorial movements for his own ends, ends quite unknown even to the ostensible leaders of those movements. On the same model, Nikolai Ishutin created Hell in the 1860s, a secret part of a Russian revolutionary group called the Organization. In recent years the National Front, a fascist group in Great Britain, has had a public message that froths against immigrants, and a private message that targets Jews.

Fifth, the Illuminati created a prototype of interlocked secret societies. Starting with Weishaupt himself, its members joined Masonic lodges, seeking to dominate them and thereby spread the Illuminati vision through Freemasonry. In the neat world of conspiracism, the two organizations are said to have achieved union in 1782 at the (real) Congress of Wilhelmsbad. That congress remains a turning point in history for many conspiracy theorists, and all the more so because it coincided with the Jewish emancipation in Austria. A clandestine nexus is also said to link the Illuminati to such real political groups as the French Philadelphes, the German Tugendbund, the Italian Carbonari, and the Russian Decembrists. The Freemasons in Italy, for example, adopted the Illuminati's technique of penetrating other lodges, its notions of radical egalitarianism, and its reliance on a secret hierarchy (in which the upper strata knows of purposes hidden to ordinary members). In all, the Illuminati broke new ground by using systematic infiltration and subterfuge to attain political goals.

In addition to its influence on real institutions, the Illuminati also "proved to be the unwilling occasion for the birth of modern conspiracy theory."[35] Alarm about Illuminati prowess surfaced even before the French Revolution; in 1788, the Marquis de Luchet published the anonymous *Essay on the Sect of Illuminists* in which he portrayed a mystical and theocratic order aiming to "govern the world."[36] While "Illuminist" refers here to a mystical kind of Freemason, and not to the Illuminati, Luchet's interpretation was quickly applied to the latter, and his exaggerating its importance had large repercussions a year later when the French Revolution erupted. By 1797, Weishaupt was accused of seeking "to rule the world by means of his Order." In another argument, the suppression of the Illuminati was denied. Anyone who believed in its termination fell for a trick by the clever Weishaupt to spread his evil message more effectively. This meant that it was ascribed a large and growing historical influence in the years to come; in particular, it would be seen as central to the French Revolution and the rise of Marxism-Leninism.

In all, the Illuminati had a powerful impact on conspiracism, for it gave some substance to the worst fears of conspiracy theorists. Previously, the enemies of secret societies

> had not asserted that a great and universal plot was to be found at its core. This now became an idea of common currency and was to be an essential key for the interpretation of many things. . . . The Illuminati was . . . the one verified example of a secret society working with subversive purposes, but it confirmed and revivified older suspicions of secret sects and societies, above all of freemasonry.[37]

The Bavarian Illuminati shows great staying power across time and space. "The shadow of the defunct order became a specter which took on a terrible reality for weak minds," notes René le Forestier, the Illuminati's chronicler. "The name of the Illuminati alone made rationalists as well as traditionalists go into delirium."[38]

To appreciate this impact, consider the Illuminati's career in the United States, where it began by inspiring a severe bout of paranoia in 1798–99, when it spurred Americans to believe that "the intrigues of secret organizations must needs be reckoned with as one of the constant perils of the times."[39] A second round took place after 1826. The onset of communist rule revived this fear in the 1920s when writers made it the progenitor of Bolshevism. And not just that. Inspired by Nesta Webster's ascribing to Illuminism the goal of nothing less than "the destruction of Christian civilization,"[40] American conspiracy theorists made it key to world problems. In 1930 testimony to the U.S. Congress, for example, Father Charles Coughlin, a radio personality with a huge audience, quoted Weishaupt to the effect that, "Destroy Christianity and civilization will be happy."[41] William Guy Carr of Canada, who wrote seven books and countless articles on this group, believed that "The Illuminati direct all evil forces."[42] The John Birch Society adopted this theme in 1966, deeming Karl Marx's *Communist Manifesto* merely an updated and codified version of Adam Weishaupt's principles. In 1968, the Birch Society interpreted the Poor People's March on Washington in the light of the siege of the Bastille in 1789, holding that "They were both planned by the same breed of conspirators, for almost identically the same purpose."[43] Even today the Illuminati remains a fearsome institution, connected by conspiracy theorists to such varied events as efforts to establish a one-world government, the development of liberal Christianity, Reform and Conservative Judaism, and the John Kennedy assassination. The Illuminati seems to have survived the Soviet collapse. Writing in 1991, Pat Robertson asserted that "Illuminism was not transitory, and Weishaupt's principles, his disciples, and his influence continue to resurface to this day."[44] However little the Illuminati succeeded in transforming society, it did create a powerful model that admirers would long emulate and enemies even longer fear.

In an almost innocent fashion, eighteenth-century thinkers developed themes of subterfuge, inner secrets, and overlapping secret societies that largely defined the subsequent career of conspiracism. One might say that just as the European philosophical tradition consists of a series of footnotes to Plato, its tradition of world conspiracy theories consists of footnotes to the Enlightenment. The consequence of these ideas would start to become apparent with the French Revolution.

THE FRENCH REVOLUTION: SECRET SOCIETY PHOBIA

We are all conspirators . . . by the wish of nature.
REVOLUTIONARY FRENCH PAMPHLET[45]

It was not merely the thrones of Europe that were shaken but civilization itself that trembled to its very foundations.
NESTA WEBSTER[46]

The growth of secret societies in the Enlightenment era, along with a parallel fear of their plots, meant that conspiracist ideas had become a serious and fairly widespread means of understanding political life by the 1780s. Cataclysm in France then enhanced the utility and scope of these ideas.

The French Revolution had a profound role in the development of conspiracism. By demonstrating the power of ideas and the potential for radical change, it ushered in a new era of human history. By winning avid supporters throughout Europe, some of them prepared to engage in clandestine activities against their own rulers, it transformed political life. From the viewpoint of conspiracism, it turned the eighteenth century's "theories of intellectual and spiritual plots into the paranoic political vision of the nineteenth."[47] If French fears from 1725 of a "famine plot" to starve the country symbolize conspiracy theories before the French Revolution—a limited scheme aiming at monetary gain[48]—fears after 1789 are captured by a supposed Philosophes-Masonic-Illuminati plot to eliminate the monarchy, the church, and private property. Just as the conspirators grew far more alarming, so did their goals—and the theories about them.

The revolution's enemies had great difficulty grasping what had happened in France, much less knowing how to fight it. The events after 1789, simply put, defied traditional classifications because it constituted the largest event of history. Many interpreters offered explanations for the causes and the course of the revolution, a process still underway two centuries later. Counterrevolutionaries and other supporters of the old order, within France and outside it, tried to account for the astonishing fall of a divinely sanctioned system to unruly mobs, even as they sought to exonerate themselves. Clearly they could not turn to religious explanations, for how could God have caused this anticlerical upheaval? Nor could any single politician, no matter how disaffected, ambitious, or evil, be accused of wreaking such havoc. Those who thought, in the Enlightenment fashion, that individual motives drive history had to confront this supreme example of good intentions going astray. If the most intelligent and virtuous of men created a monster that devoured them and countless others, clearly something too big to be accounted for the old-fashioned way had come into existence. This left a conspiratorial explanation.

Focusing on a plot also had the great virtue of causing misrule and incompetence to disappear as factors. Indeed, many royalists found a conspiracist explanation fully satisfying, for it provided them with precise enemies against whom to vent their rage while holding out the hopeful implication that eliminating those conspirators would permit a turning back of the clock.

At the same time, traditional notions of conspiracism had to change: an unprecedented event required unprecedented explanations. Who would explain this vast and confusing drama as a plot had to conceptualize a far larger and mightier group of plotters than had ever before been the case. Initial efforts to portray the revolution as the result of feuding between rival politicians or from English subsidies just did not convince. If conspiracy it was, it included many thousands of organized and mobi-

lized individuals living throughout Europe. It had to be a huge, evil, surreptitious, and almost inhumanly effective network. "The scale and violence of the changes that men were called upon to account for soon
seemed to exhaust all conventional and familiar categories of explanation. Some new dimension of understanding was needed."[49] The moment
was ripe for world conspiracy theories.

Paradoxically, conspiracism acquired force just as it became less plausible. Prior to the French Revolution, when small numbers of individuals
dominated society, plots were not difficult to execute. But ideology and
mass participation made them far less likely, and the onset of market
forces further reduced their potential. In this way, the French Revolution
had the curious effect of undermining the suppositions behind conspiracism, even as it turned conspiracism into a political force.

Three familiar secret society culprits, each allegedly working to undermine the public order, emerged as the main suspects behind these terrible
events: the Bavarian Illuminati, Freemasonry, and the Templars.

Accusations against the Illuminati began with the onset of the French
Revolution. One anecdote has Johann August Starck, a famous conspiracist, taking the waters in a resort town with a friend when the sensational news came about the fall of the Bastille. According to the friend's
recollection, on hearing what happened, the two looked knowingly at
each other, then simultaneously blurted out, "*That* is the work of the Illuminati."[50] From 1790 on, a deluge of articles and pamphlets pointed to
the Illuminati as a main organizer of the French Revolution. It hoped to
rule the world by bringing down the monarchy and abolishing private
property, the family, and religion.

As for the Freemasons, a 1791 book by a French priest, *The Veil Withdrawn*, may have been the first account to tie them to the revolution.[51]
The author found that many recent innovations in France smelled of
Freemasonry, including the geographic reorganization of the country, the
role of the security services, and the limitations on the clergy. His ideas
were subsequently repeated many times and then much embellished.

In a 1792 booklet, *The Tomb of Jacques Molay*, Cadet de Gassicourt
traced the revolution back to the Knights Templar.[52] He described in
detail how the Templars' last grand master, Jacques de Molay (d. 1314),
planned revenge against the French monarchy in his prison cell in the
Bastille and how the current revolutionaries were carrying out his will.
The Templars, according to his spectacular thesis, did not die out but

went underground and reappeared in the guise of Freemasons. Over-throwing the French king, in other words, had been plotted out 475 years before Parisians stormed the very same Bastille! Many subsequent authors accepted this thesis.[53] The Templar-Freemason connection implied a political dimension, for if surviving Templars had finally avenged them-selves against the French monarchy, the papacy, and indeed all Christen-dom, then they had a radical, even nihilistic program to forward. Cadet de Gassicourt further argued that only eight true initiates caused the rev-olution to happen; all others were dupes. He broke new ground by piling one conspiracy on another, constructing an ever more reckless edifice of secret societies, turning centuries of confusing history into a seamless account of a single conspiracy.

Then, in 1797, two original, hugely important, and remarkably similar books appeared almost simultaneously in Great Britain, both postulating a world conspiracy theory about the French Revolution that pointed to the Illuminati; six years later, a companion volume appeared in Germany.

John Robison (1739–1805), a distinguished scientific writer, wrote one of these books, *Proofs of a Conspiracy*,[54] to show that the Illuminati had not been entirely suppressed but had lived on and resurfaced as Die deutsche Union, an organization that subsequently gained predominant influence over French Freemasonry—and in turn clandestinely plotted the French Revolution. The exact transmission of influence, he specu-lated, took place in 1787, when two members of the Illuminati traveled to Paris and visited Masonic lodges. The Jacobin Club was nought but a Freemason lodge. As a result of their success, "France undoubtedly now smarts under all the woes of German Illumination." Ironically, Robison was himself a Freemason who wrote to defend the reputation of British Freemasonry from the excesses of its continental counterparts. His work found many admirers (the English writer William Cobbett declared that it "unravels everything that appears mysterious in the progress of the French Revolution")[55] and had great influence. In the United States, for example, it inspired a near-panic in New England during 1798–99 and "defined the themes that were to dominate the American literature of counter-subversion for the next century."[56] Robison also had a major influence on the man who may have been history's most important con-spiracy theorist, Augustin de Barruel.

De Barruel (1741–1820), a French ex-Jesuit and an abbot, took refuge in England after the revolution, where he met Robison and was inspired by his ideas. In 1797–98 he published the mammoth four-volume *Mem-*

oirs Illustrating the History of Jacobinism,[57] a yet more ambitious and influential study than Robison's. In it, de Barruel made a systematic and well-documented case for secret societies, having carried off the French Revolution; specifically, he saw it resulting from a plot that the Jacobins had meticulously worked out in advance. The Jacobins, in turn, incorporated three elements: Philosophes, Freemasons, and Illuminati. De Barruel's first volume, *The Anti-Christian Conspiracy*, deals with the Philosophes, showing how Voltaire and his colleagues plotted to destroy Christianity. Volume 2, *Conspiracy of the Sophists and the Rebellion against Kings*, shows how the same culprits plotted against monarchs and allied with the Freemasons to overthrow aristocratic privilege, private property, legitimate government, and Christianity. The last two volumes are jointly titled *The Impious and Anarchic Conspiracy of the Sophists*. Volume 3 concentrates on the Bavarian Illuminati and reveals their control over Freemasonry. Volume 4 ties the "triple conspiracy" into a single grand vision of history beginning with Mani, the Iranian prophet of dualism, and culminating in the French Revolution.

De Barruel popularized the ideas of his predecessors by making these more accessible and rigorous, at the same time that he extended the conspiracist argument further than any of them, the whole way back to ancient Iran. The Jacobin conspiracy for him was directed not just against Catholicism, the French monarchy, and the landowners but against religion, government, and private property as such. His was the first attempt to present conspiracy theories in an orderly and intellectually punctilious fashion. In the words of a twentieth-century historian, "the work by Barruel is a masterpiece; hatred and fear made him a poet."[58]

The *Memoirs* met a widely felt need for a unifying explanation of the French Revolution and so had an immediate and far-reaching appeal. Lengthy as the work was, it reached a vast audience. Sales boomed; author and publisher alike grew rich. By 1812, translations had appeared in Dutch, English, German, Italian, Polish, Portuguese, Russian, Spanish, and Swedish. The French edition remained in print until 1837; for many years, it was one of the most widely circulated books in Europe.

It is hard to overestimate the significance of de Barruel's highly innovative, crazed, and all-but-forgotten study. His thesis influenced generations of French thinkers, including such figures as Louis de Bonald (1754–1840), George Sand (1803–76), Gérard de Nerval (1808–55), Louis Blanc (1811–82), Hippolyte Taine (1828–93), and Charles Maurras (1868–1952). In Germany, it influenced Friedrich La Motte-Fouqué

(1777–1843), Adam Müller (1779–1829), and many others. In the United Kingdom, Edmund Burke (1729–97) lavished praise on the book ("The whole of the wonderful narrative is supported by documents and proofs with the most juridical regularity and exactness").[59]

Even those who disagreed with de Barruel had to contend with him. Percy Bysshe Shelley (1792–1822) took issue with his arguments but studied him carefully.[60] Thomas De Quincey (1785–1859) recorded his youthful struggle with de Barruel's ideas.[61] The conservative political philosopher Joseph de Maistre (1753–1821) devoted great effort to refuting de Barruel ("this rot Illuminism is an effect, not a cause").[62] Conspiracy theorists with alternate theories for the French Revolution replied to de Barruel, for example, pinning responsibility for this episode on the Jesuits. The most important refutation, by Jean-Joseph Mounier (1758–1806), appeared in 1801. In de Barruel's work, Mounier complained, "To causes extremely complicated have been substituted simple causes, adapted to the capacity of the most indolent and superficial minds."[63] De Barruel's ideas also spurred a backlash of ridicule. In a 1797 play, George Farquhar's *The Beaux' Stratagem*, Scrub exposed its underlying logic: "First, it must be a plot because there's a Woman in't; secondly, it must be a Plot because there's a Priest in't; thirdly, it must be a plot because there's French Gold in't; and fourthly, it must be a Plot, because I don't know what to make on't."[64]

De Barruel's influence went beyond the merely conspiracist. Jacques Droz has shown[65] its key role in the development of German romantic thought in politics. Viewing the French Revolution as a conspiracy inspired a mystical and reactionary movement that spawned conceptions of society and state utterly opposed to the revolutionaries' rationalism. The battle against France became a sacred act to save German culture; from here, it was only a short step to romantic conceptions of culture as an organic force. Indeed, polemics against the Illuminati and related groups served as occult sources of romanticism. Practical politics also felt the impress of the *Memoirs*. The book helped to inspire the Holy Alliance and incited the post-1815 monarchies in France, Spain, and Italy to adopt reactionary policies.

The *Memoirs* still stand out as "the great classic of conspiracy theory,"[66] "the bible of the secret society mythology and the indispensable foundation of future anti-masonic writing."[67] Even today, although his name is obscure, de Barruel's legacy remains alive, an influence on almost all conspiracist writing on secret societies. In the 1970s alone, his *Memoirs* was republished twice, and a Societé Augustin Barruel came into existence in Lyons.

An important German author contributed to the secret society thesis in the person of Johann August Starck (1741–1816) and his two-volume *Triumph of Philosophy in the Eighteenth Century*.[68] Actually, Starck had supplied de Barruel with reams of information for the third and fourth volumes of *Memoirs Illustrating the History of Jacobinism* but was disappointed in the result, so he put his own pen to paper. Like de Barruel, he argued for an unbroken line of conspirators from the Greek sophists through the Protestants to the Philosophes. He saw Masonic lodges as fronts for the Illuminati and blamed the former far more than did his French colleague.

With Starck's contribution, the British, French, and German intellectual traditions each had its premier conspiracy theorist in place. Henceforth, belief in plots became part of mainstream European political life. Together, Robison, de Barruel, and Starck created a secret society interpretation of history that remains influential and little changed to this day. Some of the specific phobias of the late eighteenth century still endure; more important, a new way of thinking had been launched.

It bears noting who was *not* blamed for the French Revolution as it was taking place: the Jews. While it is difficult to prove a negative, a foremost student of this subject, Léon Poliakov, states without equivocation that "at no time did contemporaries attribute the collapse of the monarchy or the persecution of the Church to a Jewish plot. It was only later . . . that such interpretations sprang up."[69] The reason for this lack of interest in Jews is simple to explain. During the revolutionary and Napoleonic periods, Jews were still largely excluded from society and politics, so little fear existed about them acting as a conspiratorial force. Events of the years after 1789 had importance for anti-Jewish conspiracism not at the time but decades later, when they were retroactively interpreted as signs of a conspiracy. In particular, two developments had lasting importance: the Jewish emancipation, and suspicions that secret societies had caused the French Revolution.

For centuries, Jews had lived in profound isolation from their Christian neighbors, residing in the own quarters, speaking different languages, living according to unfamiliar customs, engaging in alien trades, and pursuing a remarkably separate cultural and spiritual life. Though dispersed over large distances, Jews maintained a common culture with similar institutions, which helped isolated communities sustain their separation from the Christian majority. The longevity of this exclusion depended on both the Jewish and Christian sides' preferring it. Jews saw themselves suffering exile while awaiting redemption and eventual restoration to Zion. Christians tacitly agreed with this outlook, seeing Jews as suffering exile as a punishment for their rejection of Christ. Neither sought more contact with the other than necessary. The life of the ghetto may have been the most complete and enduring isolation of any minority from its surrounding society in all history.

This isolation began to break down in the mid-eighteenth century, in what is known as the Jewish emancipation, a century-long process. As the bonds of the church loosened, both sides took some interest in Jews' joining the mainstream. Jews found European civilization newly attractive, and liberal Christians championed the principle of equal civil rights for all. The Austrian Edict of Toleration of 1781–82 began the process of legally integrating Jews.

The French Revolution had a key role for Jews, as it did for nearly everyone else. Two events stand out. First, in a single decisive step in September 1791, the French National Assembly ended all special legal restrictions on them. This meant that however little Jews participated in the revolution, they directly benefited from it. Some observers, applying the logic of *Cui bono?*, concluded that Jews therefore must have caused the revolution.

Second, when Napoleon Bonaparte convened a group of prominent French Jews to Paris in February 1807 to assure himself of their loyalty and submission, he for no particular reason dubbed this meeting the "Great Sanhedrin," resurrecting the name of a Jewish court in antiquity and since out of use. Unknowingly, he did something fraught with significance, for enemies of Napoleon and the Jews understood this name to confirm the existence of a secret Jewish government throughout the centuries. For some, Napoleon's minor, almost bureaucratic step set off alarm bells and proved a tight nexus between Jews and the revolution. This notion of a secret council would later in the century become a central element in the *Protocols of the Elders of Zion* forgery.

It is noteworthy that decisions taken by the French National Assembly and Napoleon—and *not* by Jews—created the basis for Jews to be seen as an organized and hierarchical community seeking to gain power over Christendom. This set the pattern for the future, when time and again Jews found themselves caught up in a vortex of suspicion not of their own making.

The other major development affecting Jews concerned their connection to secret societies. The first verifiable accusation along this line dates from 1806 and involves no less a personage than Augustin de Barruel. Ostensibly, an Italian army officer named J. B. Simonini (but in reality probably the French political police) wrote a letter to de Barruel from Florence in which he praised the author for his work but asserted that the "Judaic sect" stood behind the secret society conspiracy de Barruel had so extensively documented. Philosophes, Freemasons, Illuminati, and the others plotted the French Revolution on behalf of the Jews. His letter told about Jewish plans to dispossess Christians, prohibit the Christian faith, enslave Christians, and finally set up a Jewish world government.[70]

De Barruel accepted and endorsed these ideas, then expanded on them by conjuring up a ubiquitous organization with branches in the smallest hamlets of western Europe and reporting to a council ultimately controlled by Jews. He worked out the logistics of this invisible empire in some detail (including its use of codes and relay runners) and is said to have written a major manuscript on the Jewish conspiracy, but then to have decided not to go public with it, fearing that to do so would lead to a general massacre of Jews. Instead, he provided discreet warnings to the security forces and the church. Whatever reluctance he showed, de Barruel's belief in a Jewish conspiracy did become public knowledge; coming from the author of *Memoirs Illustrating the History of Jacobinism*, it had great impact. Within a few years, many writers picked up on the idea of Jews as the revolution's ultimate plotters and as the masters of an invisible empire. The Antisemitic League in France (founded in 1889), for example, made its central premise the claim that Jews seized power in their country by means of the French Revolution.

In accusing Jews of manipulating secret societies, de Barruel took a step that had major ramifications. He made an all-important leap of logic when he determined that Jews sought world power not only in the messianic age but also right away. Further, despite having written long and impressive analyses of the Philosophes, Freemasons, and Illuminati, he imbued Jews with even more power than any of these groups, and so implied that Jews, not those others, were the most dangerous conspirators. By connecting them to the French Revolution, de Barruel brought Jews into the thick of nineteenth-century conspiracist politics, thereby paving the way for the antisemitic ideology of the 1870s. Finally, de Barruel's associating Jews with Freemasons permanently and firmly linked these two groups together in the conspiracist imagination, and so set the stage for their eventual conflation.

De Barruel did much to ensure that Jews—previously at the fringes of public life—became a prime object of European conspiracist phobia. From this time on, they stood increasingly accused of manipulating Europe's most central events. Poliakov sees in de Barruel's accusation against the Jews a possible "primary source" for the *Protocols*.[71] Norman Cohn attributes his views an even wider importance: "In its modern form the myth of the Jewish world conspiracy can be traced back to ... the Abbé Barruel."[72]

It is hard to overstate de Barruel's role in the growth of conspiracism. As brilliant as he was eccentric, he did for conspiracy theories what Adam Smith did for economics and Karl von Clausewitz did for military strategy by turning a motley of ideas into a systematic and intellectually rigorous topic of study—even if (in de Barruel's case) a wholly fictitious one. Most remarkably, this evil man and his wicked ideas did much to create both the secret society and the antisemitic myths, shaping them into the potent forces that more than a century after his death would profoundly injure Europe and the rest of the world. It is no exaggeration to state that his ideas laid some of the intellectual foundations for the views that eventually culminated in the Soviet and Nazi regimes.

FIVE

FLORESCENCE, 1815–1945

The century and three decades from the Congress of Vienna to the end of World War II marks the core of the conspiracist experience. The paranoid style moved during this period from speculation to practice, from fear to action. By the 1940s it had acquired a central role in some of the most important and terrible events in the human experience.

THE NINETEENTH CENTURY: MATURATION

There is only one power in Europe, and that is Rothschild.
A MID-NINETEENTH-CENTURY DICTUM[1]

Masonry and Marxism rule the world today.
CHARLES COUGHLIN[2]

Although remembered as a time of skepticism about the value of subversion and of honor codes ("Gentlemen do not read each other's mail"),[3] the period from 1815 to 1914 was in fact a time of much growth in the conspiracist mentality. Three main developments took place: the secret society myth spawned a great number of actual secret societies, it grew into a conspiracy theory about Anglo-American imperialism, and anti-Jewish ideas evolved into conspiratorial antisemitism. Developments during this era also revealed the complementary uses of conspiracism by Right and Left. In addition, conspiracism developed in original and significant ways in the United States.

The welter of conspiracy theories about the French Revolution had very different significance for Right and Left. The Right accepted conspiracism as it appeared: as a description of the evil works carried out by secret societies. It feared the Templars, Freemasons, Illuminati, and their offshoots. The Left then embraced these fearful specters and turned them on their head; if reactionaries fervently believed in the existence of powerful secret societies on the Left, who were progressives to deny it? Instead, they accepted the secret society myth, but with a positive spin. In a strange reversal, the Left adopted the Right's fevered exaggerations, then transformed its devils into heroic figures who stood up to the state and Church, kept bright the flame of enlightened learning, and cleared the way for revolution.

Knowing its own limits in the face of powerful states, the Left was no little impressed by a group like the Templars, which not only succeeded in maintaining its secrets for nearly five centuries but which kept anti-monarchic passions alive through all that time. Then, in an audacious move, the Left made these mythical groups an inspiration for its own activities. Just as the Jacobins supposedly plotted out the entire French Revolution, their successors turned to conspiracies to destroy the reactionary Russian and German states. Revolutionaries like Filippo Buonarroti seized upon the Templar-Freemason-Illuminati prototype of the conspiracist imagination and made it a model for their own, very real, organizations. Thus did the Left set about emulating the secret societies that existed only in the minds of rightist paranoids.

As networks of surreptitious organizations came into existence, fantasy became real. If secret societies made up of Templars, Freemasons, and Illuminati remained imaginary, actual political movements did take on conspiratorial forms. As secret societies attempted to cooperate across national boundaries, they confirmed the deepest fears of conspiracy theorists. Conspiracy theorists no longer lived in cloud-cuckoo-land; their fears, once imaginary, had become real; the Left had, obligingly, followed their script. The Right's fear of secret societies had become a self-fulfilled prophecy. Obsessions became self-validating: life imitated art. J. M. Roberts explains this subtle development: "[T]hough secret societies existed in large numbers in Western Europe between 1750 and 1830 and strove to influence events, their main importance was what people believed about them. This always mattered more than what they did and their numbers and practical effectiveness were in no way proportionate to the myth's power."[4]

Then, to close the circle, police reports and confessions about real secret societies appeared retrospectively to confirm all the fears about Freemasons and Illuminati: and if these were valid in the nineteenth century, why not in the eighteenth too? The circle closed especially tightly when conspirators, inspired by the sensational programs found in de Barruel et al., proclaimed their goals to be the same as those of imaginary secret societies. For example, a defector from the Carbonari announced that his organization's goals were precisely those of the Illuminati: the global destruction of religion and state.

The real secret societies divide into three main categories: socialist, nationalist, and anarchist. The conspiratorial Left came into being with François ("Gracchus") Babeuf (1760–97), organizer of a 1796 effort to turn the French Revolution in the direction of radical egalitarianism, the Conspiracy of Equals. Inspired by Babeuf, Louis Auguste Blanqui (1805–81) coined the phrase "dictatorship of the proletariat" and devoted his life to achieving it through conspiratorial means; toward this end, he wrote books, went to jail, fled to exile, and fought governments.

In 1879, thirty Russian radicals founded a conspiratorial group, the People's Will (*Narodnaya Volya*), with the goal of bringing down the tsarist regime. This they failed to do, but they did assassinate Alexander II. "It was the first political terrorist organization in history and the model for all subsequent organizations of this kind in Russia and elsewhere."[5] People's Will had lasting importance. It predicated its actions on intellectuals, deciding what the "people" wanted better than they themselves did, and thereby created a new basis for conspiratorial violence as well as the methods that Lenin would later draw on to organize the Bolshevik putsch.

Clandestine nationalist organizations proliferated throughout Europe in the nineteenth century, spurred by a vivid sense of the injustice implicit to rule by foreigners or an ethnic minority. Associated with the overthrow of a stifling order, these groups imbued conspiracy with a romantic quality. Pierre Joseph Briot (1771–1827) relied on his Masonic experience to establish the Carbonari, the murky opposition to Napoleon in Italy that started sometime before 1810 and later served as the backbone of Italy's nationalist movement. Giuseppe Mazzini (1805–72), the founder of Young Italy, wrote a passage that summed up its outlook: "There is no more sacred thing in the world than the duty of a conspirator, who becomes an avenger of humanity and the apostle of permanent natural laws." The two Young Bosnians who conspired to assassinate Archduke Ferdinand later adopted this passage and drew sustenance from it.[6]

Filippo Buonarroti, an Italian, was the outstanding nationalist conspirator—a man who organized secret societies across much of Europe. His presence looms large over nearly five decades of conspiratorial activity, starting with the French Revolution (he participated in Babeuf's Conspiracy of Equals) and lasting long after his death. Although Buonarroti achieved few of his goals, he became the bogeyman of the paranoid minded, doing "more than anyone to give reality to the spectre of the universal conspiracy."[7]

These and other conspiratorial groups created an atmosphere rife with tension. Scholars dispute exactly when it reached its apex. One historian sees the Restoration as "the moment when the myth of the secret societies came to a climax" and deems it "at the peak of its strength" between 1815 and 1848.[8] Another notes that "the secret society mania . . . was if anything rather more pervasive at the end of the nineteenth century than thirty or forty years earlier."[9] The latter is probably the more accurate assessment, if only because the number of real conspiracies picked up with the century's passing. Consider assassination: conspirators found the murder of political leaders to be effective, and they made use of it with increasing frequency through the century. One listing shows a mere 19 political assassinations in the 76 years before 1867; in contrast, 69 assassinations took place in the subsequent 46 years,[10] a sixfold increase.

Until the middle of the nineteenth century, fears of a world conspiracy were largely confined to secret societies. At that time, however, two offshoots emerged that would eventually push the anti-secret society fears to the side: anti-imperialism and antisemitism. What began with an exclusive focus on Freemasons and other private groups eventually came to include public institutions as well. This change not only brought the Left in as a full partner in the conspiracist mentality but later also extended to the Right as well (think of the militiamen in the United States today).

Curiously, these fears of government focused almost entirely on Great Britain and its daughter country, the United States; other states barely registered.

This line of thinking transfers the clandestine nature of the secret society to the state: MI5 and the CIA become the new brotherhoods, complete with handshakes and pledges of silence until death. Secret societies are thought sometimes to take over great democratic powers. Thus did Germans interpret Woodrow Wilson's Fourteen Points, an outline he offered in 1918 to define the settlement following World War I, as a "Masonic peace program."[11] Or they saw Freemasonry as "the General Staff of Marxism."[12] As befits leaders of clandestine organizations, Anglo-American leaders make self-serving deals among themselves. During World War II, "it was believed by many Indians, and quite sincerely, that the help of the United States to begin with, and finally its participation, were secured by Mr. Churchill by bribing President Roosevelt."[13] Russians suspect George Bush of making a deal with Mikhail Gorbachev in 1989: get rid of communist rule, and communists can take over state property, ensuring their own wealth. Two years later, Bush personally profited from the Kuwait war: "two large companies owned by the sons of President Bush and his secretary of state, James Baker, have been established. . . . Bush was rewarded with a ton of gold, which he took back with him [from his trip to Kuwait in 1993]. This gold is his own."[14]

How did conspiracism make this leap so that it included fear of entire regimes? Two quite different sources fed this fear: a historic mistrust of Anglo-Americans, and Leninist ideology.

MISTRUST OF ANGLO-AMERICANS. A French rivalry with Great Britain that goes back to the Hundred Years' War (1337–1457) also included an impulse to blame sundry problems on London. "Perfidious Albion," a French expression, summed up the mistrust of a conniving, duplicitous, conspiratorial Britain. With the French Revolution, this antipathy reached the precision of conspiracy theories, as French leaders on all sides found it useful to blame England for their troubles. Even as royal circles muttered about English money fueling the revolution, Maximilien de Robespierre and the other revolutionaries developed an elaborate conspiracy theory (which Napoleon later perfected). To ensure its global empire, they said, London had to keep its continental rivals off the high seas; this it did by stirring up trouble for those rivals at home. This conspiracist explanation conveniently opened the way for governments to condemn all dissent as agentry for Great Britain.

These conspiracy theories of the 1790s had great staying power, persisting through the imperialist rivalries of the nineteenth century and even through the British and French alliances of the world wars. As late as 1954, Paris saw Iraqi maneuvers against Syria as an underhanded effort by London to expand its sphere of influence. A decade later and still in the same spirit, Charles de Gaulle resorted to a mildly conspiracist pretext to shut the door on British efforts to join the Common Market.

Over time, fears of Perfidious Albion spread to other countries, including Russia and the United States. In Germany, a sterling list of intellectuals repeated the argument that London caused European conflicts in order to profit from it and step closer to its goal of world domination. No less a personage than the philosopher Immanuel Kant (1724–1804) promoted Robespierre's conspiracy theory portraying England as an avaricious and aggressive force that deployed virtually unlimited means to achieve its aim of conquest and self-enrichment. Friedrich List (1789–1846), the economist and advocate of protectionist doctrines, interpreted British liberalism as a means to attain financial control of its rivals, a theme that later became standard fare in Germany. The historian and publicist Heinrich von Treitschke (1834–96) saw Britain as a parasite that spread war for its own profit. Eventually this view became widespread.

Although Germans had developed a similar fear and mistrust about the United States by the 1820s, it was not until a century later, in the aftermath of World War I, that it turned into a conspiracist attitude.[15] The German Right and Left both discerned the awesome behind-the-scenes power of "finance capital" over the policies of the United States; indeed, Woodrow Wilson entered the war to ensure the repayment of loans to a few Wall Street bankers. The Communist party deemed Wilson's peace plan a conspiracy to strengthen the winners' economies at Germany's expense, while the Dawes Plan of 1924 (which reduced German reparations) was denounced as a conspiracy to enslave Germany permanently. The League of Nations served as a clever mechanism to eviscerate German nationalism.

LENINISM. The suspicion that wealthy elements of society use the state to forward their own selfish purposes is an old one. In the phrase of Thomas More (1478–1535), "Everywhere do I perceive a certain conspiracy of rich men seeking their own advantage under the name and pretext of the commonwealth." Around 1900, however, this suspicion became the basis of a new and eventually powerful conspiracist ideology.

The Leninist corpus contains a conspiracy theory at its heart: financiers and manufacturers group together to extract riches not rightfully due them by keeping down workers' wages and controlling the government. The second point is of particular interest here. In capitalist countries, the state is said to represent business interests, which it helps by repressing the working class, offering hidden subsidies to corporations, creating loopholes to allow cartels, and funneling tax money to businesses. This subservience also extends to foreign policy. In particular, the capitalist need for inexpensive raw materials and labor, combined with their desire for monopolistic control of markets, drives imperialist states to fight wars of expansion. In a 1902 study of lasting importance, John Atkinson Hobson (1858–1940), a leftist English economist, argued that while imperialism makes little sense for Great Britain as a whole, it greatly benefits "certain sectional interests that usurp control of the national resources and use them for their private gain." This occurs because "certain well-organised business interests are able to outweigh the weak, diffused interest of the community." Hobson argues that, in keeping with business needs, "the modern foreign policy of Great Britain has been primarily a struggle for profitable markets of investment"—and the same goes for all the other imperialist states. He concludes by arguing that the financiers control diplomacy among European states in the European theater as well.[16]

Hobson's writings much influenced Vladimir Ilyich Lenin (1870–1924) and through him the European Left and Soviet state propaganda. (Is this yet another, particularly subtle, form of British imperialism?) In his 1916 study, *Imperialism*, Lenin describes imperialism as a system whereby the capitalist states, at the behest of monopolist combines, expand to take over the world; thanks to their success, less than 10 percent of the world's population "plunder the whole world" by clipping coupons from bonds. The key point here is that "monopoly capitalists" run the foreign policies of their governments by creating an "epoch of finance capital and of monopolies which introduce everywhere the striving for domination."[17]

The Left thus reinterprets some of the oldest activities of government as conspiracies. War results not from ambitious monarchs or conflicting nationalisms but from the greed of capitalists. The centuries-old European drive for geographical expansion turns into a conspiracy of investors. Beginning with collusion among manufacturers, the Left ended by postulating that all the governments of Europe engaged in conspiracies. It needed only a few steps, in other words, to go from a conspiracy of secret societies to one of states. Hobson and Lenin thus added a new dimension to the conspiracist imagination, leaving the confines of a clandestine organization or a religious minority dreaming of power, now to include the world's strongest states. Since about 1900, conspirators are thought already to be in power.

This change had several implications. It had to precede the extension of conspiracism from the Right (which controlled nearly all governments) to the Left (which opposed them). It also heightened the fear of conspiracy in two ways. First, His Majesty's government is more to worry about than a group of fly-by-night plotters. Freemason lodges are more worrisome as capitalist gathering spots for mapping out state policy than as hotbeds of dissent and change. Second, the Left put the fear of conspiracy into an ideological context, thereby magnifying it. "Whereas the right wing sounded somewhat quaint when speaking of 'Anglo-Saxon' world domination, the Left modernized the subject with the concept of imperialism."[18]

More recently, as workers have prospered in the industrial democracies, the class-based analysis of Marxism-Leninism has become less and less convincing. To salvage the basic notion of a business-driven conspiracy, the Left has needed to amend its old doctrines. In the most persuasive of these updates, *dependencia* theory, thinkers like André Gunder Frank and Immanuel Wallerstein substitute geography for class. They sketch out a systematic effort by industrial states to control the economics of weaker countries and argue that Western wealth derives from the exploitation of poor countries.[19] Another updating, the theory of organized capitalism, sees "an economic order organized in cartels" that is highly concentrated and protected by state intervention.[20] It too perpetuates the notion of a business plot.

The United Kingdom from the start had a unique place in the constellation of nonsocialist conspirators because of historic French suspicions, sharpened by Robespierre's thesis of British sabotage, plus Leninist theories of a business plot. Eventually, when Britain in its post-World War II weakness could no longer shoulder all these suspicions, the leftist conspiracy theory shifted easily to the United States.

In similar fashion, anti-Jewish bias has changed with the times. Although it dates back over two millennia, much longer than the fear of secret societies, conspiratorial antisemitism originated just over a century ago. It has had two main forms, rightist and leftist.

ON THE RIGHT. The process of emancipation that began in earnest with the French Revolution continued for decades. Not until the 1860s did Jews enjoy legal equality in most of Europe (and even then, not in the Russian Empire or parts of the Balkans). Jewish integration was usually not the result of popular sentiment, but accomplished by an edict from on high, so it rested on weak foundations. In itself, the emancipation did not arouse alarm, but as substantial numbers of Jews escaped the ghettos of Europe and joined the mainstream of European life, they quickly shed their centuries-old reputation for poverty and backwardness. As Jews acquired wealth and a disproportionately visible role in the public arena, they became a prime focus for the paranoid imagination. Jews might abandon the traits that had made them so very conspicuously different through the ghetto centuries, but now their success at modern activities made them newly conspicuous in a different way.

Some Christians, mostly rightists, looked fearfully at this integration, imagining it as a step toward Jewish domination. They responded by reviving old Christian fears of Jewish messianism, which they now found newly credible. Jews, hitherto isolated and weak, for the first time became plausible candidates as world hegemons. Initially they were seen conjoined to a secret society, especially the Masonic; before long, Jews were seen as either conspiring on their own or manipulating others, such as Freemasons, imperialists, or totalitarians.

A conspiratorial antisemitic literature came into existence about 1870. "In the Jewish Cemetery in Prague," written pseudonymously by a German, Hermann Goedsche, and published in 1868, was an imaginary report on a once-a-century meeting of the twelve tribes of Israel, detailing their plots to take over the world.[21] Though unabashedly fiction, by 1872 this tale was transmuted into fact, and it became all the scarier with the telling and retelling. Over time, the many speakers coalesced into a single chief rabbi. His supposed presentation, "The Rabbi's Speech," became a mainstay of antisemitic literature.

These themes crystallized in the *Protocols of the Elders of Zion,* a long pamphlet that appeared around the turn of the century. Called by one author "the world's strangest book,"[22] the *Protocols* purports to be the authentic transcript of the first Zionist Congress convened in Basel, Switzerland, in August 1897 by Theodor Herzl, as taken down by a tsarist spy who attended the meetings. In fact, the *Protocols* is a forgery. Many details point to this, from the history of the manuscript to the structure of the text to its many contradictions. Its writing took place in Paris, the product of many hands, about the time of the Dreyfus Affair (1894–99), and most probably toward the end of that period. Cobbled out of such disparate sources as Goedsche's obscure novel and a liberal French political satire,[23] the *Protocols* appears to have been sponsored by the chief of the Okhrana office in Paris, Pyotr Ivanovich Rachkovsky.[24] His purpose for the document seems not to have been to influence public opinion but to prove to Tsar Nicholas II that Russian liberals were agents of the Jews.

While the *Protocols* deals with a number of topics—the ugliness of liberalism, how Jews will gain power, and what they will do with it—the plans of Jewish leaders to dominate the world take center stage. These are intricate and long-range. The Jewish leadership boasts that it is "invincible" and explains its goal of putting together a "Super-Government Administration" that will "subdue all the nations" in pursuit of the ultimate objective of "sovereignty over all the world."[25]

The publishing history is obscure, but the *Protocols'* first printing appears to have been in serial form in Russian in *Znamya*, a St. Petersburg newspaper, in issues published between 26 August and 7 September 1903. The first book version came out two years later as an appendix to the third edition of a book by Professor Sergei A. Nilus of Moscow, *The Great in the Small: Antichrist Considered as an Imminent Political Possibility*,[26] in which he told of his conversion to Orthodox Christianity. Although the forgery received a strong initial reception (the metropolitan of Moscow had it read in all the churches), it then languished, answering needs yet not widely felt. Only with the dislocations of World War I and the Russian Revolution did a receptive environment develop for the *Protocols'* messages about the evils of liberalism and a Jewish drive to dominate the world.

The great importance of the *Protocols* lies in its permitting antisemites to reach beyond their traditional circles and find a large international audience, a process that continues to this day.[27] The forgery poisoned public life wherever it appeared; it was "self-generating; a blueprint that migrated from one conspiracy to another."[28] The book's vagueness—almost no names, dates, or issues are specified—has been one key to this wide-ranging success. The purportedly Jewish authorship also helps to make the book more convincing. Its embrace of contradiction—that to advance, Jews use all tools available, including capitalism and communism, philo-Semitism and antisemitism, democracy and tyranny—made it possible for the *Protocols* to reach out to all: rich and poor, Right and Left, Christian and Muslim, American and Japanese.

The *Protocols* and the other texts of conspiratorial antisemitism recurringly emphasize certain themes, especially the ubiquity, size, organization, and near-success of Jewish plotting.

• Jews always scheme. Antisemites imagine the existence of a cosmic battle in which Jews at all times and places engage in a clandestine drive for power. Heinrich Himmler saw his SS troops fighting a battle that had started with the origins of human life. The astonishing title of a tract by one of Hitler's early mentors, *Bolshevism from Moses to Lenin*,[29] captures this idea of continuity: Moses was a communist, Lenin a Jew. Another book title referred to a "two-thousand year conspiracy system."[30] A Canadian author blithely states that "The Long Range Plan for the ultimate subjugation of Spain started, as in other countries, soon after the death of Christ."[31] The conspiracy to install a "Jewish caesar" explains why Jews were persecuted in Egypt and Persia. In recent times, the Irish nationalist Eamon de Valera was said to be a Portuguese Jew, and Jews funded the Irish nationalist movement. Albert Einstein's theory of relativity amounted to Jewish science and extended the battle beyond the planet earth.

• Jews are everywhere. Weishaupt and Cagliostro were Jewish. One Russian antisemite claims that Hitler, Eichmann, Goebbels, Hess, and Streicher were all Jewish; only Goering was not. Franco, Churchill, and Roosevelt were too.[32] American antisemites in the 1930s insisted that Jews constituted 40 percent of the American population (the true figure was about one-tenth as much) and that Franklin Delano Roosevelt (real name: Rosenfelt) and all his cabinet members were Jews, not to speak of the entire Supreme Court, General MacArthur, and the leadership of the Post Office, the police, and even the Boy Scouts. In a bizarre echo, the Soviet media thirty years later pronounced the United States home to 20 to 25 million Zionists, who made up 70 percent of the country's lawyers, 60 percent of its physicists, and 43 percent of its industrialists; in addition, Zionists owned 80 percent of news agencies around the globe.[33] The Nazis invested huge efforts in proving the Jewish origins of every significant figure in the Soviet Union—as well as their aides, down to the typists. In brief, anyone who disagrees with an antisemite—even a fellow antisemite—gets dubbed a Jew.

• Jews are behind every institution. Jews founded all the other secret societies, including the Templars, Freemasons, and Illuminati. Henry Ford discerned a Jewish control of "Gentile Fronts" running the financial world. Jews founded Christianity and continue to control its institutions, including the papacy.

• Jews obey a central authority, the shadowy "Elders." This collective authority maintains strict control over all Jews at all times. It has taken various forms over two millennia: the Sanhedrin in ancient times, the rabbis in the medieval era, the Alliance Israélite Universelle in the nineteenth century, and several organizations (the World Zionist Congress, the American Jewish Joint Distribution Committee, and the American Israel Public Affairs Committee) in the twentieth. The Alliance Israélite Universelle, a Paris-based charitable institution with an innocuous charitable mission, boasted a name that sounded to conspiracy theorists like the confirmation of their nightmares. Looking to the future, some conspiratorial antisemites believe that Jews hope to crown their own king to rule the earth.

• Jews are close to success. Antisemites point to a number of key Jewish (or formerly Jewish) figures of the past two centuries who either reduced Christian strength or empowered Jews. The Rothschilds used their financial hold over governments to make them go to war with each other; Karl Marx founded an atheistic ideology and movement;[34] Benjamin Disraeli directed the resources of the British empire; Theodor Herzl founded Zionism, a program of Jewish nationalism; Leon Trotsky helped bring Bolshevism to power; Sigmund Freud's psychoanalysis endorsed irrationalism; and Henry Kissinger put the resources of the United States at Israel's disposal.

One's own country often remains the only bulwark against Jewish hegemony. In the 1930s, French antisemites portrayed France alone standing up to le péril juif. In the 1960s, Soviet counterparts presented Jews as already holding power in the West, leaving the Soviet Union as almost the only remaining barrier to their world conquest. A three-volume Japanese forgery prominently advertised in 1993 was titled *Get Japan, The Last Enemy: The Jewish Protocols for World Domination.*[35]

ON THE LEFT. Although more central to the Right's message than the Left's, antisemitism was very much present among progressives in the nineteenth century. Militant atheists (following Voltaire's example) blamed Jews for having spawned Christianity. Sophisticates recoiled against the way Orthodox Jews live and look. Liberal nationalists worried about the Jews' having an only partial loyalty to the nation. Ex-Jews (like Karl Marx) adopted antisemitism as an instrument of their own assimilation. But more important than any of these reasons was that socialists frequently made Jews part of the ruling class, thereby including them among the exploiters who must be fought. As Jews became financiers, large-scale merchants, and captains of industry, the Left portrayed them as middle-men, compradors, and other economic "parasites" who introduced capitalist innovations and controlled high finance.

For one or another of these reasons, virtually every major figure in the early history of socialism—including Friedrich Engels, Charles Fourier, Ferdinand Lassalle, Marx, and Joseph Proudhon—showed a marked antipathy to Jews. This attitude imbued the Left with a bias that would come into its own in the Soviet Union.

In this context, Mayer Anselm Rothschild (1743–1812) and his descendants played an outsized role. The elder Rothschild founded a financial firm in Frankfurt that his five talented sons took over and expanded to Vienna, Naples, Paris, and London. The Rothschilds' ability to work across borders, even as they allied with mutually hostile governments, their role in the development of a modern industrial economy, plus their great eminence and their extraordinary and visible wealth, made them an archetype of Jewish power that seemingly transcended national boundaries. The family's success raised the specter of a Jewish drive to dominate all Europe, perhaps the world. It also earned them the criticism of revolutionaries who pictured them as colluding with the forces of reaction. Most of the late nineteenth-century fortunes (such as those of the Rockefeller, Carnegie, and Harriman) get traced back to the Rothschilds. (But, curiously, not the late-twentieth-century ones: Bill Gates and Warren Buffett may be too new to be synthesized within the conspiracy theory.)

The most important consequence of this left-wing conspiracy may concern the accusation that the brothers Rothschild instigated wars to sell arms and make loans to both sides, and so to profit from the misery of others. First heard with reference to the Battle of Waterloo in 1815, the calumny quickly became endemic on the Left. J. A. Hobson argued in 1902 that if "the house of Rothschild and its connexions set their face against" war, no European state could defy them,[36] implying that it prefers war.

With time, this accusation of warmongering passed to the Right as well, so that the Rothschilds eventually served as a bogey for extremists of all persuasions. Then accusations against them were extended to Jews in general. During the Boer War (1899–1902), much commentary in Britain blamed the fighting on "imperialist Judaism." By World War I, this explanation also attracted rightist support (Hitler made it central to his argument). The idea that Jews profited from both sides in a conflict resurfaced prominently in the Iraq-Iran war of 1980–88, when the central

Jewish leadership was accused of "prolonging the war by its own design."[37] Today the Nation of Islam maintains that Jews "appear, seemingly, in every conflict as suppliers of either *or both* sides."[38]

This new form of Jew-hatred contained dangers yet greater than its prior versions. If Jews, now emancipated and at least partially assimilated, can be thought to wield such awesome power, then they pose a far greater threat in paranoid eyes. Just as Lenin was inspired by the Left's turning the anti-secret society into anti-imperialism, so was Hitler inspired by conspiratorial antisemitism. The rise of these ideologies brought conflagration closer. Before examining the bloody climax of conspiracism in the world wars of the twentieth century, however, we take a detour to the United States, that most remote and favored of countries that ought not to have a history of conspiracism but does.

Americans are, in the view of the eminent historian David Brion Davis, "curiously obsessed" with conspiracies.[39] Their objects, he notes, have included fears "of the French Illuminati, of Federalist oligarchs, of Freemasons, of the money power, of the Catholic Church, of the Slave Power, of foreign anarchists, of Wall Street bankers, of Bolsheviks, of internationalist Jews, of Fascists, of Communists, and of Black Power."[40] As this listing suggests, the United States both offered a smaller-scale version of what happened in Europe (fearing the Illuminati, Freemasons, Catholics, and Bolsheviks) but also came up with its own enemies (Slave Power, Black Power). In general, though, Americans weaned themselves from European influence over time, and their conspiracy theories increasingly differed from those of Europe in terms of institutions and content. It is striking to note how the same shapes and themes took hold in a relatively libertarian and nonhierarchcal society with (at least until the New Deal) a small and fragmented government. How did this happen?

In the Enlightenment period, American colonists showed an endemic suspicion of petty conspiracies by outside powers. Bernard Bailyn, an authority on this era, remarks that "the fear of conspiracy against constituted authority was built into the very structure of politics,"[41] and there is much evidence to support this view. The Salem witch trials of 1692 and the French and Indian War of 1755–63 resulted from such fears. Bailyn writes that overwhelming evidence of a conspiracy "was signaled to the colonists after 1763, and it was this above all else that in the end propelled them into Revolution."[42] The Stamp Act of 1765, which taxed virtually all documents, as well as newspapers, playing cards, and the like, was interpreted in the American colonies as a British conspiracy to take direct control over them. Why? Because the very resentment of this tax in the colonies suggested an intention by the British authorities to stimulate a rebellion, thereby allowing them to reduce the colonies militarily.

By similar logic, many colonists saw the Boston Massacre of 1770 as a planned event, "a deep-laid and desperate plan of imperial despotism."[43] Americans even became obsessed by fears that the British government sought to reduce the colonists to slavery. In the words of Samuel Seabury, leaders of the independence movement asserted "over, and over, and over again" that the British had laid a regular plan to this end.[44] These and other factors convinced the colonists of King George III's intent to undermine their freedoms and chain their economy to Britain's; to prevent this nonexistent plot, they went to war. During the War of Independence, Americans held British leaders personally responsible for a troubled relationship. The British reciprocated these worries. In the words of a historian, "the idea of conspiracy proved as appealing to ministers [in London] as it had to [royal] officials in America."[45]

The assumption of conspiracy was nearly universal during the early national and antebellum periods, when it "generated countersubversive discourse that contributed to the making of the new republic's culture."[46] George Washington warned of "the mischiefs of foreign Intrigue" in his Farewell Address of 1796.[47] President John Adams alerted his countrymen to the "hostile designs and insidious acts" coming from abroad,[48] and did something about it in 1798 by passing the Alien, the Alien Enemies, and the Sedition acts. Alexander Hamilton described Adams as presuming that "every citizen who is his enemy, is the confederate of one or another of those foreign powers" ostensibly endangering the United States.[49]

Fear of the Slave Power, an alleged Confederate plan to seize the Federal government and ban free labor, was a significant factor in the Northerners' readiness to go to war against the South. On the other side, Southern whites developed a conspiracy theory about Northerners' instructing slaves to rebel and kill their masters. These mutual fears helped bring on the Civil War.

Americans had established political institutions to combat perceived conspiratorial threats in the early nineteenth century, before Europeans had done so. The Antimasonic party, a prominent political organization between 1827 and 1836, was perhaps the most singular of these, created as it was for the express purpose of combating Freemasonry. The suspicious disappearance in September 1826 of one William Morgan, a renegade Freemason, and his presumed murder, brought the party into exis-tence. Building on the ready-made ideas of Robison and de Barruel and dwelling on alleged crimes committed in lodges, Antimasons claimed to uncover a conspiracy to overthrow the existing order in the United States and replace it with a Masonic monarchy. They also worried about a "Masonic way to a Masonic heaven, and blood and massacre and destruction to all who subscribe not to the support of the Monarch."[50] In 1832, a minister called Freemasonry the "darkest and deepest plot that ever was formed in this wicked world against the true God."[51] The party enjoyed some electoral successes, especially in the elections of 1832 (when it polled a quarter of the New England vote), but its blatantly inaccurate fears (e.g., that the Boston Freemasons had amassed an arsenal to outfit an army of two thousand; an inspection turned up forty-three swords and thirty-four spittoons) with time caused the party to collapse.

The American party, commonly known as the Know-Nothings, emerged from an elusive collection of secret societies in response to increased Catholic immigration to the United States at midcentury. Ini-tially a secret society, complete with initiation ceremonies and secret passwords, the Know-Nothings insisted that nonmembers were to know nothing of the organization (hence the name). Running on an anti-Catholic platform, it quickly emerged as a force and made its mark in the elections of 1854, electing governors, legislatures, or both, in seven states, only to collapse just as swiftly by 1860. Its demise did not mean the end of anti-Catholic sentiments, however. The American Protective Association, at one point claiming two and a half million followers, hewed to terrible conspiracy theories about Catholics, as did the Ku Klux Klan and other organizations.

If more liberty and less inherited privilege did not curb conspiracism among Americans, they did stay aloof from European-style content, perhaps because the American identity builds not on shared ancestry (which excludes Jews) but on shared ideals (which includes them). Further, in a country of so many ethnicities, none of them naturally becomes a central focus. Instead, Americans developed indigenous conspiracy theories expressing an abiding concern with the violation of their ideals of democ-racy. The ultimate horror lies in elite power—a small, unelected minority representing un-American interests that takes over the Federal government and uses it against the people—such as the Slave Power, the Money Power, or the Mormons. This inclination points to two distinctive qualities of American conspiracism: populism and fear of one-worldism. The populist (or nativist) tradition sees a conspiracy carried out by big business, big government, and big labor. William Jennings Bryan (1860–1925) was perhaps the outstanding populist. Blaming the problems of farmers and miners on Wall Street and European capital, he nearly rode a campaign against Money Power in 1896 to the White House. Other outstanding populists include the Louisiana politician Huey Long (1893–1935), Father Charles Coughlin, and Patrick Buchanan.

One-world phobia grew out of a sense of American exceptionalism: we have it so good here that others must seek to steal our happiness. The country's global significance implies that its opponents must be correspondingly evil. "The enemy's mission, like that of America itself, was universal in scope."[52] This fear translates into an abiding concern that some group of foreigners, helped by traitorous Americans, plots to take over the government of the United States. The theme runs through American conspiracism. The 1790s saw alarm about the Bavarian Illuminati, the Know-Nothings worried about the pope, the Red Scare of 1919–20 and McCarthyism worried about the Soviet Union, and the United Nations is today's worry. In the world war period, however, this line of thinking did little to help Americans concentrate on the dangers posed by real conspirators in Russia and Germany.

THE WORLD WARS: IN POWER

Other centuries have only dabbled in conspiracy like amateurs. It is our century which has established conspiracy as a system of thought and a method of action.
SERGE MOSCOVICI[53]

The three decades after 1914 witnessed the apogee of conspiracist fears and influence. The end of World War I left the great powers of Europe, Germany most of all, devastated; at the same time, revolution in Russia prompted widespread anxieties. These twin disasters, plus the widespread suffering and the massive dislocation they caused, spawned an environment of deprivation and anxiety uniquely favorable to world conspiracy theories. The antisemitic and anti-secret society traditions, hitherto little more than hothouse growths, now developed with the most consequential totalitarian movements of modern times, the communist and fascist.

Conspiracism reached the apex of its importance, helping to cause a magnitude of destruction unparalleled in human history. Indeed, the conspiracist mentality had a prominent role in many of the many tragedies of this period, each of which took the lives of millions: the programmed Soviet famine of 1932–34, the Soviet terror of 1937–38, the Jewish Holocaust, and the Eastern Front of World War II.

Blaming the Jews increased dramatically after World War I. The war itself evinced a variety of conspiracy theories. Throughout the West, but in Germany most of all, the unparalleled disaster of the trenches required explanation. How could these most civilized countries engage year after year in such brutal combat with each other? Antisemites had the answer. As defeat loomed in Germany, the Right asserted that conflict harmed all sides except the Jews, whom they accused of provoking the war, benefiting from it, extending it, and then causing Germany to lose it. Jews had to be involved in so great a catastrophe, for no one else was clever and ruthless enough. Only Jews had ambitions so great that the war would serve their interests. Surprisingly large numbers of Europeans found this a convincing explanation.

Russia's revolution and civil war then made things worse, as alarmed rightists portrayed the new Bolshevik government as a major step toward Jewish world power. In addition to identifying virtually the entire communist elite as Jewish, which it was not, this myth operated against the backdrop of the increasingly fevered atmosphere of the Romanov dynasty's final days (vehement statements by Rasputin; the tsar's reading the *Protocols*; the tsaritsa's placing her favorite charm, the swastika, all over the Romanovs' final residence). Jews were then accused of killing the tsar and his family. These circumstances help explain why the White, or anti-Soviet, forces massacred over one hundred thousand Jews in southern Russia between 1918 and 1920—probably the largest number of Jewish killings before the Nazi Holocaust.

Then, primarily through the *Protocols of the Elders of Zion*, the Whites spread these charges to an international audience. In a desperate bid to involve the outside world in their battle against the Bolshevik regime, Russian émigrés pressed the *Protocols* on West Europeans: this issue concerns you, they insisted, for if you do not act soon, the Jewish conspiracy will bring cataclysm to your country. Their account was full of specifics about individual Jewish bankers (Jacob Schiff of New York, in particular) and the precise amounts they spent on fomenting the revolution. Alfred

Rosenberg, a Baltic German, served as their most important emissary, interpreting the Bolshevik seizure of power as the "Russian-Jewish Revolution" and claiming that Jews and Freemasons now "stood at the peaks and behind the scenes of today's world politics."[54] So successful was this anti-Bolshevik campaign, that "It is rare to find an anti-Semitic source after 1917 which does not stand in debt to the White Russian analysis of the Revolution."[55]

The myth of "Judeo-Bolshevism" struck a chord in the outside world and spread widely. In the United States, for instance, fascists argued that "Communism is World Jewry in action."[56] The British antisemite Henry Hamilton Beamish flatly declared in the early 1920s that "Bolshevism was Judaism."[57] Further afield, when only thirteen years old in 1919, the later King Faysal (1906–75) traveled extensively in Europe representing Saudi Arabia and there apparently learned about Bolshevism as a Jewish conspiracy. Many decades later, Faysal still insisted that "Zionism is the mother of Communism. . . . It's all part of a great plot, a grand conspiracy. Communism . . . is a Zionist creation designed to fulfill the aims of Zionism."[58]

But the identification of Judaism and Bolshevism had its most profound consequences in Germany, where it provided a seemingly credible base to the otherwise highly speculative Nazi claims about Jewish ambitions; Russia seemed to provide an actual case of the conspiracy in action. Already in the early 1920s, Hitler presented communism as a Jewish conspiracy for world power. Indeed, Richard Pipes sees in this the key justification for Hitler's genocidal attack on the Jews, then concludes that the Holocaust was "one of the many unanticipated and unintended consequences of the Russian revolution."[59]

The decade following World War I was a time when the concepts behind conspiratorial antisemitism spread widely, promoted by a range of German groups (the All-German Association, the German Folks' Defensive and Offensive Alliance, the National Socialist German Workers' Party, the League of the Imperial Hammer, the Association against the Presumption of Jewry, the National Socialists)[60] and a rash of blockbusters such as Henry Ford's *International Jew* (which sold a half-million books within a few years) and Friedrich Wichtl's widely read screeds.

Of them all, by far the most important was the German-language edition of the *Protocols of the Elders of Zion*. Its first Western publication was in Germany in January 1920, as part of a much longer antisemitic tract.[61] The text initially had limited impact. Only when The *Times* of London discussed the book respectfully in May, referring to its "uncanny note of prophecy" and appealing for an impartial inquiry into its charges,[62] did the forgery take off, becoming a bestseller in Germany. The *Times* endorsement in effect legitimated conspiratorial antisemitism throughout Europe.[63] The Hohenzollern family helped defray publication costs, and Kaiser Wilhelm II had portions of the book read out loud to dinner guests. Henry Ford recommended the book, giving it not just new publicity and expanding its reach, but also making antisemitic conspiracism a respectable force in the United States. Alfred Rosenberg's widely distributed analysis of *Protocols*[64] gave the forgery a huge boost. Even Winston Churchill briefly joined this bandwagon, blaming the Russian Revolution on Jews. By 1926, one study concluded that "no piece of modern literature has even approximated the circulation of *The Protocols*."[65]

Although exposure of the book's forged nature in 1920–21 somewhat reduced its appeal (both *The Times* and later Ford retracted their endorsements), the book remained a powerful force among extreme rightists, who showed themselves immune to logic and proof. This immunity encouraged Adolf Hitler and the Nazi movement, who earlier had shown some apprehension, to endorse the *Protocols* and make it a centerpiece of their ideology. It was proclaimed in *der Führer*'s speeches (from August 1921 on) and studied in classrooms. Joseph Goebbels, the Nazi propaganda chief, endorsed the forgery at the height of World War II: "The Zionist *Protocols* are as up-to-date today as they were the day they were first published."[66] In Norman Cohn's words, the book served as the Nazis' "warrant for genocide."

The cumulative impact of these books, plus the many that had gone before, was to make antisemitism part of the established political landscape and thereby create a receptivity to antisemitic claims. The notions of "Jewish peril," "Jewish finance," and the "Jewish press" had become so familiar and axiomatic that antisemites found they had only to assert and repeat, not to prove. Antisemitism had become an established, if still disreputable, body of thought accessible to nearly everyone. Through these efforts, antisemites succeeded in several countries partially to undo the Jewish emancipation, and Jews in many places now suffered increased restrictions.

The Russian Revolution transformed the place of conspiracy theories in public life. When the Bolsheviks seized power, conspiracism for the first time became the ideological platform of a powerful state. The conspiracist mind-set pervaded the political culture of the Soviet Union. Lenin launched the notion that whoever did not join the Communist party or blindly follow its orders was a "counterrevolutionary" working for enemies of the Soviet state. Under Stalin, this paranoia became institutionalized in both its anti-imperialist and antisemitic variants. Never again could one ignore the outlandish ideas espoused by a fringe group; now the danger always lurked that it could take power and turn those ideas into the bases of state policy. The rise of such rulers as Adolf Hitler, Mao Zedong, and Ruhollah Khomeini, not to speak of their many epigones from Japan to Egypt, Italy, and Argentina, many times over confirmed this danger.

ANTI-IMPERIALISM. On coming to power, Lenin insisted that outside powers were conspiring to bring down the Soviet Union, even though none had made a serious effort to do so; had they tried to, they would have succeeded. (The Soviet archives recently revealed that Lenin had approved the Allied landing at Murmansk, long used as proof of Western efforts to overthrow his regime.) Despite this benign environment, Lenin constantly inveighed against "capitalists" and "imperialists." Throughout the Russian civil war (October 1917–November 1920), for example, he portrayed the White armies as the agent of foreign powers; one unit he specifically accused of being the tool of "Anglo-French stockbrokers."[67] The rebellion of sailors at the Kronstadt garrison in early 1921 he ascribed to French plotting.

Joseph Vissarionovich Stalin (1878–1953) had long seen the world through a conspiracist lens, but his fears reached new levels in the latter half of 1932, when, having faced some setbacks in his efforts at total control of the Soviet Union, he started seeing himself as the victim of a massive anti-Soviet conspiracy. Incapable of accepting that he was being criticized for real errors, he turned his critics into conspirators who sought to assassinate him, wreck the economy, bring down the regime, and reverse the revolution. Some of these hostile elements he imagined to be acting on their own behalf, but many more of them he connected to the capitalist powers, which he portrayed as so fearful that the successes of the Soviet experiment would undermine their own system that they took desperate measures to snuff it out. He conjured up a "capitalist encirclement" whose numbers varied from one incident to another, but nearly always included the British and German governments (more rarely, the Polish, French, American, or Japanese). Distantly echoing Hobson, he spoke of the "English bourgeoisie" as the ultimate enemy.

Rather than attack the revolution militarily, he argued, and repeat an attempt that had earlier failed, enemies of the state tried to bore from within. They infiltrated agents into the country and these recruited assassins, deviationists, provocateurs, and saboteurs. Stalin interpreted anything untoward—industrial accidents, fires, agricultural diseases, even inferior workmanship—as sabotage directed from abroad, and many Russians lost their lives to pay for these mistakes. As scriptwriter, Stalin showed flare, accusing doctors of injecting their patients with syphilis, artisans of hiding swastikas in teacup patterns. He discovered that such famous foreigners as T. E. Lawrence and Raymond Poincaré belonged to an "Industrial Party" that aimed to overthrow the Soviet government. He located conspiracies among those closest to him; no one was safe, and over the years, one by one, most of them disappeared. Commissar of Foreign Affairs Vyacheslav Molotov, a slavishly devoted yes-man, had to be an agent of American imperialism, as Nikita Khrushchev later explained: "When Molotov was in the United States he traveled from Washington to New York by train. Stalin reasoned that if Molotov traveled by train, then he must have had his own private railway car. And if he had his own private railway car, then where did he get the money? Hence, Molotov must have sold himself to the Americans."[68]

Conspiracy theories also served abroad. When Soviet forces occupied the Baltic states in 1940, they did so to put an end to intrigues there "by which England and France are attempting to sow discord between Germany and the USSR."[69] After the war, Stalin thirsted for tensions with the United States, the new conspiratorial enemy. Some analysts believe that Stalin in his final days was preparing the Soviet population for war with the West.

ANTISEMITISM. Moscow also displayed a pronounced antisemitism that lasted, with the partial exception of three periods, through the entire Soviet era. The first exception was in the immediate aftermath of the Bolshevik revolution; when the new state rejected all of the tsarist legacy, it naturally rejected antisemitism too ("Antisemitism is the counterrevolution," Lenin would often say),[70] even going so far as to make antisemitism a criminal offense. Second, Stalin permitted an easing of persecution during the dark days of World War II, so as not to offend his American ally. Third, for ten months in 1947–48 Stalin supported the creation of the state of Israel and helped it fend off an Arab assault, seeing Israel as a useful club against British imperialism and its Arab agents. According to *Pravda*, "Western imperialism was responsible for the Arab invasion of Palestine."[71] This attitude remained at least partially in place until late 1952. Stalin supported Israel despite its Jewish and Zionist character; life for Soviet Jews did not improve as a result of this foreign policy decision.

Other than these brief moments, Soviet Jews lived in an unremittingly hostile environment. As Stalin reintroduced Russian nationalism in the 1930s, he also included its anti-Jewish dimension. The state repressed Jewish culture. The Great Purge of 1937–38, with its inordinate emphasis on attacking a Jew, Leon "Judas" Trotsky, and its heavy toll on party members, took on a pronounced anti-Jewish quality. His daughter Svetlana's marriage to a Jew raised suspicions in Stalin's mind of Zionists plotting to infiltrate his family. Conspiratorial antisemitism made great progress during the nearly two years of the Nazi-Soviet pact, to the point that Soviet media complimented the Nazis for their war on the Jewish religion.

In the immediate postwar years, Tito briefly filled the role that Trotsky had earlier had (and was portrayed as a puppet of the Jews), then was replaced in this capacity by Zionists. Indeed, Soviet propaganda frequently drew a connection between Trotskyism and Zionism, precisely to establish just how serious a danger the latter presented. From 1948 until his death five years later, "Stalin became increasingly fixated on the Jews, following in a different way the path taken by his erstwhile partner, Hitler."[72] He feared that Zionists wanted to rip off pieces of the Soviet Union, starting with the Crimea. The great show trial of the anti-Zionist campaign took place in Czechoslovakia, where Stalin personally scripted the 1951–52 prosecution of Rudolf Slansky and eleven other Czechoslovak communist politicians of Jewish origin. They stood accused of espionage and sabotage on behalf of many parties, starting with the "Zionists." Reviving Nazi slogans, the trial proceedings sometimes painted the Zionists as merely the "most reliable running dogs" of American imperialism, at other times as an evil of earthshaking scope. In all, this much-publicized event had the effect of resurrecting conspiratorial antisemitism after its apparent burial with the Nazis.

Stalin's final conspiracy theory, cut short by his death (and so the only one he did not see through to its murderous end), was directed against Jews. In the "Doctors' Plot" announced in January 1953, he had the mostly Jewish physicians attending to the Soviet leadership accused of murdering two prominent figures and planning, in collusion with the Western powers and Israel, to kill four others. From then on, for the last six weeks of Stalin's life, "the stories about the traitorous Jewish doctors and their Jewish and Russian accomplices proliferated in every section of Soviet society."[73] Had Stalin lived, all the Jews of Russia would probably have been forced to Siberia, where few would survive the maltreatment and cold. A conspiracist hysteria had once again taken hold, but Stalin's death in early March cut it short. It appears that this campaign was initi-ated to lift up the Russian population at the Jews' expense, for after it took its deadly toll, "the most downtrodden of Russians would rejoice in the fact that he was not a Jew."[74]

In assessing Stalin's antisemitism, two points stand out. Although it almost ended in genocide, Stalin's antisemitism differed from Hitler's in not serving as the ideological pillar of his regime, but could be turned on or off, depending on circumstances. Second, until the Doctors' Plot, it involved anti-Jewish bias more than conspiratorial antisemitism.

In Germany, military defeat and hyperinflation combined to create an acute sense of despair after World War 1. The real danger of a communist takeover then made the widespread fear of conspiracies nearly universal. As a result, hoary ideas acquired a startling new importance and abstract notions became operational.

Conspiratorial antisemitism stood at the heart of National Socialism and provided a key mechanism for Adolf Hitler (1889–1945) to reach power. The Nazis added several novel elements of their own to its estab-lished themes. First, they combined racism with conspiratorial anti-semitism: Jews gain power by encouraging a mix of races, which leads to moral and physical degeneration, thereby weakening the racially pure ruling class of Aryans.

Second, Germans have a unique motive for antisemitism, the *völkisch* nostalgia for Wagner's heroically pagan epoch of Siegfried, Tristan, and the Niebelung. That wondrous age ended when the Jews imposed the effete outlook called Christianity, a variant of their own religion, on Ger-mans. As German speakers (Hitler included) developed a longing for the time before Christianity, the Jewish conspiracy came to include Jesus, the Church fathers, and the popes. Erich Ludendorff, Germany's outstanding general in World War I, portrayed Christianity as nothing but propa-ganda for Jewish world hegemony.[75] His wife Mathilde viewed the phrase "Thy Kingdom come" in the Lord's Prayer as a declaration of "Jewish world domination" in the messianic age.[76] The Ludendorffs and the Nazi party culminated this trend by taking steps to replace Christianity with their own religion, antisemitism. Even foreign acolytes accepted such ideas. "This business of Christianity is nothing but Jewish propaganda," echoed an American Nazi leader. "My religion is National-Socialism."[77]

Third, the Nazis insinuated conspiracism into the entirety of German life. Administratively, an "institutionalizing of the conspiracy myth" took place,[78] with a host of agencies, boards, offices, and other bureaucratic entities dealing with everything from republishing antisemitic "classics," to organizing boycotts, to building a machinery of death. Culturally, where possible, conspiracy theories were absorbed into the substance of the matter; such was the case in philosophical and historical studies. Where not possible, it became a matter of Nazi art, Aryan mathematics, or German athletics set against their Jewish counterparts. By bringing conspiratorial antisemitism under the state's authority, the Nazis gave it a presence and authority far beyond anything that had ever come before.

Fourth, Hitler eliminated the apologetic and defensive tone that prior antisemites had adopted. Before him even the most virulently hateful writers felt compelled on occasion to say something positive about Jews. They betrayed a tentativeness, a fear of going beyond the limits of respectable opinion, of losing their following. Hitler had no use for such hesitation or kindness; he hated Jews in the extreme and in every way.

Fifth, antisemitic tracts published over previous decades had laid every calumny at the feet of Jews, but not one of them clearly called for the killing of Jews. Only in the 1920s did the Nazis and their allies introduce this element. Claiming that the Jewish conspiracy aimed not just at world power but at "annihilation of the northern peoples"[79] justified their own response in kind. The most original element of the Nazi movement, then, was to turn prejudice and fear into murder; the "final solution" remains its highest creative achievement.

Hitler's ideas had a deep impact on the Right not only in Europe but in Japan, the Middle East, and the Americas. In the United States, for example, conspiratorial antisemitism hitherto had had little appeal, but now little *Führer*s closely mimicked their German leader. Hundreds of hard Right groups emerged in the Depression years, including the German-American Bund, Father Coughlin's Christian Front, and William Pelley's Silver Shirts. Those Nazi sympathizers blamed the 1929 stock market crash, plus the economic crisis that followed, on "international financiers," meaning Jews. The heroic Charles Lindbergh accused Britons and Jews, in collusion with the Roosevelt administration, of pushing America to war with Germany. Nazi acolytes insisted that the war resulted from the work of Jewish "war mongers" and especially that of "international Jewish bankers."[80] Wall stickers proclaimed, "Jews caused this war. Make them pay for it."[81]

As for the fear of Freemasonry, though it did not experience an upsurge as dramatic as did antisemitism, it had been growing since 1914. Just a year later, Germans already portrayed their wartime predicament as the result of a Masonic conspiracy, for example, blaming Freemasons for the assassination of Archduke Ferdinand. These ideas were then stoked by some powerful books. Friedrich Wichtl's *World Freemasonry—World Revolution—World Republic*,[82] "the best-known and most influential work to propagate an antimasonic conspiracy theory myth," came out in 1919 and had an "astonishing diffusion."[83] Also in that year appeared the important screed by Karl Heise, *Entente, Freemasonry and World War*.[84] *Annihilation of the Freemasons by Unveiling Their Secrets*, by Erich Ludendorff[85] of World War I fame, appeared a few years later with a huge distribution and inspired a small library of responses.

The Nazis subscribed to secret society myths; after Jews, Freemasons were the second group to be persecuted.[86] Still, they were second, turning up in Hitler's public statements mainly as an instrument of Jewry's world conspiracy. "Semitic Freemasons were the main agitators of the [First] World War. Secretly concealed Masonry is Jewry's best weapon."[87] The verbal assault began even before 1933, and so active were the security services' antimasonic units that by August 1935 the party newspaper could announce "the end of Freemasonry in Germany."[88] After that, the services still kept a close watch on ex-members to make sure they did not reach positions of responsiblity. Foreign Freemasons often came up in speeches and in the media. One newspaper implausibly announced in 1937 that American Freemasons had donated eighteen bombers to the Loyalist forces in Spain (and then used this alleged donation to help justify German help to the Insurgents). When the war began, the Nazis busied themselves with destroying lodges in "Greater Germany." Masonic sources report that in Germany alone, 76,000 out of 80,000 members were killed, though others show smaller numbers. Nazi plans for the occupation of Great Britain indicated that Masonic lodges, along with Jewish organizations, would be among the first institutions targeted for "special attention."[89]

As for the "imperialist" powers, the Nazis turned a century's tradition of German conspiracist thinking about Great Britain and the United States into operational policy. Echoing old myths, Hitler and his henchmen vehemed against Perfidious Albion, portrayed the British Empire as an octopus, and asserted that the United States joined in World War I as the result of a plot by American capitalists. Concerning present-day politics, Berlin had the temerity to accuse the Anglo-Saxons of seeking "world domination" and portrayed the U.S. government as an agent of "finance capital." The decline of Nazi fortunes in 1944 prompted Goebbels to draw on twenty-year-old themes and warn his countrymen of American plans to achieve world power by enslaving the Germans.

As in the past, Germans painted deep and nefarious connections between the liberal democracies and Jewish power. Winston Churchill and Franklin Delano Roosevelt either served Jewish interest or were transformed into Jews. Real Jews, such as the Rothschilds, Bernard Baruch, and Felix Frankfurter, were ascribed great ambitions and enormous power. Beyond these individuals, whole countries became symbolically Jewish: "Uncle Sam has been transformed into Uncle Shylock."[90] The conjunction of Anglo-Saxons and Jews became a major theme of German propaganda: "Like a kraken, that many-armed beast of the ocean, this land [of America] stretches its arms in all directions, grasping hold of islands, countries, and peoples and suffocating them in its embrace. Yet behind this monster appears the grotesque face of the wandering Jew, who sees it as nothing less than a precursor to the implementation of his ancient and never-abandoned plans to rule the world."[91] Of course, Jews took the blame for American entry in World War II, a theme that reverberated strongly on the Right in the United States itself.

When in power, Hitler acted inconsistently toward secret societies. In *Mein Kampf* and for years afterward, he decried communism as a Jewish attempt at world hegemony, yet in 1939, he signed a treaty of friendship with Moscow. He remained more true to his anti-British and anti-American conspiracy theories, though here too he at times indicated a willingness to coexist. Hitler could afford inconsistency on this score. Just as Stalin picked up or discarded antisemitism as it suited him, so did Hitler change policies toward non-Jewish enemies, dealing with them as practical politics required.

In the period 1933 through 1945, operational conspiracism reached its apex as two totalitarian leaders drenched in its phobias and hatreds challenged the world order. Relations between history's two most powerful and ambitious conspiracist rulers followed an unpredictable pattern of cautious entente followed by unremitting hostility. It began with lots of insults mixed with quiet cooperation; for example, Stalin facilitated the Nazi ascent to power in 1933 by refusing to let the German Communist party ally with the Social Democrats. Already in April 1936 the two sides signed an economic agreement; thereafter, Stalin worked hard to reach a political accord with Hitler. "We must come to terms with a superior power like Nazi Germany," an aide quotes him saying.[92] In early 1938 Stalin initiated diplomatic contact with Hitler and did him more favors, completely staying out of the Czechoslovak crisis and letting collapse the Republican forces in Spain. In August 1939, the two sides signed their notorious non-aggression pact, and neither stopped the other from invading and conquering far-flung territories over the next twenty-two months. Quite the contrary, the two confirmed their alliance by signing the Soviet-German Boundary and Friendship Treaty in September 1939 and a trade agreement in February 1940.

Despite the great advantages of a truce with Moscow at a time when Germany was unable to defeat Great Britain, Hitler reneged on his agreement with Stalin and attacked the Soviet Union in June 1941. This, the two-front war that German strategists rightly dreaded, constituted a mistake unrivaled in the history of warfare.[93] But with Hitlerite and Stalinist fears of conspiracy given free rein, how could the two avoid a clash? In the end, they had to go to war; the only question was when and under what circumstances.

As is, the surprise attack produced the largest and most decisive theater of World War II, the Eastern Front; it also led to the largest, most vicious, and most destructive battleground of human history. The clash of these two totalitarian leaders, both inspired by conspiracist ideas and deploying gigantic modern armies, gave rise to a supreme contest of wills in which leaders and soldiers gave no quarter. At its start, the Nazi-Soviet battle included some 8 million troops; at its peak, the combatants' number reached as high as 15 million. The confrontation included the Battle of Kursk in July 1943, the largest set-piece in history, with 2 million soldiers and six thousand tanks. The city of Leningrad alone lost 1.5 million residents and soldiers. At its conclusion, the Eastern Front left an estimated 3 million dead on the Nazi side and 27 million on the Soviet (one-third of them soldiers, the rest civilians).

Grotesque as these numbers are, they hide the purposeful terror that the two conspiracy theorists imposed on each other's armies and peoples. The Nazi command in particular instructed its forces to exterminate the Slav and Jewish enemies, encouraging and justifying some of the most horrific and large-scale atrocities ever committed in war. These took place not as aberrations committed in the heat of combat but as systematic extensions of the ruler's will. In turn, the Soviet forces responded with unrestrained ferocity, amazing the Germans with their determination. Further, the war dead number far fewer than those killed by governments outside of battle. At the low end, excluding war losses, one estimate puts the total number of Stalin's victims in the quarter century 1929 through 1953 at between 19.5 and 22 million, of which not less than one-third were sentenced to death or died.[94] At the high end, R. J. Rummel counts the total number of Soviet victims killed by their own government at 62 million.[95]

The parallel between the two greatest killers in history is no coincidence. Stalin and Hitler "were both conspiracy theorists who ended by seeing mass murder as the only way to liquidate the imaginary plots that threatened them."[96] Accordingly they initiated the greatest killing fields of all time. They had much else in common, and these similarities helped pave the way for the pact of 1939. Beyond their hatreds and brutality, the two also shared a common phobia of world conspiracies, as well as an inclination to engage in conspiracies of their own. "Both were enemy-obsessed. Both were terroristic and practiced torture in their prisons. Under both regimes state terrorism was linked with a theory of international conspiracy: a Jewish anti-Aryan conspiracy in Hitler's case and anti-Soviet one in Stalin's."[97]

Did they believe in the conspiracy theories they inflicted on the outside world? No; Dmitri Volkogonov believes Stalin used these for his own purposes. By way of proof, he points to the charges of an "anti-Soviet conspiracy" leveled against top generals in 1941; Stalin crossed out the accusation and wrote, "None of this nonsense," then replaced it with the charge that they "showed cowardice, lacked authority and efficiency, permitted the breakdown of command."[98] Yes, say Christopher Andrew and Oleg Gordievsky; there is "little doubt" that Stalin "believed his own conspiracy theory. So, in one form or another, did most of the Party hierarchy. Indeed, their ideology almost obliged them to do so."[99] Others are not sure. Nora Levin reflects: "How much of this alleged threat Stalin himself believed and how much he exploited craftily for internal purposes is difficult to assess. Many observers have reported his growing paranoia and obsession with personal as well as national security, which reached a bizarre pitch of suspicion in the so-called Doctors' Plot of 1953."[100]

Did Hitler believe in a Jewish conspiracy? No, Walter Laqueur argues: "Hitler, Goebbels, Goering, and their ilk thought the Jews racially inferior and hated and despised them; but they never believed in a giant plot. . . . [T]here was the feeling that the *Protocols* and the other conspiracy theories should not be taken at face value."[101]

In contrast, Ron Rosenbaum sees a complex mental process. It begins with what seems like a cynical calculation that what is important is not to believe but *to be seen to believe*—that the counterfeiting of belief counts for more than the sincerity of belief. But if there is calculation initially, what follows is the "remarkable process" whereby the actor-deceiver becomes carried away, becomes a believer in his own deception—possessed by himself.[102]

Norman Cohn considers the contradictory evidence and concludes:

> It has sometimes been argued that Hitler was simply a super-Machiavellian, a man without convictions or loyalties, an utter cynic for whom the whole aim and value of life consisted in power and more power. There certainly was such a Hitler—but the other Hitler, the haunted man obsessed by fantasies about the Jewish world-conspiracy, was just as real. What one would like to know is just how far the near-lunatic was active even in the calculating opportunist.[103]

Generalizing, it seems likely that Stalin and Hitler mostly did believe in the conspiracy theories whose gruesome consequences they inflicted on the world, but not necessarily in every detail. Humans are complex amalgamations, easily able to mix self-serving motivations with profound credulity, and these two monsters could certainly entertain a mix of purposes.

Which did more to foster conspiracism around the world; the Soviet Union or the Third Reich? The former, without a doubt, and it advanced both the antisemitic and the secret society variants. Nazi conspiracism was ideologically more central, rhetorically more venomous, and operationally more vicious than the Soviet variant, but the Nazi reign lasted only a few years and ended by being thoroughly discredited. In contrast, the Soviet Union survived three generations and never suffered the same ignomy. Even after its collapse, Lenin's state continues to enjoy much the better reputation.

Thus did conspiracism play a major role in the many tragedies of this most tragic century.

SIX

MIGRATION

TO THE

PERIPHERY,

SINCE 1945

With the important exception of the Soviet Union and other totalitarian states, conspiracism lost its central role in European and American life after 1945, and the Soviet collapse between 1989 and 1991 reduced the impact of conspiracism even more. But reduction hardly means disappearance. Rather, the urge to imagine plots found refuge in two main locales: at the political margins of Western life and at the geographic margin of Western states.

THE TOTALITARIAN LEFT

We believed that every Western country hated us and wished to see our doom.
PAVEL SUDOPLATOV, STALIN'S OFFICER IN CHARGE OF SPECIAL OPERATIONS[1]

The founding conspiracist premise of the Soviet Union—that capitalists working through the British and American governments are the greatest menace to human welfare—also became fundamental to the ruling ideologies of the many other communist states that came to power after World War II.

Although the Soviet Union sponsored conspiracism from its inception until its expiration, several changes took place over time: antisemitism grew stronger, cynicism replaced conviction, and, from the late 1940s, slightly different conspirators emerged as Israel replaced local Jews and Washington replaced London.

ANTISEMITISM. The death of Stalin in 1953 (who was dispatched not by a conspiracy by his doctors, it bears noting, but perhaps by his closest aides) caused conspiratorial antisemitism to go somewhat into eclipse. His obsessions continued to affect state policy for decades longer, at least until the 1980s and the early Gorbachev period. Under Nikita Khrushchev, conspiracy theories about the global ambitions of Zionism (and its local agents) became standard fare. At the same time, and somewhat in contradiction, Jews and Israel were increasingly portrayed as agents of the Western powers; as such, they were said to threaten the very existence of the Soviet people. The Soviet authorities supported such accusations with forgeries, rumors, and other forms of disinformation.

Events in the Middle East then turned this somewhat abstract phobia into operational enmity. From 1955, the Soviets invested heavily in the regimes of Gamal Abdel Nasser and other Arab leaders, so that Israel's astonishing military victory over Egypt, Syria, and Jordan in June 1967 left the Kremlin enraged with Zionism. In contrast to the early Marxist-Leninists, who deemed Jewish nationalism too insignificant to devote even an article to it (Lenin apparently referred to it just fifteen times in all the writings of his *Collected Works*), Zionism became a centerpiece of Soviet propaganda starting in August 1967. A founding document of this campaign set its tone: "An extensive network of Zionist organizations with a common center, a common program, and funds much greater than those of the Mafia 'Cosa Nostra' is active behind the scenes of the international theater."[2]

Retroactively justifying pre-1917 Russian antisemitism, the Soviet media presented this now as a form of class struggle against the "barbarous exploitation by the Jewish bourgeoisie." It also began reproducing pre-1917 antisemitic literature, usually making the cosmetic change of replacing "Jew" with "Zionist," but not always. The KGB purged itself of all known Jews by the spring of 1953 and never let them back in. How could it when it saw Zionism as a main instrument, if not the main one, of ideological subversion?

In ways, Soviet use of antisemitism resembled its role in Nazi Germany.[3] Just as there, a huge literature on this subject came into being, produced now at the pace of about one book every two months. A number of individuals acquired renown as antisemitic specialists, including Vladimir Begun, Yuri Ivanov, Lev Korneyev, A. Z. Romanenko, and Yevgeny Yevseyev. The content was also reminiscent: Jewish business interests control a Zionist apparatus that dominates the world's financial, political, and cultural institutions. The uses of antisemitism also recalled that of the Nazis: both states affixed this label on dissidents, Western powers, and other enemies. Soviet sources developed a theory that Judaism requires the genocide and enslavement of non-Jews, thereby making Zionists the objective allies of Nazism. This explains how Jews could be accused of cooperating with the Third Reich (in actuality, of course, it was Stalin, not Zionists, who allied with Hitler).

These accusations grew with time. During Stalin's era and until about 1967, Israel was usually seen as but a pawn of the great powers. Even weeks after the Six-Day War of June 1967, Leonid Brezhnev declared to Arab leaders that "American, German, and British imperialism is the factor that pushed Israel to carry out this aggression. This needs no proof."[4] But Israel later grew to the point that it was seen as the force standing behind the great powers: "Zionist agents" were accused of "penetrating foreign intelligence services" and through them influencing the policies of the United States and Great Britain.[5] Already in 1963, a major work equated Judaism with fascism and posited Jewish readiness to gain world hegemony through such evil means as mass murder.[6] Zionists were said to control the oil companies and the military-industrial complex in the United States. The KGB interpreted Watergate as a Zionist conspiracy to foil détente.

ANTI-IMPERIALISM. With the decline in Great Britain's world presence following World War II, Americans inherited much of the anti-imperialist suspicion hitherto directed against it. In fact, this transfer has a specific date: 21 February 1947. On that day, the first secretary of the British embassy in Washington went to the Department of State, where he delivered two similar notes from His Majesty's government—one concerning Greece, the other Turkey. Both conveyed an identical, urgent appeal: unless the U.S. government took over their defense from Britain, Soviet-backed forces would soon conquer the two countries. In one of the key foreign policy decisions of American history, President Harry Truman promptly accepted this responsibility. In retrospect, the short trip to the State Department that winter day a half-century ago marked a passing of the baton and the emergence of the United States as the leading Western power.

One side effect was to transform America's place in the conspiracist imagination; if London dominated it during the two centuries before 1947, Washington has done so since. In many cases, the same themes remained intact, with only the country changed. Their many shared characteristics—language, political system, legal heritage, industrialization, wealth, political stability, great power status, naval orientation—made it easy to shift the supposed attributes of one "Anglo-Saxon" power to the other. Indeed, the United States was moved so smoothly into Britain's nefarious role, that the transfer had a feeling of inevitability. But it was not predestined, for the two states had very different records in one key area: London had recently controlled the largest empire in history, while Washington had almost always (the major exceptions occurring around 1900) aggressively pursued a policy of anti-imperialism. Such details, however, hardly mattered for conspiracy theorists.

The Soviets created the mold, and other communist movements and regimes followed. Virtually without exception, all made the paranoid style central to their message. In Kim's Korea, Mao's China, Pol Pot's Cambodia, Hoxha's Albania, and Castro's Cuba, an inordinate fear of conspiracies characterized the system itself, not just individuals at the apex of power. All parroted anti-imperialism, and nearly all followed suit with antisemitism. Predictably, East Germany, with its many unreconstructed Nazis in high positions, stood at the forefront of conspiratorial antisemitism, but even distant regimes in Vietnam and China dutifully chimed in with fearful analyses of Zionism. The workers' vanguard carried hateful fantasies about Jews to many places in which they had previously not been known.

Anti-imperialism had a more central role, however, for Soviet ideology is premised on combating capitalist efforts at world hegemony. Wherever Marxist-Leninist regimes came to power, a version of the Stalinist paranoia soon followed. In Czechoslovakia during the early 1950s, for example, a former member of the security ministry told of potential state enemies seen "everywhere": "anyone with the remotest connection to the West," including former members of the Boy Scouts, Rotary Club, Salvation Army, YMCA, and churches, was "a possible spy."[7] The Cultural

Revolution in China reached greater heights of hysteria: mere knowledge of a foreign language or a visit abroad constituted evidence of espionage.

Although conspiracism's fatalities decreased with Stalin's death, conspiracism itself did not abate; to the contrary, it kept expanding, as did the number of communist or pro-Soviet regimes. In the 1970s, at the height of Soviet power and reach, the anti-imperialist conspiracy theory had acquired an extraordinary presence. Lenin's conspiracist tracts had become sacred texts for hundreds of millions—Chinese, Russians, Germans, Vietnamese, Poles, Cubans, Yemenis, and many others—while their leaders emulated his tactics. The 1970s also witnessed the largest post-Stalinist bloodlettings, and many of them involved fears of conspiracy: the Cultural Revolution in China, the Khmer Rouge genocide in Cambodia, the Pakistani assault on Bengal, and the Derg's programmed starvations in Ethiopia.

Leninist states then encountered a series of sharp reversals and changes of course. After Mao's death in China, totalitarianism gave way to a milder form of market-oriented authoritarianism. Conspiracism experienced a major decline about 1985, when Mikhail Gorbachev came to power in the Soviet Union and instituted a policy of *glasnost,* or openness; the obsession with imperialist enemies became an early casualty of his rule. Some Leninist regimes lost power (as in Nicaragua). Then came the *annus mirabilus* of 1989, which saw the virtual disappearance of the Soviet bloc and, with it, history's most protracted and influential force promoting conspiracism. The Soviet collapse at the end of 1991 much reduced the power of operational conspiracism, marking a major turning point in the fortunes of this way of thought. A vast, organized campaign of anti-Israeli and -American allegations came nearly to an end. Although Soviet acolytes clung to power in Cuba and North Korea, their conspiracist ideologies carry about as much weight as do their economies.

TO THE POLITICAL MARGINS

Our wonderful race is on the brink of total
extermination.
STORM, A SWEDISH NEO-NAZI MAGAZINE[8]

World conspiracy theories had lost operational importance in Western Europe and North America by 1945. What James H. Hutson calls the "migration of jealousy to the margins"[9] removed them mostly to the fringes of the West's body politic. Still, conspiracism persists in a wide range of lesser ways.

After an extraordinary thirty-year career at the dizzying heights of power, the hidden-hand mentality collapsed in Western Europe in the aftermath of World War II, losing its place in respectable discourse, the leading media, and the corridors of power. Hitler and Stalin had established the hideous price of conspiracy theories running rampant; the horrors they inflicted on their own and foreign populations finally ended conspiracism's two-century growth. The destruction of the Nazi state, along with many of its allies, then solidified these changes.

Under American tutelage, Western Europe established democratic and liberal institutions that took hold and became proof against operational conspiracism. Millions of Nazi sympathizers and Soviet fellow travelers did not experience an overnight change of heart, but they recognized that the great majority of their fellow citizens had turned their backs on conspiracism and that the public mood no longer indulged their fears and accusations. Conspiratorial antisemitism became so disreputable in the postwar years that a foremost historian of this phenomenon could write in 1968, "Today, the Jews are no longer accused of weaving a permanent plot against mankind, of unleashing revolutions and historical catastrophes. They are no longer attributed with supernatural powers. Any display of fanatical or 'paranoid' antisemitism by an individual . . . is dismissed by public opinion as a freak or even a psychosis."[10] Such changes, however, "were too good to last."[11] With time, conspiracism made a comeback; three decades later, in an age when fascist politicians such as Jean-Marie Le Pen in France and Jörg Haider in Austria win a sixth of the national vote and take office in some municipalities, Poliakov's musings sound quaint and naïve. Richard Levy, an American scholar, more clearly sees the enduring place of Jew-hatred: "antisemitism today is not simply an old relic of history, the obsession of lunatic individuals and groups, but rather an evolving ideology with a long past to draw upon and political functions yet to perform. It will not conveniently disappear."[12]

Along with antisemitism comes the inevitable anti-imperialism, now directed against the United States. German rightists note the dominance of American popular culture and interpret it as a purposeful effort to bleach out the German character. Their leftist counterparts point to the international financial system as proof that Americans have inherited

Nazi ambitions to control the world. Both sides suspected an American plot to turn Germany into the preferred battlefield for a nuclear exchange with the Soviet Union.

Alarm about Muslim immigration to Western Europe now ranks as one of that region's top social problems, so that anti-African and -Asian sentiments have emerged as political forces. Responsible analysts even raise the prospect that major states like France will become Muslim in orientation.[13] Even so, conspiratorial antisemitism retains its old role: "fascist groups may have found new targets for their anti-immigrant rhetoric, but they have not adjusted correspondingly the targets of their conspiracy theories," which remain preoccupied with Jews.[14] The Right talks about issues of the moment to attract followers, but hard-core members remain fixated on Jews. The public message stresses problems associated with the immigration of Muslims, but in the privacy of its councils the leadership obsesses over Jews rather than Pakistanis, Turks, and Algerians. The antisemitic conspiracy theory seems destined to remain a force among extremists of various persuasions, no matter how extraneous to their mundane concerns.

From time to time, it also impinges on the mainstream. A deputy of the France's National Front spoke on the floor of the European Parliament about Jews' carrying out the Russian Revolution and trying to take over in France. The Italian labor minister blamed the fall of the lira on "New York's Jewish lobby."[15] The Belgian foreign minister reminded all that the anti-secret society tradition also lives on in vestigial form, blaming European financial woes on "a kind of plot" carried out by Anglo-Saxon "organizations and personalities who prefer a divided Europe, condemned to a secondary economic role."[16] This said, the operational influence of such ideas remains small; conspiracism does not seriously threaten the body politic. Western European governments no longer act on conspiracist beliefs; the core is solid.

The same cannot be said of the countries in Europe's east, for peoples indoctrinated with conspiracism do not easily give up their prejudices. Serbia's descent in the 1990s into poverty and atrocity was accompanied by a pervasive conspiracism centered on Freemasonry. Typical of this muddled mind-set, an Orthodox priest had this to say about Tito, the dictator who had closed all the lodges in Yugoslavia: "You know, Tito was a Mason and so is the Pope and all the Catholic bishops. After Mahatma Gandhi was killed, Tito became the head of the Masons. . . . We know Tito was secretly buried in the Vatican."[17]

As *glasnost* relaxed controls in Russia over private expression and the media, it led to a spectacular increase in right-wing conspiracist thinking. The antimasonic edifice that exiles in the interwar years had built, with elaborate theories about Freemasons bankrolling the 1917 revolution, came back to life, but now it also served to explain the 1989 counterrevolution. New groups (like Pamyat), publications (*Nash sovremennik*), and politicians (Vladimir Zhirinovsky) did away with Soviet circumlocutions about Zionists and capitalists. Picking up from the Whites' conspiracism of seven decades earlier, they now focused directly on Jews and Westerners. The Soviet state had vilified Jews for decades as anti-Soviet; the Right now built on this antagonism but reversed it, portraying Jews as the carriers of the communist infliction. The Jew became an impersonation of evil who adopts the guise of a Freemason, liberal, or communist, but ultimately always forwards a specifically Jewish agenda of seizing power.[18] To substantiate these ideas, practically every major figure in modern Russian history was assigned a Jewish or Masonic affiliation (including Aleksandr Kerensky, Aleksandr Solzhenitsyn, and Gorbachev).

A new set of theories quickly appeared to the effect that *perestroika* (economic and political restructuring) was a Western plot to weaken Russia. Gorbachev served as a Western agent and Yeltsin took money from Western financial interests for wrecking the ruble (thus making former Soviet corporations cheap to buy). These and other fanciful worries impeded political development: "the flowering of conspiracy theories in Russia indicates the severity of the psychological dislocation in the country. The swirl of such theories makes it difficult for democratic politics to take root and makes it likely that an increasing number of Russians will call for 'strict measures' to restore order and curtail reforms that are being promoted by the West."[19]

True to this 1992 prediction, the communist Gennady Zyuganov came in second in the presidential elections of 1996, running on a conspiracist platform. Zyuganov had reached the Central Committee in Gorbachev's time, and from that position did all he could to maintain the old system. As Russia recuperated from the Soviet era, he forwarded J. A. Hobson's familiar conspiracy theory, but now on a truly vast scale: since the great schism of 1054 (when the Orthodox church separated from the Catholic), the West, led by the Jews who dominate its finances and decision making, had sought to keep Russia weak and poor, and thereby exploit its economic resources. This greed accounts for Western opposition to the Russian Empire in the nineteenth century and for its anti-

Soviet policies in the twentieth: "From age to age the West, like an insatiable Moloch or a giant whirlpool, has been sucking into its womb useful raw materials and a cheap colonial labor force, new territories and spheres of influence, goods, money, ideas, and brains."[20] Somehow Zyuganov also manages to blame Jews for wrecking the Soviet experiment. In contrast to such patriots as Comrade Stalin, Marshal Zhukov, and the legendary worker Stakhanov, Jews tried to export the revolution and thereby brought down the Soviet Union. Such thinking, or at least a watered-down version, clearly resonates among Russians. A 1996 poll found that over 60 percent of them agree with the notion that "the West is pursuing the goal of weakening Russia with its economic advice."[21]

So deeply did conspiracism penetrate Russian life that even anticommunists adopted it. Anatoliy Golitsyn, a KGB agent who defected in 1961, told of a game plan developed at a Moscow conference in May 1959 at which the KGB developed a "strategic disinformation" plot that called for the appearance of weakness to lull the West into complacency, and thereby achieve the long-sought Soviet goal of global power.[22] In a 1984 book, Golitsyn spelled out his thesis about Moscow purposefully creating the illusion of having a range of problems, such as the the disputes with Yugoslavia, Albania, and China; Romanian independence; Prague spring; the Polish labor union Solidarity; power struggles within communist parties; de-Stalinization; economic weakness; and the dissident movement. In fact, he claimed all these were nothing but Moscow-run plots. The renowned dissident Andrey Sakharov, for example, was "still a loyal servant of his regime, whose role is now that of a senior disinformation spokesman for the Soviet strategists."[23] Ignored in the Soviet Union, these sensational claims had some impact on rightist thinking in the United States, though Golitsyn persisted with them even after the Soviet Union collapsed, and eventually lost most of his audience.[24]

Many Russians, in other words, have voluntarily maintained the very conspiracism that had so long been imposed on them. This should not come as a complete surprise, for the former Soviet Union is the only place where the government sponsored conspiracy theories and endlessly repeated them on a daily basis for three generations. Other peoples also experienced a comparable immersion—notably Germans during the twelve-year *Reich* and Chinese during the twenty-seven-year Maoist era—but none so long as those living in the Soviet Union. Such a legacy probably contributes to the difficulties that nearly 300 million residents of the former Soviet Union have in leaving conspiracism behind.

What of the United States, the country with its different but frequent conspiracy theories, the exception that seems to prove the rule? In the aftermath of World War II, American conspiracism changed in two important ways: the Right saw Washington as ever more of a problem, and American ideas acquired influence around the world.

WASHINGTON AS PART OF THE CONSPIRACY. The vivid fear of Soviet subversion in the United States that once alarmed Americans virtually disappeared after 1970, replaced by a fear of Soviet arms; this change makes it difficult to recall the earlier worry. Nor was the fear of subversion a folly, for Leninism did in fact attract a wide range of highly placed Americans (including nuclear scientists, State Department officials, and artists) who with near impunity organized in underground cells from the 1930s on and engaged in espionage for Moscow or in other forms of conspiracy. The occasional exposure of this network (in famous spy cases such as those of Alger Hiss and the Rosenbergs) led to the flourishing of two complementary conspiracy theories in the 1950s, one concerning communists in the United States, and the other about Moscow's agents and dupes inside the country.

In 1938, a time of cresting totalitarianism in Europe, the House of Representatives established the Committee on Un-American Activities to investigate "the diffusion within the United States of subversive and un-American propaganda."[25] But only with the cold war did this concern become an issue with national repercussions. Senator Joseph McCarthy (Republican of Wisconsin) gave its most famous exposition in a 1951 Senate speech during which he asked and answered his own question:

> How can we account for our present situation unless we believe that men high in this Government are concerting to deliver us to disaster? This must be the product of a great conspiracy, a conspiracy on a scale so immense as to dwarf any previous such venture in the history of man. A conspiracy of infamy so black that, when it is finally exposed, its principles shall be forever deserving of the malediction of all honest men.[26]

With great fanfare and the usual conspiracist disregard for evidence and procedure, McCarthy then proceeded to use his control of the Permanent Investigations Subcommittee to uncover American communists in government, show business, the academy, and other leading positions. Some individuals named were indeed communists, but many were not.

McCarthy's sensational charges and uncontrolled methods may represent the most visible example of conspiracism's entering American mainstream politics. Only three years later, however, his campaign was defunct, felled by its own tendentiousness: the very prominence of his charges proved to be their undoing, for he needed to substantiate them and could not.

In the wake of this failure, an alternate conspiracy theory gained currency, one stressing not "the shabby people who staff the official apparatus of the Communist Party" but "well-intentioned people (in the PTA and similar organizations) who have been brainwashed with Communist ideas."[27] This theory focuses on the Council on Foreign Relations (CFR), a New York club that brings together Americans with an earnest interest in the outside world. Looking at its membership rolls, conspiracy theorists noted that its members staffed many of the highest positions in each presidential administration, Democratic or Republican, as well as many other key positions throughout American life.

Finding a hierarchy where none exists, reading discipline into a voluntary organization, the Right fingers the CFR as the "invisible government" that really runs the United States. What does the council use its immense power to achieve? Conspiracy theorists deem its goal "to get Americans to the point where entering a world government would seem as natural and American as baseball and apple pie."[28] This has other, more ominous implications: to "convert America into a socialist state" and achieve the Stalinist goals of "collectivization and subjugation of the human race."[29] Some leading members of the invisible government "know exactly what they are doing" in bringing America under the Kremlin's thumb;[30] but the great majority (and especially in the case of some anticommunist CFR members) do not realize they are working for its ends.[31] Yet others who have no taste for one-world government get coopted: "all it takes is a quiet word from the right person to destroy the future of any public company that is carrying a substantial debt."[32] Such power also explains why the national media never permit criticism of the CFR.

While membership in the CFR "has become a prerequisite for running for the presidency,"[33] the CFR's power reduced even the president to a figurehead. In the case of Dwight Eisenhower, the John Birch Society found that in return for his having "been guided by, and taken orders from, the Communist bosses, . . . the Communist push was behind him every step of the way" of his career. In all, he was "the most completely opportunistic and unprincipled politician America has ever raised to high office," and he played a leading part in "treasonous developments."[34] In the view of a right-wing priest, John Kennedy was "more or less a victim of his job in the White House. He had a lot of enemies and his wires were tapped all the time."[35]

Two other developments complemented the fear of communism: the increased roles of the Federal government and Jews. From FDR's New Deal in the 1930s until the election of Ronald Reagan in 1980, the steady and massive increase in central government activities spawned a right-wing reaction. For it, Washington was a font of evil. As Washington took more in taxes, emasculated the power of states, enforced civil rights provisions, and placed more restrictions on gun ownership, its actions fueled conspiracism, to the point that some imagined Feds controlling the minds of U.S. citizens: "certain insidious, subtle techniques are used to gain the subject's trust and to actually interfere and change the thought processes and attitudes."[36]

Libertarians, not usually a group associated with conspiracism, also tend to interpret the American role in the world in a suspicious way. Bureaucrats in Washington, they argue, fomented hostile relations with foreign states that would otherwise coexist peacefully with the United States: cold wars with the Soviet Union or People's Republic of China, hot wars with Nazi Germany or Iraq. Why? Foreign adventures served as a way to augment the bureaucrats' power at home to tax, censor, and diminish the role of states. This self-aggrandizing conspiracy makes Washington, in the view of some libertarians, the greatest menace in the world. Libertarianism's leading intellectual concludes, "Taking the twentieth history as a whole, the single most warlike, most interventionist, most imperialist government has been the United States. . . . [In contrast,] the Soviets arrived early at what Libertarians consider to be the only proper and principled foreign policy."[37] The same suspicion continues in the post-cold war era. Responding to the notion of U.S. global leadership, the libertarian CATO Institute commented that while this notion "sounds benign, today's proponents of global leadership envision a role for the United States that resembles that of a global hegemon."[38]

Antisemitism gained force as Jews in the 1930s acquired a new role in American political affairs, both visibly and behind the scenes. That role continued to grow, so that by the 1990s (if one includes women) the Senate had a *minyan*. Jews at one time or other filled almost every cabinet post. Jewish money was said to amount to half of that given to presidential candidates. The American Israel Public Affairs Committee gained a reputation as "perhaps the most effective pressure group in Washington."[39] The hard Right reacted to these developments by calling the Federal government ZOG (or Zoglandia), an acronym for Zionist Occupied Government. In a typical statement, an Oregon-based armed group, Posse Comitatus, declared in 1985 that "Our nation is now completely under the control of the International Invisible government of the World Jewry."[40] Echoing Hitler, it also worried about Jews' using this power to eliminate the Aryan race.

In sum, the Right's long-time suspicion that unseen forces controlled the Federal government increased in the 1930s due to three main developments: the fear of communist subversion, major extensions of Federal government power, and the entry of Jews into American public life. These trends seemed to reach fruition in the 1950s in the form of famous spy cases, a Republican president who accepted the New Deal, and the full acceptance of Jews in American public life.

INFLUENCE ON OTHER COUNTRIES. In the United States, conspiracy theories inspire the disaffected and titillate the sensible, neither of whom dispose of operational power, but both of whom spark conspiracism in others, especially those beyond American borders. Ideas and terminology flow to like-minded extremists in Europe, Japan, South Africa, and other places. ZOG has gone international, the English acronym now being used in Sweden, Switzerland, and elsewhere. Even ideological enemies pick up American ideas: a Soviet conspiracy theory about the Freemasons, Trilateral Commission, and Bilderberg Club (another elite club) giving orders to sovereign states came directly from the American far Right.

U.S. conspiracism spreads via three main avenues: political organizations, publications, and the Internet. Conspiracist American institutions have begun building international networks. Lyndon LaRouche has active outposts in Latin America and Australia. Louis Farrakhan not only makes quasi-state tours in several parts of the world but heads affiliated groups in Canada, the West Indies, Great Britain, and Ghana. A well-known antisemite, Masami Uno, heads the Liberty Lobby's Japanese branch. The Militia of Montana has contacts with Australian counterparts.

The United States has far and away the most complete freedom of expression of all the countries in the world (one survey of censorship calls it "libertarian to the extreme"),[41] so conspiracist ideas banned elsewhere for their violent and noxious qualities find American publishers. This pattern applies especially to pro-Nazi materials, banned in many countries but completely uncensored in the United States. Most printed Nazi materials in Germany during recent years have come from Gary Lauck's press in Lincoln, Nebraska, or other American sources; Lauck's stint in a German jail from March 1995 for activities perfectly legal in the United States confirmed the exceptional nature of the First Amendment freedoms and pointed to the alarm in foreign states about the American role in spreading conspiracism. American materials are often translated and published abroad, where they sometimes have a larger impact than at home. Gary Allen's obscure scribblings for the John Birch Society reached a massive audience in Japan thanks to Kinji Yajima's nearly literal translation of his works. Lyndon LaRouche's fantastical notions about Western powers' dividing the Middle East into small states won a respectful hearing at the upper reaches of the Iranian government.

Finally, Americans have a two-way role on the Internet. Most conspiracist materials on the system originate in the United States, and then are disseminated around the world. Conversely, the World Wide Web permits those living in countries with censorship to get their message out via the United States. Jailed for spreading his Holocaust denial and conspiracist writings in Canada, Ernst Zündel set up a "Zündelsite" in the United States, where, beyond the reach of the Canadian authorities, he broadcasts his ideas in English and German.[42] Zündel has even managed to turn himself into a symbol of free speech; so that his message not be stifled, at least two universities host mirror sites, that is, computers containing the same information as the original Zündelsite.

The influence of American conspiracism fits into a larger context of American popular culture. Previous great powers had wide intellectual, artistic, and religious influence (think of Greece, China, Iran, or France), but none of them directly reached the masses as does the United States. The beginnings of this influence go back to the motion pictures and songs of the 1920s; today it includes fast food, dance fads, clothing styles, rock videos, computer games, and much more, including conspiracy theories.[43]

There is a final, ironic and sad, group that sometimes resorts to conspiracism—Jews, the victims of so many conspiracy theories at so monumental a cost to themselves. Indulgence in this particular vice is rare, but exceptions do exist, primarily among fringe groups of the religiously Orthodox.

On the secret society side, two American rabbis express conspiracist fears. Meir Kahane, founder of the Jewish Defense League (a group of toughs in the United States) and Kach (a quasi-fascistic political party in Israel), reverses the classic anti-Semitic myth: Jews are not the source of such corrupting modern ideas as capitalism and democracy but their victims. He characterizes these as gentile notions that damage the moral fiber of Jews and eventually will lead to the religion's demise. Concurring, Marvin Antelman offers a more elaborate thesis: the Illuminati stand ultimately behind the fracturing of (Orthodox) Judaism into its Conservative and Reform branches, splits that he sees as a blatant effort "to undermine Judaism" and thereby "destroy Jews and Judaism." Antelman traces Illuminati influence to such influential figures as Jacob Frank (c. 1726–1791), a would-be messiah, and Moses Mendelssohn (1729–1786), the intellectual leader of Jewish emancipation. He draws a direct line from the Illuminati to the communists and concludes that "The same radical clique that gave the world Socialism and Communism want [sic] to see the Jewish religion and its people destroyed."[44]

More remarkable yet, some Jews discern a Jewish conspiracy! A number of *haredi* (ultra-Orthodox) groups see Zionism as a plot of Satan. Believing that only the messiah can revive the Land of Israel, they understand Zionism as a conspiratorial human effort to preempt and pervert the divine will. This outlook leads such anti-Zionist groups as the Satmar, Toldot Aharon, Yerushalayim, and Natorei Karta routinely to compare the Israeli authorities to the Nazis and the KGB (or, in a different twist, Christian missionaries)—all groups with a proved intent to see Judaism disappear. Theirs amounts to a bizarre form of conspiratorial antisemitism for Jews.

TO THE NON-WESTERN WORLD

The hallmark of an insecure culture is to rely on rumor and see conspiracy in the eye of every man.
FOUAD AJAMI[45]

The most fertile ground for conspiracism since 1945 has been outside the West. This comes as something of a surprise, for world conspiracies are by no means a universal way of thinking; rather, they originated in very specific circumstances in Western Europe. No other region developed this way of thinking on its own, but many found it attractive enough to import it, or large portions of it, from Europe.

This fits a common pattern, whereby little—whether artifacts or ideas—gets invented more than once. Just as copper, gunpowder, modern medicine, and the personal computer spread from their place of origin to other parts of the world, so did concepts like monotheism, romantic love, the symphony orchestra, representative democracy, and conspiracism. Each has its requisite elements: a symphony orchestra must have violins and flutes, and conspiracism must include Rothschilds and Rockefellers. It appears (in the absence of scholarship on this subject) that world conspiracy theories first spread to non-Western regions in the nineteenth century, where they had a wide appeal. Conspiracism particularly resembles nationalism and communism, in that all three ideas originated in Western Europe, where they caused great tragedies, then atrophied in their birthplace even as they went on to great careers in other regions. Of course, the conspiracist tradition has not been received the same everywhere; for example, it has particularly flourished in the Philippines, Iran, and Haiti.

That the outside world takes its conspiracy theories from the West has two general implications. First, it means that the non-Western conspiracy theorist accepts the West's bogeys as his too, and so tends not to focus on his own enemies. The non-West thereby dismisses itself as insignificant: Chinese do not fear Japanese world hegemony, Japanese do not fear Chinese secret societies, Muslims do not fear Hindu Elders, Hindus do not fear Pakistanism. Western influence not only enthralls peoples around the world to European fears but imbues non-Western conspiracism with a particularly unreal quality; its alleged enemies are strangers who live far away.

Second, borrowing conspiracism from the West makes it derivative elsewhere. Conspiracy theorists around the world share a common ancestry in the Crusades, the Enlightenment, the French Revolution, and the two world wars. Prime Minister Tojo and Ayatollah Khomeini may never have heard of Robespierre, much less de Barruel, but they nonetheless derived much of their thinking from the major currents of European thinking, including the dual conspiracist themes. Interestingly, it was the Left (and not, say, Christian missionaries, White Russians, or Nazis) that took the lead in spreading both antisemitism and anti-imperialism. Once absorbed in non-Western countries, these conspiracist traditions lose their associations with Left or Right.

Noting the harm that conspiracism does to the non-Western world, a conspiracy theorist might conclude that Westerners knowingly passed along this outlook with a mind to hobble its rivals—and of course some do. "The real conspiracy lies in the fabrication of the plot theory," writes the press secretary to Jordan's King Husayn.[46] A Turkish daily explains that "to create confusion, theories are drawn up about plots and conspiracies in suspicious and dark rooms."[47]

Conspiratorial antisemitism today is far more virulent outside its place of origins than in it. Note the recent career of the most widely available antisemitic publication, the *Protocols,* which has largely dropped out of sight in the West while becoming an important source of information in other parts of the world. Published in many non-Western languages, including Persian and Chinese, it has appeared in Brazil, India, and Australia and reached best-seller status in Japan and Lebanon. More separate translations and editions of the forgery have appeared in Arabic than in any other language, and it enjoys high-level official sponsorship in a number of Muslim countries, including Saudi Arabia and Iran.

A brief look at the career of conspiratorial antisemitism in selected regions suggests its current standing. Antisemitism's worldwide expansion began with the Middle East, Europe's closest neighbor and the one non-Western region where Jews are politically active. This form of conspiracism dates to the 1920s, when a combination of the Balfour Declaration and the availability in Arabic of the *Protocols* prompted both the fear of Jews and a conspiracy theory to channel it. I have written a large book on conspiracy theories in the Middle East, half of which concern Jews and Israel, in an attempt to understand this phenomenon and assess its implications.[48] Here I note only how specific European themes have a history of reappearing, sometimes down to minor details, in the Middle East.

Augustin de Barruel received a letter in 1806, ostensibly from an Italian military officer named J. B. Simonini, in which he was informed that eight hundred clergy in Italy, including bishops and cardinals, were actually Jews.[49] This old canard still echoes today in the Middle Eastern press; the *Syrian Times,* an English-language newspaper published in Damascus, announced on 14 May 1994 that "30 percent of Protestant bishops in the U.S. are originally Jews who did not quit Judaism."

Walther Rathenau, Germany's Jewish foreign minister, famously asserted in 1909 that "Three hundred men, all of whom know each other, guide the economic destinies of the Continent."[50] His comment continues to resurface in the West,[51] often with an antisemitic twist, and in the Middle East: Gamal Abdel Nasser once stated, for example, that "three hundred Zionists, each of whom knows all the others, govern the fate of the European continent.[52]

Nesta Webster, a scholarly conspiracist, wrote in 1924 that anti-semitism is "a misnomer coined by the Jews in order to create a false impression," for it incorrectly refers to Arabs as well as Jews, thereby confusing matters.[53] Nearly a half-century later, a Sudanese scholar likewise argued that Zionists, in an attempt to improve their own standing, "coined the word 'antisemitism' to mean 'anti-Jewish.'"[54]

Adolf Hitler declared that "99 percent of the press of England is to be found in Jewish hands."[55] Similarly, President Ali Hoseyni Khamene'i of Iran called Zionists the "ringleaders of the world's media" and declared that Zionists run the "world propaganda network."[56]

The image of Jewry as an octopus with international reach developed in Europe and was then adopted in the Middle East, where it now appears everywhere from political cartoons to the front cover of the *Protocols*. A 1930s French edition of the *Protocols of the Elders of Zion* shows an octopus astride the globe; so does the cover of the *Protocols* published in Cairo in the 1970s.

As these examples suggest, Arabs and Iranians have absorbed some of the most extreme elements of European conspiratorial antisemitism, and these have found large and appreciative audiences. What in the West remains the province of hate groups and other minorities is there the stuff of presidential speeches, the national media, professorial analyses, and major sermons.

In the Muslim world, influence customarily travels from the Middle East to other regions. In keeping with this general pattern, antisemitic ideas have spread from Egypt and Iran to countries like Malaysia, a minor hotbed of conspiratorial antisemitism. The government there has a penchant for banning cultural artifacts deemed too friendly to Jews, so that the New York Symphony Orchestra found itself prohibited from playing Bloch's *Shlomo*, and the movie *Schindler's List* could not show. Henry Ford's long-forgotten tract, *The International Jew*, lives on in Malaysia, even as Prime Minister Mahathir Mohamad contends that "Jews and Zionists" seek to remove him from office and destabilize Malaysia.[57] He also blames criticism of him in the Chinese-language press to Jewish control of the media. It has reached the point that antisemitism is almost endemic to the Muslim world.

Antisemitism also spread beyond the Muslim world to countries lacking significant contact with Jews. In Thailand, for instance, King Rama VI (r. 1910–25) drew on his eight-year education in England to write *The Jews of the East*, in which he attacked the Chinese minority in his country by drawing on the example of Jews in Europe. About the same time, among Chinese intellectuals "Contempt for the Jews, and even a feeling of hatred towards them, remained vivid for decades."[58]

But these were minor and nonconspiratorial forms of anti-Jewish sentiment. True antisemitism outside the Western and Muslim worlds exists only in Japan, where fascination with *yudayaka,* or the Jewish peril, has existed since the 1920s. On two occasions—during the World War II era and from the mid-1980s—Jews have come to represent liberalism among those who hate it. The *Protocols* reached Japan in the aftermath of World War I and became state dogma as the alliance with Nazi Germany gained importance. In part because its ideas so closely resembled Japanese anti-Christian polemics of an earlier period, it won an immediate audience, which grew as Japan plunged into ultranationalism and alliance with Nazi Germany.

As antisemitism in Japan developed into the "belief in a global Jewish conspiracy bent on destroying Japan,"[59] the 1937 attack on China was in part justified as a fight against this Jewish conspiracy, while confrontation with the United States was portrayed as a battle with Jewish "hegemony" in that country.[60] In 1941, one Japanese writer held that "The degree to which countries retain a democratic character is precisely the degree to which they are subject to the Jewish dictatorship."[61] Late in the war, antisemitism had progressed so far that leading newspapers interpreted Italy's surrender to the Allies as a Jewish plot, and some even read history backwards to see Commodore Perry's expedition as a Jewish invasion of Japan.[62] More broadly, Jews were viewed as the puppeteers behind Stalin, Chiang K'ai-Shek, Roosevelt, and Churchill, as well as the Christian religion. Not content merely to repeat Western themes, the Japanese formulated original ones of their own. One writer, for example, presented Jews as the Japanese *Doppelgänger:*

> No country has a more profound relationship with the Jews than Japan. The relationship can be traced back to ancient times. . . . What is known as Judaism today is actually a counterfeit religion forged by Jewish priests who dressed up the Satanic god Yahweh in the garb of the Sumerian sun god and other gods. . . . [W]hat is known as Jewish culture developed diabolically as a counterfeit expression of Japanese Sun Goddess culture.[63]

Conspiracy theories about Jews waned after the war but returned to prominence decades later, when they served as vehicles to define Japanese identity (most notably in the 1971 book, *The Japanese and the Jews*) and express fears of the United States. Antisemitism revived in a serious way during the mid-1980s. Masami Uno's two 1986 books blamed Japan's economic recession on the Jews who run virtually all American corporations, and he predicted a Jewish tyranny running the world from the Third Temple in Jerusalem.[64] He also argued that the two-party democracy in Japan was part of a Jewish plot to destroy Japan. His books sold over a million copies.

Uno's success made antisemitic conspiracism socially acceptable, and a flood of even more extravagant works followed. Judaism caused all the evils of Western civilization, including colonialism and Nazism. Jews, not the U.S. government, defeated Japan in World War II. A powerful Jewish "shadow government" runs the United States and conjured up the Kuwait crisis in 1990–91. "Jewish money" caused the Tokyo stock market's steep drop in 1992—part of a pattern to weaken Japanese companies and so render them vulnerable to foreign purchase. Jews control Japan's Ministry of Finance, as reflected in the "Jewish" marks on Japanese paper currency. One author traces the Jewish plot against Japan back to the Nara Period (A.D. 710–784). As antisemitic theories attained popularity and sales, book stores set up "Jewish corners" to handle a profusion of books on the subject.

Along with antisemitism, anti-imperialism continues to flourish in the non-Western world. Soviet incitement against London and Washington also had far-ranging impact, affecting not just Marxist-Leninist regimes but winning a substantial body of acolytes among intellectuals, artists, and other alienated Westerners. These added their eloquence to the Soviet drumbeat, and the result was an impressive extension of imperialist phobia around the world.

Latin Americans long labored under the sway of an anti-imperialist conspiracy that owes much to the guild mentality (that there is only a finite amount of wealth in the world) and a series of disappointments through the twentieth century. Yankee imperialism was widely accused of stealing the affluence that until World War I seemed near at hand. The connection between U.S. perfidy and Latin failure is direct: one got ahead because the other was left behind. Indeed, American success at purloining Latin riches is said to be "the main cause, and probably the only one, for North American wealth and Latin American poverty."[65]

This suspicion of U.S. plots led Latin Americans down many colorful and unexpected paths. Accusations about a CIA connection were not just bandied about but widely believed. A Peruvian Marxist writer devoted a whole book to proving that the Shining Path movement in Peru is not a fringe Left group but a CIA-sponsored operation seeking to destroy the social base of the Peruvian Left and weaken the country.[66] For weeks in 1980, Mexico's media reported in front-page headlines that a drought in that country, the worst in twenty years, resulted not from unfavorable meteorology but from American airplanes' diverting hurricanes from Mexico. Why? One reply saw the effort as part of a campaign to get tourists to choose Florida as their vacation spot. When the American press called José López Portillo, Mexico's exceedingly corrupt president from 1976 to 1982, one of the world's richest men, he in turn accused the CIA of spreading this "infamous lie" and asked, "That's what it was created for, wasn't it?"[67]

For decades, such reasoning prevailed on Left and Right, was scrawled on graffiti-strewn walls, and was heard in literary salons, rarely to be challenged. Recent years have seen impressive changes, however, as the rapid spread of democracy and capitalism imbues Latin Americans with more wealth and a greater sense of their own potential. They are now less prone to blame others and more inclined to take responsibility for themselves. Conspiracism has abated.

In contrast, Haiti remains mired in the old ways of conspiracist thinking. When the American ambassador in late 1993 showed the movie of John Steinbeck's *Of Mice and Men*, he chose it for the simple reason of availability. But nothing is simple in Haiti, by far the poorest and most troubled country of the Western Hemisphere. The audience understood the movie's story (about Lennie, a dimwitted farmhand who mistakenly kills a young woman, then gets killed in turn by his friend George, who thereby protects him from the wrath of an angry mob) as allegorical. Questions then arose as to the exact nature of the allegory: "Was the U.S. Embassy saying ousted President Jean-Bertrand Aristide had acted clumsily and should be literally or figuratively killed? Or was Lennie meant to portray the potential fate of Lt. Col. Michel François, the powerful police chief who is helping block the return of Aristide? Who was George? Or was the message hidden, and had they missed it completely?" A U.N. official commented that "No one would believe it was simply a movie, shown for enjoyment." Such overanalysis and suspicion typifies Haitian life: "It is this propensity for finding layers of meaning where none are intended that has helped keep Haitians so divided and unable to talk to each other."[68] Unlike most other countries, where Jews and imperialists are thought to conspire, conspiracy theories in Haiti involve the Vatican and the United States. Also unusual is the small scale of Haitian worries: not the globe but Haiti itself.

In the Philippines, almost anything can be and is laid at the feet of the U.S. government, the colonial power from 1898 to 1946. A secret U.S. agreement with the Nacionalista party, long the dominant force in Filipino politics, supposedly prevented the National Assembly from legislating the country's independence. Decisions taken in Washington resulted in Ramon Magsaysay's defeat of Elpidio Quirino in the 1953 presidential election. The U.S. government decided Ferdinand Marcos had to go after his wife, Imelda, invited the American ambassador's "special girlfriend" to a party at the presidential residence. One writer summarizes the situation:

> It probably hasn't occurred to many Americans that the United States might be contemplating an invasion of the Philippines. But anyone who has grazed through an armful of Manila's more than thirty daily papers knows that conspiracies involving the United States are a staple of this city's political culture. . . . [Paranoia] is a manifestation, in part, of a colonial mentality in which Filipinos are perceived as powerless and Americans as larger than life.[69]

In India, so long dominated by Great Britain, the Western conspiracy remains much feared. In a typical assertion, the ex-speaker of the Uttar Pradesh assembly speaks of "an international conspiracy to create instability" in India by funneling money to various religious fundamentalists who divide the country along caste and communal lines, thereby "shaking the foundations of secular India."[70]

The Muslim world and Christendom have engaged in a millennium-long confrontation, so, to Muslims, "imperialist" sounds similar to "Crusader," giving the modern power relationship an old-fashioned feel. The profundity of this rivalry not only provided the basis for a common bond with the Soviet Union but suggests that not all that much will change in the post-cold war era. Fundamentalist Muslims and autocrats like Saddam Husayn and Mu'ammar al-Qadhdhafi display an extraordinary range of conspiracist fears about the United States and Great Britain, to the point that this seriously gets in the way of intelligent policymaking.

In contrast, conspiracist fears of the West have been little in evidence in Japan and China. Meiji-era Japanese faced probably the most rapid

change in lifestyle of any people anywhere. Having totally excluded foreigners between 1638 and the mid-1850s, they suddenly had to cope with
an influx of Western influence, and at the high tide of European imperialism in the late nineteenth century. Still, the Japanese did what had to
be done. Inspired by the slogan *fukoku-kyohei*, "rich country-strong army,"
politicians and intellectuals alike engaged in a protracted and successful
effort to understand what had gone wrong, then set to righting it. With
the exception of the interwar period, the Japanese have not had to rely
on conspiracy theories about imperialism, though a significant minority
of Japanese see trade tensions with the United States through the prism
of American efforts to weaken Japan and thereby control it.

The same general indifference goes for China, where, as Mary Wright
observes, "The foreign menace is always seen as a symptom of the Chinese state's failure to maintain universal harmony by performing its
proper functions, never as the cause of the domestic failure. Until well
into the twentieth century, no Chinese conservative, however xenopho-
bic, attempted to lay the responsibility for China's domestic disasters at
the door of foreigners."[71] Even in the communist period, conspiracy theories roughly fit this pattern, with the major exception of the Cultural
Revolution. Mao Zedong worried more about petty conspiracy theories
than about world-shaking ones. When the Great Leap Forward led to
economic catastrophe, for instance, he insisted that the problems resulted
from counterrevolutionaries who undermined production, but without
linking them to foreign states. He only occasionally raised fears of British,
Russian, and Japanese conspiracies. American plots did not come up
often, and toward the end of his life, his enmity with the Soviet Union
grew so deep that he turned to the United States for help against it. In
the post-Mao period, the recourse to conspiracy theories has been both
occasional and vague—more a mechanism to control the population
than a serious effort to identify enemies.

The last half-century has seen a dramatic, if uneven, shift in the power
and scope of conspiracism. A force that once nearly ruled the world now
stands outside the citadels of power in the West; conspiracy theorists
have a loud voice but find themselves unable to shift policy. In other
parts of the world, however, most notably the Middle East, politics have
become thoroughly enmeshed in conspiratorial explanations.

SEVEN

TWO

CONSPIRACIST

TRADITIONS

Conspiracy theories tend to focus on four peoples: Jews (who number about 15 million), Freemasons (5 million), Britons (60 million), and Americans (260 million). In total, these four groups constitute some 6 percent of the world's population, leaving 94 percent of humanity rarely seen as conspirators. Why this particular foursome? Connections imagined between these groups and their special characteristics explain why they serve as scapegoats of such exaggerated fears.

COLLUSION

The First World War saw a reactivation of the conspiracy theory myth. In the course of the wider development, its two historical precursors, the myth of a Masonic conspiracy and of a Jewish world-conspiracy, became ideologically compressed.
ARMIN PFAHL-TRAUGHBER[1]

Beginning as distinct outlooks, the antisemitic and anti-secret society traditions over time increasingly tended to accept the other's ideas. In the process, they reinforced each other and harmed both Jews and "insiders."

In each tradition of antis, a small minority finds the other utterly mistaken. Some antisemites dismiss secret societies as vehicles of the Jewish conspiracy. Henry Ford regretted that Freemasons and Illuminati had been blamed for plots in fact hatched by Jews (in part, perhaps, because he himself belonged to a lodge). Conversely, some enemies of secret societies dismiss Jews as decoys, possibly dupes, and portray antisemitism as a diversion from the real menace. On the Left, Leninist theory (if not Soviet reality) portrays bias against Jews as a distraction designed to keep the masses from ascertaining the class enemy, their true opponent. On the Right, Senator Joseph McCarthy and Robert Welch, founder of the John Birch Society, promoted a radical anticommunism shorn of antisemitism. Welch blamed antisemitism within the Birch Society on "agents provocateurs" hired by his conspiratorial enemies, the Insiders.[2] Some Birch Society writings even portray antisemitism as a plot by which secret societies deflect suspicion from themselves. "Antisemites have played into the hands of the conspiracy," writes Gary Allen of *American Opinion*, "by trying to portray the entire conspiracy as Jewish."[3] Using the same words, William Guy Carr earlier wrote that antisemitism "plays right into the hands of the Illuminati."[4]

Confusing matters further, a curious subliterature accepts the *Protocols* but ascribes them not to Jews but to the Illuminati. Nesta Webster took the first steps. She found "striking" similarities between the Illuminati literature and the *Protocols*, devoted eight pages to documenting these parallels, and concluded that they prove "a clear connection between the Protocols and the former Secret Societies working for World Revolution, and also between the Protocols and Bolshevism."[5] Carr went further: the first person to publish the *Protocols* in a book, Sergei Nilus, "played right into the hands of the Illuminati conspirators" by ascribing the *Protocols* to Jews rather than the Illuminati. The *Protocols* is correct, he writes, "if the word 'Elders' is changed to read 'Illuminati.'"[6] This notion lives on: a former U.S. naval intelligence agent recently argued that the *Protocols* "were written intentionally to deceive people. For clear understanding . . . any reference to 'Jews' should be replaced with the word 'Illuminati' and the word 'goyim' should be replaced with the word 'cattle.'"[7]

Such efforts to keep the other conspiracist tradition at arms' length are fairly rare and usually unsuccessful; the Birch Society for all its efforts could not resist the siren call of antisemitism. Several factors overcome this purity of outlook and bring the two together: parallel histories, basic themes, mutual influences, shared beliefs, and overlapping culprits.

PARALLEL HISTORIES. The conspiracist traditions evolved in similar ways over the centuries. The premises of hate were established in the Crusading era—1096 for the Jews, 1307 for the secret societies. The Enlightenment saw the development of world conspiracy theories. The French Revolution created an unprecedented hunger for the sort of explanation that secret societies provide, and modernization during the nineteenth century gave antisemitism a comparable boost. By the 1890s, both traditions were fully formed and found their classic expositions. Curiously, both were done by Russians: as the Okhrana office in Paris forged the *Protocols of the Elders of Zion*, Lenin penned his theories about "monopoly capitalism."

But both sets of writings had to wait two decades before circumstances—World War I and the Russian Revolution—spurred a paroxysm of conspiracist thinking that placed these ideologies in charge of powerful states. Hitler and Stalin each drove his respective strain of the conspiracy mentality to its logical conclusions: one killed millions of Jews, the other millions of Ukranians, *kulaks* (peasants deemed enemies of the regime), and "saboteurs." Culminating nearly millennial-old hatreds, the two fought the largest-scale and most horrible battle of human history on the Eastern Front of World War II. The war marked a unique and harrowing moment—when world conspiracism came close to world domination. Antisemitism lost ground in the West after 1945, and both traditions diminished further in the 1980s as the Soviet Union imploded. Today both retain their greatest significance outside the West, and particularly in the Middle East.

The two conspiracist traditions adapted over time, keeping their basic outlooks intact while making the necessary changes to retain widespread appeal. Thus, anti-Jewish fears began with the Jewish religion, then switched to the Jewish "race," and subsequently the Jewish state. Secret society foes began with the Knights Templar, then moved on to the Freemasons, Illuminati, and the Anglo-American governments.

BASIC THEMES. But these are mere adjustments to changing circumstances; the language, spirit, and content of the two conspiracist traditions changed little across time and place. Basic themes reappear time and again. In eighteenth-century France, fears of a plot to starve the country lasted for decades almost without change as individuals of all classes similarly perceived provocations (a disruption in the grain supply), villains (men of power and their entourages), and denouements (the villains' discovery). Steven Kaplan concludes, "The actors, modes of expression, and contents of each episode bear a striking resemblance to each other. It is as if Frenchmen were somehow constrained to see the world this way. The repetition of the same pattern of perception and evaluation in each crisis experience suggests that the famine plot persuasion was built into the structure of the collective mentality."[8] Similarly in the United States, the conception of the Great American Enemy—the Bavarian Illuminati, Wall Street, and international communism—has common elements from the end of the eighteenth century to the present. American history displays, according to David Brion Davis, "a continuity in the imagery of subversion that bears no necessary relation to any given enemy." Those images include Trojan horses, entering wedges, blueprints for the destruction of liberty, and lists of names of supposedly loyal leaders who are exposed as the tools of a hostile power.[9] Antisemites also share much in common, as Robert Wistrich notes: "we find across the cultural and political divides an astonishingly similar conspiracy theory of history, society and politics, integrated into a closed system of belief and salvationist politics whose eschatological drive is always directed against the Jews.[10]

This continuity provides an important element in common between the two traditions. "Again and again," Norman Cohn writes, "one comes across the same weird, apocalyptic atmosphere, hints of some gigantic final battle in which the demonic hosts will be eliminated, the world released from the strangling octopus, a new age brought to birth."[11] The conspiracist mentality, Serge Moscovici adds, "is like a piece of clothing cut from the same material, according to the same pattern." He points to conspiracism's "hopeless monotony" through time; "the whole world draws from the same archaic depths."[12]

MUTUAL INFLUENCE. Having developed so much in parallel, it comes as little surprise to learn that the two traditions have often affected the other. Augustin de Barruel applied his ideas about secret societies to the Jews. Freemasons had a highly conspicuous role in early antisemitic literature. Lenin provided the precedent for Hitler. The *Protocols* provided a new way of seeing secret societies.

The two schools of thought also share specific elements in common. Four of these have particular importance: an abnormal animosity, a disdain of logic, a willingness to see most conspirators as dupes, and an inclination to see them on the verge of power. First, both antisemites and those fearful of secret societies fear that an apparently benign group has malign plans for world hegemony. Each school insists it has found the root cause of most of the world's problems, and both suspicions derive more from theoretical hatreds than from personal experience or conventional dislikes. They trace those ambitions to ancient times and imagine secret conclaves (the Elders of Zion, the World Masonic Council). Both overestimate the conspirator's powers in comparable ways; thus do Jews and Americans alike stand accused of causing earthquakes.

These abnormal hostilities can lead to abnormal acts. Conspiracy theorists ultimately hope to isolate and persecute all Jews, usually to the point of not permitting them to escape their predicament through conversion. The irradicably evil nature of the Jewish identity holds even against the wishes of the individual Jew. The Nazi race laws assessed the percentage of a person's Jewish ancestry and on that basis alone (as opposed to current religious affiliation) categorized individuals. Similarly, although moderate forms of anti-secret society phobia see Freemasons and Insiders as merely misguided individuals who, upon repentance, can be welcomed back to the fold of a common humanity, the full-bodied version brands conspirators in the antisemitic manner and never releases them. They, their children, and subsequent generations remain branded as parasites and enemies of the people. That was the fate of class enemies in systems ruled by Stalin, Mao, and Pol Pot of Cambodia. In short, the fears, logic, enemies, and solutions of the two traditions resemble each other quite closely.

Second, the two traditions disregard the constraints of logic. Time and place hardly matter: Jews are blithely located where they do not live, Freemasons and Illuminati blamed for conspiracies occurring long before either group came into existence. Both traditions ignore inconvenient matters of fact. If Jews are so powerful, why were so many of them killed in pogroms and then in the Holocaust? What sort of world-challenging power lets one-third of its people be murdered? The Jacobins outlawed Freemasonry in 1792, so how could a joint Jacobin-Freemason conspiracy have pulled off the French Revolution? Similarly, the Bolsheviks banned lodges, rendering outlandish a Masonic plot behind the Russian Revolution.

Third, they both see the majority of members as dupes. Most Jews are the victims of the Jewish conspiracy. The same goes for secret societies, both the Freemasons ("an overwhelming majority of Masons haven't the faintest idea of what their organization is really about") and the Illuminati ("many outstanding citizens . . . are blissfully ignorant that they are serving the cause of Satan").[13] Britons and Americans are the victims of financial interests: the Right accuses them of establishing a New World Order and the Left of gaining worldwide economic hegemony.

Finally, both types of conspiracy theorist believe its main nemesis has already achieved power. Antisemites read the French and Russian revolutions as Jewish success stories, as they do the creation of Israel and the makeup of the U.S. government. While enemies of secret societies see different forces conspiring behind the scenes—Illuminati in the French Revolution, capitalists in the Russian, British and American interests behind Israel, and the Money Power taking over in Washington—they agree on the key point of conspiratorial success.

The alleged culprits behind the two conspiracy theories are so similar that those who blame one usually blame the other one too. Most famously, they see Jews and Freemasons as colluding; in addition, they believe Jews join forces with either "imperialist" or totalitarian states.

FREEMASONS. Freemasons and Jews constitute the most lasting and significant combination. Seen as jointly opposed to the Church and aspiring to world domination, they often meld together into a single unit in the conspiracist imagination.[14] Jews are generally seen as too few in number to dominate by themselves, so they turn to Freemasons as their main source of agents.

Although the first known instance of a Jew's joining a lodge took place in London in 1732, there were few Jewish Freemasons until decades later, when Jews flocked to the craft to gain social respectability and to network. In general, British and French organizations accepted Jews far more readily than did German ones.

So much for fact. Already in 1778, a monk in Aachen anachronistically declared that "the Jews who crucified the Savior were Freemasons, Pilate and Herod [were] the directors of a [Masonic] lodge."[15] In retrospect, the year 1782 tends to be seen as the moment when Jews captured Freemasonry, for two events took place then: Freemasons held the Congress of Wilhelmsbad, a much-publicized meeting at which they abandoned the claim of descent from the Templars; and the Illuminati moved their headquarters to Frankfurt, which happened to be home to the Rothschild clan, and henceforth relied on Rothschild funding. The Jesuit de Barruel said Jews founded the Freemasons, a notion that subsequently became commonplace. Some Americans in the Antimasonic party saw Freemasonry as a "system of wickedness, which can be summed up in three words—Judaism, Paganism, and Idolatry!"[16]

The bulk of such accusations date from 1848, when the prominent role of Jews in the epochal events of that year prompted an anonymous German pamphleteer to ascribe those revolutions to Jews and Freemasons (perhaps Protestants too). But the distinctly antisemitic tone of Freemasonry in Germany meant that this and subsequent German accusations fell on deaf ears until after World War I. Only when translated into French[17] did tracts joining Jews and Freemasons find an audience. Indeed, they inspired a voluminous French literature on Freemasonry as a Jewish conspiracy aiming at world power. A relentless drumbeat followed. In 1852, Benjamin Disraeli connected Jews to secret societies in his own eccentric but important way:

> Destruction of the Semitic principle, extirpation of the Jewish religion, whether in the Mosaic or in the Christian form, the natural equality of man and the abrogation of property, are proclaimed by the secret societies who form provisional governments, and men of Jewish race are found at the head of every one of them. The people of God co-operate with atheists; the most skilful accumulators of property ally themselves with communists; the peculiar and chosen race touch the hand of all the scum and low castes of Europe![18]

An antisemitic study of 1869 deemed Freemasonry "an audacious work of Judaism, an artificial Judaism to recruit strange men—and especially Christians—to the Jewish race." Freemasonry, it said, uses Christian-style grades and symbols to fool innocent Christians and better hide its real aims. Its lodges are the "indispensable substitutes for the Synagogue."[19]

This theme became a veritable obsession. In 1880, a French priest asserted that Jews had hardly entered Freemasonry when they took it over, for Jews "have a natural instinct to dominate."[20] The first international antisemitic conference, held at Dresden in 1882, issued a manifesto that referred to a Jewish takeover of Freemasonry. Whole books delved into the intricacies of this control and discovered differing but compatible connections. One common theme had the Alliance Israélite Universelle, a Jewish philanthropy, running the Freemasons. Edouard Drumont, the so-called pope of antisemitism, filled his influential tracts from the 1880s on with references to "Jewish Freemasonry." In 1893, a French archbishop declared that "everything in Freemasonry is basically Jewish, exclusively Jewish, passionately Jewish, from the start to the end."[21] By that time, according to the historian Jacob Katz, it had become "impossible"for French antisemitic writers not to attack Freemasons as well.[22]

The Dreyfus Affair of 1894–99 further emphasized the Jewish-Masonic connection. Paris in the late 1890s was also the time and place where the tsar's secret police fabricated the *Protocols*, with its many allusions to Freemasonry. Indeed, the first publication of the *Protocols* in 1903 calls this document the *Minutes of the Meeting of the World Union of Freemasons and Elders of Zion*. The Russian term *Zhidomasonstvo* ("Jewmasonry") codified this alleged union, and Tsaritsa Alexandra wrote in her diary in 1918 that the tsar "read to us the protocols of the free masons."[23] Assuming the Protocols to be genuine, Nesta Webster concludes that *"they are the revised programme of illuminized Freemasonry formulated by a Jewish lodge of the Order."*[24]

Notions of Jewish-Masonic collusion took on enhanced importance in Germany in the wake of World War I. Many Germans argued that their country's war defeat resulted not from military failure but from a "stab in the back" *(Dolchstoss)* administered by Jews, Freemasons, socialists, Bolsheviks, and others—anyone but the actual leaders of Germany. In this context, the union of Jew and Freemason proved powerfully persuasive. The very day Kaiser Wilhelm abdicated the throne, a newspaper announced that "the war of 1914 was begun by international Jewry, international Freemasonry, and international plutocracy, then carried through for a distinct aim: to annihilate the German empire."[25] Friedrich Wichtl argued in a much-read book that Freemasons, and especially the Jews among them, had instigated both the war and the Russian Revolution.[26] Taking this a step further, the newly revised *Protocols of the Elders of Zion* blamed the war on Jews alone, turning Freemasons into their pawns. (The translation of the *Protocols* into German altered the Russian text of some twenty years earlier in many ways, taking recent events into account and making the Freemasons far more prominent.) Erich Ludendorff, the general turned antisemite, argued that non-Jews who join the Freemasons become "artificial Jews."[27]

Nazi propaganda accepted this fusion, prominently railed against it, and decreed Freemasonry a Jewish offshoot. A barrage of books and pamphlets stressed their joint activities against the monarchy and their betrayal of Germany in the war. Nazis then took advantage of this alleged connection to close all the Masonic lodges in Germany in mid-1935. By this time, Katz explains, there was "an almost complete identification" of Jews and Freemasons.[28] To this day, many Europeans and Americans assume that Freemasons and Jews are somehow connected. Soviet propaganda went so far as to have Freemasons worshipping the Star of David.

IMPERIALISTS. Since the eighteenth century, conspiracy theorists have speculated without end about Jews conspiring in combination with a government, most often the British one. Frederick II of Prussia (1712–86) saw Jews playing a key role in the limits placed on the power of the British king, then joining with Britons in corrupt and martial activities to extend their joint influence to the Continent.[29] Jews were key to the British victory over Napoleon. The undermining of German crafts in the late nineteenth century by British industry stimulated a belief that economic liberalism was a Jewish-British trick. The *Protocols* refer to the "kinship between the English and the Jews."[30] One French author describes London as the city where "the kings of Israel sit" and portrayed Jewish bankers in control of the British Empire.[31] The Boer War confirmed the widespread opinion that British soldiers and Jewish money were closely allied; Lenin charged Cecil Rhodes with being "mainly responsible" for the war,[32] and others connected him to Jewish financiers. The same ideas echoed in the United States. One opponent described President Grover Cleveland as "the agent of Jewish bankers and British gold."[33] In Russia, one of the first editions of the *Protocols* portrayed Zionism as always "friendly to English foreign policy."[34]

These ideas gained new currency after the trauma of World War I, and London's issuance of the Balfour Declaration in 1917, calling for "the establishment in Palestine of a national home for the Jewish people," did nothing to diminish them. World historian Oswald Spengler saw the British and the Jews working in combination to keep Germany weak. Influential antisemitic writings portrayed King George V as the Jews' supreme ruler and argued that the English and Jews jointly planned World War I to further their plot for world domination. Henry Ford's *Dearborn Independent* dubbed London the Jews' "capital" before World War I.[35] Joseph Goebbels, the chief Nazi propagandist, called Britons "the Jews among the Aryans," and Heinrich Himmler drew a closer connection, portraying the British as descendants of Jews. Such ideas live on today in conspiracist circles: Lyndon LaRouche places a British-Jewish alliance at the center of his conspiracism and the Ku Klux Klan promotes it as well.

At times, and especially in the aftermath of World War I, other states were seen joining with Great Britain and the Jews. Colonel McCormick's *Chicago Tribune* connected Jews, Anglo-Saxons, and communists in a single plot. Many Britons saw Jews and Germans allied together. German slogans during World War II harped on an alleged pact between the Western democracies generally and world Jewry. Ludendorff deemed a secret Jewish government to be working with, if not dominating, London and Paris; he also saw it behind the revolution in Russia. The 1935 French edition of the *Protocols* contains an introduction that has the German, British, and American governments all benefiting from a Jewish connection.

When in 1947 the United States inherited Britain's traditional role of maintaining the international status quo, it also inherited the role of alleged ally to the Jews. That this transfer nearly coincided with the state of Israel's birth enhanced the importance and mystery of the U.S.-Israeli bond for conspiracy theorists. So close do they see it that the United States inspires an opprobrium reminiscent of that previously reserved for Jews. Actually, this merging began at the top of the twentieth century. As early as 1906, one German author stated that "in a certain sense, one can now characterize the Jews as the representatives of Americanism here. Judaization is actually Americanization"; a few years later, the renowned German scholar Werner Sombart more succinctly called the United States "a state of Jews [*Judenstaat*]."[36] André Glucksmann, a French philosopher, sees anti-Americanism inheriting the features of classic anti-Jewish bias, with its notions of power unseen and violent forces beyond control. "The reproaches are the same. . . . The words are just different."[37] Similarly, Paul Hollander, an analyst of attitudes toward the United States, notes that "to a large degree anti-Americanism represents a transfer of hatred from Israel to the United States since these two countries are closely allied and identified with one another."[38] The columnist Richard Grenier goes so far as to state that "everything bad is the fault no longer of the Jews, but of America."[39] Dan Diner concludes that "anti-Americanism resembles anti-Semitism structurally."[40]

The notion of a rapacious octopus spanning the globe, its tentacles sucking in all good things, offers visual evidence of the interchangeability of Jews and the imperialist states. The great German dramatist Johann von Schiller (1759–1805) first conjured up this image and applied it to Great Britain. With time, the octopus imagery was applied to the two parties acting together: an American tract of 1894 showed a ten-armed octopus-like creature reaching from the United Kingdom bearing the sobriquet "Rothschilds."[41] It can also apply just to Jews: Soviet propaganda spoke of "the espionage octopus of Zionism," and the British far Right called Zionism a vast empire whose "tentacles" menace the entire world.

TOTALITARIAN MOVEMENTS. Anticipating the wild exaggera-
tions to come, Tsar Nicholas II wrote in 1905 that 90 percent of the revolutionaries in Russia were Jewish, a much-quoted hyperbole[42] that would
become enshrined in subsequent decades as individuals of Jewish background[43] did play a disproportionately important role in the Russian Revolution. More broadly, communism was in large part formulated by Jews
or former Jews, starting with Karl "Mordechai" Marx, then Otto Bauer
and Rosa Luxemburg in Germany, Bela Kun in Hungary, and Leon Trotsky, Pavel Axelrod, and Grigori Zinoviev in Russia.[44] Antisemites extrap-
olated from these individuals to create an alluring but false law: Jews by
nature are Bolshevik. Even so great a figure as Winston Churchill at one
moment accepted the reality of a Jewish-communist nexus:

> This movement among the Jews is not new. From the days of
> Spartacus-Weishaupt, to those of Karl Marx, and down to Trot-
> sky (Russia), Bela Kun (Hungary), Rosa Luxemburg (Germany),
> and Emma Goldman (United States), this worldwide conspiracy
> for the overthrow of civilisation and for the reconstitution of
> society on the basis of arrested development and envious malevo-
> lence, and impossible equality has been steadily growing. It has
> been the mainspring of every subversive movement during the
> nineteenth century.[45]

In the perverse logic of conspiracism, enemies are really friends. That six
million Jews lost their lives at the hands of Nazi murderers to conspiracy theorists proves not the absolute polarity of these two groups but their con-
nectedness. A whole leftist literature has developed around the
contention that, in an effort to get Jews to Palestine in the 1930s, Zionists
worked hand in glove with Nazi Germany; in particular, Jewish financiers
supposedly aided Hitler's rise to power. Lenni Brenner offers scholarly
support for this thesis,[46] and Jim Allen provides its literary expression;[47] the
Soviet government enshrined this noxious theory as official ideology.
Neo-Nazis go a step further and declare that Zionists killed Jews in the Holocaust. LaRouche bends words so far as to posit that Jews were the only Nazis.

Who runs the show? As much as they believe in a joining of forces
between Jews and others, conspiracy theorists dismiss the notion of balance and mutual benefit as naïve. Someone must be in charge, but who?
Are Jews the puppeteer and secret societies the puppet? Or is it the other

way around? Such questions befuddle many conspiracy theorists. An influential antisemite noted in 1880 that "the Jews inspire and direct everything" but also that Freemasonry "inspires and directs everything" and admitted this to be "a dilemma": "either it is Masonry that has seized of the Jew and exploits him and pushes him in front; or it is the Jew who has taken hold of Masonry and made it the stepping board and instrument of his designs."[48]

A century later, the same dilemma continues to torment, but now the key issue concerns the U.S.-Israel bond: does the American Israel Public Affairs Committee call the shots in Washington, or was the Jewish state created to further imperialism's interests in the Middle East? One thesis has the imperialists protecting Israel; another has the Zionists running America. One minute, the U.S.-Israel relationship is more intimate than the facts warrant; then the two countries turn into opponents. In general, Americans are more susceptible to the idea of a Zionist plot,[49] and Muslim Middle Easterners put slightly more credence in the imperialist thesis.[50] Even scholars admit bafflement before this issue. Yasumasa Kuroda of the University of Hawaii, for example, states that "at times it has been difficult to tell which country is being manipulated."[51] So widespread are these conspiracist ideas that former secretary of state Dean Rusk felt impelled to repudiate them in his memoirs: "That Israel is not an American satellite is a point many Arabs unfortunately miss. But the opposite is true as well: The United States is not an Israeli satellite, a point that Americans sometimes miss."[52]

Other conspiracy theorists know exactly who uses whom. Devoted antisemites portray all secret societies—Freemasons, Illuminati, Communists, the British and American governments, even Jesuits—as Jewish creations. For them, the ancient roots, cohesive ties, and religious aspirations of Jews make them necessarily the senior partner in any joint venture. Further, while Jews can plausibly fill high positions in secret societies, how are the latter to infiltrate Jewish institutions? After all, one never hears of Christians' penetrating the Elders of Zion.

Those preoccupied with secret societies insist rather on foreign governments as the ultimate powerbrokers. Most of the time they see Washington calling the shots in Jerusalem, but some dwell on the British role. Lyndon LaRouche and his followers see London controlling not just the Jews but also their Muslim cousins. In their view, it "has maintained control of the Mideast in the post-World War II period" by sponsoring both "Zionist expansionist cults" and "Islamic-formatted and Arab-radical terrorism."[53]

Standing back from the details and reviewing a quarter millennium of conspiracism, two trends become apparent. First, what began as two wholly discrete sets of fears has gradually, irregularly, but steadily merged. Antisemitic and anti-secret society phobias began as unrelated phenomena with different appeals; over time they became ever more similar. The immediate aftermath of World War I—that terrible time of crisis for the West and great innovation for conspiracism—marked the moment when the two traditions perhaps became more merged than distinct. The partial explanations of old no longer sufficed. Radical dangers called for a single meta-conspiracy theory combining the antisemitic and secret society myths. Confusion reigned. Lenin and King George V of England both now became simultaneously Freemasons and Jews (of course, neither was either). The new Bolshevik leadership interpreted the British occupation of Palestine in December 1917, just one month after it got to power, as a direct threat to itself. Hitler rose to power interpreting nearly everything in antisemitic terms, then added on an anti-secret society outlook. Conversely, Stalin was a thorough anti-imperialist who at the end of his life (in the Doctors' Plot) was on the verge of launching a massive assault against Jews.

Second, the antisemitic tradition appears to have gained in importance at the expense of its anti-secret society counterpart. Conspiratorial antisemitism started later but continues longer. Jews have a cohesion and a seriousness that secret societies and even governments lack. Also, Jews fight back—organizing, lobbying, taking out full-page ads in newspapers—which gives them an authenticity and reality that secret societies lack.

Indeed, the antisemitic version so predominates by now that the anti-secret society theme sometimes drops out of sight. The world knows well about the Nation of Islam's views on Jews (who control the U.S. Congress, Hollywood, the academy, and the medical profession), but few realize that its theology places yet more stress on Freemasons (believed to control the whole white race). Likewise, while Pat Robertson was roundly criticized for implicit antisemitism in his *The New World Order*, that book contains page after page of explicit and wild-eyed fear of Freemasons and the Council on Foreign Relations; no one seems to notice or care about the latter. Analysts go so far as to dismiss the fear of secret societies as an "old conspiracy theory predating 'the international Jew' theory,"[54] implying that it is defunct.

This blindness leads to a peculiar mistake: an assumption that all conspiracist references concern Jews. Aware of antisemitic conspiracism, uninterested in the anti-secret society variant, Dennis King insists in his study of Lyndon LaRouche that references to the British as the ultimate conspirators are really "code language"to refer to Jews.[55] In fact, they are references to the British. In a study of the American militia movement, Kenneth Stern writes that its "leaders are careful to talk about 'international bankers' or the 'Federal Reserve' or the 'Trilateral Commission' or 'eastern elites.' But these are code phrases, carefully picked by the leadership, to pull people into their movement without greeting them with overt anti-Semitism." Stern further contends that the militia movement believes in a Jewish conspiracy, "even if some call it something else and never mention Jews."[56] Both these authors make the mistake of thinking that today's Right feels a need to hide its antisemitism with euphemisms. There was indeed a time when euphemisms like "international bankers" were needed, but in today's uninhibited climate that is no longer the case.

Michael Lind offers a most interesting case of confusion along these lines. When Lind found that leading conservatives (William F. Buckley, Jr., Norman Podhoretz) failed adequately to condemn Pat Robertson's conspiracism (as displayed in his book, *The New World Order*), Lind not only turned against his former conservative mentors but harshly denounced conservatism as an intellectual movement. He took special interest in Robertson's tract, analyzing its sources and implications in no fewer than three articles and in a book chapter. Yet for all his close scrutiny of Robertson, Lind's blindness to the anti-secret society tradition causes him fundamentally to misunderstand *The New World Order* by turning it into a singleminded attack on Jews. Lind makes three mistakes. He reads anti-secret society statements as anti-Jewish ones; thus, he insists that Robertson's warnings about a New World Order constitute a step toward "legitimizing the paranoid worldview of the opponents of ZOG."[57] He dismisses or ignores Robertson's many sympathetic, even laudatory references to Jews and Israel.[58] Strangest of all, he drags Jews into Robertson's text where they are simply absent. For example, when quoting Robertson's writings, Lind inserts references to Jews in square brackets;[59] he also makes Karl Marx into a Jew.

When, due to Lind's accusations of antisemitism, Robertson had to reply, he seemed genuinely baffled as he unequivocally denounced antisemitism: "I deeply regret that anyone in the Jewish community believes that my description of international bankers and use of the phrase 'European bankers' in my book refers to Jews. . . . I have never intentionally used what some would describe as code words to portray Jewish business interests. I condemn and repudiate in the strongest terms those who would use such code words as a cover for anti-Semitism."[60] His apology is credible, for Robertson mentions Jews only in passing. Indeed, Lind himself documents how Robertson excises the antisemitism of the sources he otherwise very closely follows. There are mentions of Jews in *The New World Order*, to be sure, and the Rothschild family in particular, but they appear as part of the secret society myth, not as a code word for Jew-hatred. It bears noting that even Jews of an anti-secret society disposition point to the Rothschilds as conspirators; James Perloff notes that he himself "is partly of Russian-Jewish lineage," but this does not prevent him from raising the usual conspiracist tropes about the Rothschild family.[61]

CONTINUITIES

[R]eplacing the term "International Jewry" with the myth of "World Zionism" . . . was simply old anti-semitic wine in new anti-Zionist bottles!
ROBERT WISTRICH[62]

It is quite remarkable that the antisemitic and anti-secret society traditions should have almost merged, for they have differed in important ways throughout their long histories.

First, the antisemitic myth is a cohesive one, focusing on a small and virtually unchanging group of people. Conspiratorial antisemites locate one cohesive Jewish plot through history, starting with Herod and lasting until the present. Antisemites perceive differences among Jews as a superficial; they all answer to the same central authority. *"We have in our service,"* the *Protocols* boasts, *"persons of all opinions, of all doctrines, restorating monarchists, demagogues, socialists, communists, and utopian dreamers of every kind."*[63] In contrast, the secret society phobia is directed against groups of every description: religious and anti-religious (Jesuits and Illuminati), moderate and extremist (Freemasons and Jacobins), capitalist and socialist (arms dealers and Communist party agents), great powers and fly-by-night individuals (the British government and witches), rich and poor (Trilateral Commissioners and Catholic immigrants), educated and ignorant (Philosophes and mafia). Further, some accused secret society conspirators are alive (members of the Council on

Foreign Relations), some disappeared centuries ago (Templars), and others never existed (Rosicrucians).

Just as Jews share much in common, so do antisemites. In contrast, the secret society enemies are as varied as the objects of their fear. Those preoccupied with Templars see the world very differently from those phobic about the U.S. government. Antisemites work together much better than do the foes of secret societies. Anti-secret society theorists cannot even agree among themselves whether the secret societies collude or fight. Those who believe they cooperate see a single group driving history over the past for two hundred years. For Nesta Webster, "the Russian Revolution . . . was a *direct continuation of the French.*"[64] Similarly, for Pat Robertson, "The satanic carnage that the Illuminati brought to France was the clear predecessor of the bloodbaths and successive party purges visited on the Soviet Union by the communists."[65] In contrast, others see secret societies at each others' throats and find in their conflict the motor force of history. As a character in Ishmael Reed's novel puts it, "beneath or behind all political and cultural warfare lies a struggle between secret societies."[66] The notion of Freemasons in conflict with each other has wide appeal, with some opponents going so far as to understand the world wars in terms of German versus Russian Freemasons, and others portraying modern history as a "war between English and French Freemasonry."[67]

Second, while antisemites reflect the serious and cohesive body of Jewish thinking, making their politics almost invariably focused, venomous, nasty, serious, and dangerous to its targets,[68] secret society conspiracists range from the murderous to the humorous. In some cases, they turn toward an "occult conspiracy" myth that veers into the magical, permitting one ancient tradition to pile promiscuously onto another— Egyptian, Iranian, and Indian mystery religions, the kabala, Pythogoreanism, Gnosticism, astrology and alchemy, tales of Druids— forming a woolly, indiscriminate whole. This anything-goes atmosphere then attracts mystics, charlatans, and thrill seekers.

In other cases, flippancy and humor take over, along the lines of a tongue-in-cheek 1894 *New York Times* editorial:

> the chief disintegrating force of the modern world is the passion
> for collecting postage stamps . . . [T]he postage stamp collector is
> infinitely more to be feared than is any other variety of political
> or religious fanatic. . . . [T]he chief aim in life of the stamp col-

lector is to alter the political map of the world. . . . to promote in every possible way the breaking up of kingdoms and republics and the formation of new ones. . . . These collectors have completely subordinated patriotism and morality to the gratification of their ruling passion. Acting together with perfect unanimity, they can surely accomplish vastly more than the Freemasons, the Jesuits, and the combined secret societies of Europe.[69]

A century later, as the Soviet bloc was breaking up, The *American Philatelist* echoed this thesis: changes in world politics make for good stamps, so stamp collectors must be the cause of unrest. "Why should Western Europe be uniting just when Eastern Europe is dividing? Who benefits from the process of change itself? Who else but stamp collectors."[70] In *Pale Fire*, a highly literate parody of conspiracism, Vladimir Nabokov writes an execrable thousand-line poem about the banalities of middle-aged suburban life, then provides a bogus critical apparatus (foreword, commentary, index) that turns the poem into an adventure tale of the lost kingdom of Zembla.[71] The humorously named National Insecurity Council ("a cabal of rogue journalists with headquarters somewhere on the West Coast") published *It's a Conspiracy! The Shocking Truth About America's Favorite Conspiracy Theories!*[72] Those favorites include everything from Henry Ford's Nazi connections to the faking of Elvis Presley's death. The humorist Calvin Trillin pokes fun of those who think Indiana road signs are part of a conspiracy.[73] A breezy paperback aimed at the young has Noam Chomsky in cartoon introduce his conspiracy theories.[74]

The secret society tradition offers vicarious thrills and risqué pleasure without danger, somewhat like *manga*, the violent or sexual comics that staid Japanese businessmen read during their commutes. The Templar myth, for example,

> is not and has never been a wicked and destructive fantasy of the type of the Protocols of the Elders of Zion, or like the old witch-craft hysteria. It has proved to be an eccentric but harmless theosophical dream, sometimes exploited by charlatans to the detriment of the credulous, but not used to encompass evil ends. . . . The note of bizarre play-acting has never been absent from Templarism, and, indeed, in this lack of "seriousness" some of its crazy charm lies.[75]

Secret society phobia can thus be innocuous, a happy insanity, something antisemitism cannot be.

The intense focus on Jews, secret societies, and Anglo-Saxons means ignoring 94 percent of humanity. Of particular note among those left out are three of the great powers that tried to dominate Europe between 1618 and 1991, the extreme Left and Right, universalist religions, and the entire non-Western world.

EUROPEAN GREAT POWERS. Starting with the Thirty Years' War (1618–48) and ending two and a half centuries later (with the Franco-Prussian War of 1870), French leaders such as Cardinal Richelieu, Louis XIV, Napoleon, and Napoleon III repeatedly tried to establish France as the hegemonic power in Europe. In the course of this effort, they precipitated what might be called the first two world wars, those of the Spanish Succession (1702–13) and of Napoleon Bonaparte (1792–1815). Subsequent French history somewhat parallels that of Great Britain. In the nineteenth century, the two states built up the largest global empires, both were battered by the World Wars, and since 1945 they have similarly decolonized, built up nuclear arsenals, and enjoyed the prestige that goes with sitting as a permanent member of the United Nations Security Council. If anything, France has more wealth and military power than Great Britain, and it exercises a far more independent foreign policy. Yet France has a low to nonexistent profile among conspiracy theorists.

From Bismarck to Hitler, 1870–1945, Germans strenuously and increasingly challenged the world order, thereby precipitating World Wars I and II. Yet hardly any conspiracy theories discuss the Hohenzollern aspirations for a "place in the sun," Ruhr region corporate efforts to gain market share, cultural imperialism in *Mitteleuropa*, much less Nazi ambitions at world conquest. The rare anti-Teutonic conspiracy theory finds Germans working in conjunction with either Jews or Anglo-Americans. For example, the Germanophobe Nesta Webster in 1921 fingered a German conspiracy as more certain and basic than these others, but she always had Germans working in collusion with them. In the course of a single study, she variously discerned an alliance between "Prussian militarism and international finance," between "German Imperialism and Jewish intrigue," and between "German Atheism and Jewish antagonism to Christianity."[76]

Russia seems to be accepted as geographically the world's largest country, as though that were a given and not the result of many centuries of territorial aggrandizement. Or, if questioned, this size is explained in defensive terms, as though invasions by the Mongols, Napoleon, and Hitler account for the need for a glacis. (If this were truly the case, Belgium would outsize Russia.) In the post-Soviet era, Russian intentions to retain control over the "near abroad"—the other republics of the former Soviet Union—arouse few concerns internationally and no conspiracy theories.

LENINISM AND NAZISM. The Communist and Nazi movements amounted to the two greatest world conspiracies of the human experience. Lenin saw "our revolution" not as something limited merely to Russia but as "a *prologue* to the worldwide socialist revolution, a *step* toward it."[77] For him the events of 1917 did not constitute the "Russian Revolution" but rather, in the words of one historian, the "worldwide revolution that happened to have had its start in Russia. . . . Lenin was first and foremost an internationalist, a world revolutionary, . . . [who] would have been prepared to lead the revolution in any country where the opportunity presented itself."[78] His was truly a world conspiracy. So was Stalin's. The Soviet propaganda machine articulated his dream of an "All-European Union of Soviet Socialist Republics," to be followed by what a poet called "only one Soviet nation." The Soviet Union subsequently acted on these dreams by meddling in countries as far away as Cuba, Angola, and Vietnam. Hitler also had world domination in mind, as he repeatedly indicated. For example, on declaring war against the United States, he spoke of the "historic struggle" that would be "decisive not only for the history of Germany but for the whole of Europe and indeed for the world."[79]

Conspiracy theorists barely notice these developments. Quite the contrary, the cognoscenti pooh-pooh allegations about these global ambitions: Winston Churchill met with much disdain in the 1930s when he talked of the "jackboots," as did Ronald Reagan in the 1980s with his one-time reference to the "evil empire." Both totalitarian movements may have relied on semiclandestine structures and made overt plans for world hegemony, but they attracted less notice than empires put together in a fit of absent-mindedness (Great Britain), hardly existent (the United States), or completely fantastical (Jews).

Strangely, the Right tends to see the totalitarians not as autonomous forces but as agents of Jewish or capitalist conspirators. Antisemites like Henry Ford believe that "The so-called 'dictatorship of the proletariat' is really and practically the dictatorship of Jews."[80] Similarly, secret society-phobes like the John Birch Society argue that "what you call 'Communism' is not run from Moscow or Peking, but is an arm of a bigger conspiracy run from New York, London and Paris"; the apparent Leninist rulers are nothing but "hired Communist thugs."[81] Dan Smoot, an American rightist, portrays Israel and the Soviet Union as "pursuing a common objective . . . to isolate all Arab countries from the United States and drive them into the Soviet orbit."[82] In other words, the Soviet empire threatens only when linked up with the fearsome Jews or Anglos.

Even Stalin failed to see a Nazi conspiracy staring him in the face. As millions of German troops gathered on his border, he found ways to explain away this very real threat. (For an inquiry into this misperception, see appendix B.) Yet more bizarre was how each totalitarian movement insisted that Jews stood behind the other. Nazis concocted "Jewish Bolshevism," charging that the Soviet Union was a tool of international Jewry. The Kremlin later (after the 1967 Arab-Israeli war) responded with the obnoxious specter of "Jewish Nazism," deemed the most pernicious form of Nazism. These contradictory but compatible claims had the effect of further merging the two conspiracist traditions.

UNIVERSALIST RELIGIONS. Universalist religions—and militant ones most of all—logically should be more suspect than an exclusivist one like Judaism. Buddhists and Hindus, numbering in the hundreds of millions, would seem to make for a more likely conspirator than do Jews, who number a fraction as many. But this is not the case, for (unlike Jews) they neither lived cheek-by-jowl with Europeans nor did they symbolize the cutting edge of modernity.

It is noteworthy how little attention Protestants pay anymore to Catholicism, given the religious wars of previous centuries, the centralized nature of the Church, and the hundreds of millions of Catholics. To be sure, a fanatical sort of anti-Catholicism does remain alive in tiny circles, but it lacks wide appeal. Alberto Rivera, an American who fraudulently claims to be an ex-Jesuit, puts out materials that accuse the Jesuits of standing behind *The Communist Manifesto*, the Russian Revolution, and Hitler, and one of his tracts avows that a computer in Vatican City lists the name of every living Protestant, thus preparing the ground for a new Inquisition.[83] He also portrays ecumenicism as a means to cause Protestantism to wither away. His collaborator, Jack Chick, raises the alarm about Washington's intentions: "I can believe we're going to sign a concordat with the Vatican. And if we do, we're going to be hauled away in trucks in all directions. We'll be taken away . . . to mental institutions somewhere up in Alaska. The Catholics are going to eat us up."[84] Louis Farrakhan's publications call the pope the worldwide leader of organized crime. But the very unfamiliarity of these themes points to their lack of appeal and their unimportance. Fears of Protestant conspiracies are even less apparent, though Jehovah's Witnesses are sometimes seen as a Jewish offshoot and made part of the Jewish conspiracy.

Confirming that Catholic and Protestant conspiracy theorists do not really fear each other is that each connects the other to Jews. Father Coughlin's Christian Front disparaged the Protestant movement by asserting in 1938 that "the Jews were behind [Martin] Luther."[85] In the same spirit, William Guy Carr announced that "[John] Calvin's real name was Cohen" and that the Geneva reformer's movement was in fact a Jewish plot to divide Christians.[86] More colorfully yet, a Daughter of the American Revolution declared about that same time that "Pope Pius is a Jew, I tell you. He and the Jews pooled $5,000,000 to stop Hitler. You think the Pope was elected by the College of Cardinals? Nonsense. The Pope was put there by the international Jewish bankers. They hold a $15,000,000 mortgage on the Vatican!"[87] Curiously, even Catholic conspiracism acknowledged the truth of this accusation; Father Coughlin admitted that "the first thirty-three popes were Jews. Among the last ten popes we've had, three were predominantly Jewish."[88]

Islam ranks a bit higher as conspirator, no surprise given the long history of Christian-Muslim hostility, Islam's reputation for aggressiveness, and the extreme volatility of Middle Eastern politics. Here, however, Westerners fear a Muslim conspiracy less than they do two other forms of hostility: *jihad* (sacred war) and demographics. *Jihad* involves all-out bellicosity, not a conspiracy. In this spirit, two British authors write that "Islam is on the move again. It could prove as frightening to the West, and perhaps as economically disruptive, as the stolid Soviet empire ever was."[89] Jim Rogers of Columbia University goes further, seeing Islam as a greater problem than Muscovy: "Westerners think modern history is the 50-year story of the Cold War. That was an interesting, important struggle, but it's only a sideshow compared with the conflict of the past 1,300 years between Islam and Christianity."[90]

Nor is the demographic concern conspiratorial. Muslims number nearly one billion and enjoy a huge demographic growth rate; millions have immigrated to Western Europe and North America, where, in contrast to the small and diminishing numbers of Jews, their numbers are starkly growing. Quite a few Europeans view this as the top social problem and even see a danger that their country will lose its historic identity and become Muslim.[91] Along with Britain's National Front, many right-wing groups identify Islam as "a deadly enemy of the white race."[92] Such sentiments lead a Norwegian analyst to predict that "as fear of Islam is more and more replacing communism as the perceived main threat to Western Civilisation, Islamic conspiracy theories are likely to become more and more elaborated and appealing."[93] But Muslims have little prospect as arch-conspirator. Who can blame the French Revolution on them, much less modern capitalism? As Muslims become more numerous and important, they seem to become adjuncts of Jews and secret societies, not their replacement. Europe's long fascination with the latter two is likely long to remain in place.

For confirmation, note the career of Vladimir Zhirinovsky, the often clownish but briefly successful leader of Russia's misnamed Liberal Democratic party. He had a conventional conspiracy theory to explain the Soviet collapse in 1991 (Americans instigated the non-Russian republics to revolt, finding this cheaper and less dangerous than confronting Russia militarily). But he spun a far more original theory about Russia's future enemy, one that bears special note because it has little to do with Jews, secret societies, or imperialists: "today the threat to Russia comes from the south. From Afghanistan, which is already attacking Tajikistan; from Tehran, which is planning the Pan-Islamic seizure of massive stretches of land; from Ankara, where plans for a Great Turkish State have long been ready."[94] Zhirinovsky based his foreign policy and much of his political career on this proclamation of a Muslim plan to "smash Russia"[95] and argued that Russia should preempt with a military strike of its own. One analyst doubts that Zhirinovsky strongly held this view but did so for opportunistic reasons: he "has no convictions of his own. He badly wants to be president of Russia, and he thinks that a set of rabidly anti-Islamic foreign policy positions will help him attain power."[96] If so, Zhirinovsky made a mistake, for the Russian public hardly responded to the notion of a Muslim threat, and his political career declined.

NON-WESTERN WORLD. With rare exceptions, the rest of the world is seen as not having the means or imagination to stage an assault on Europe and North America. Japan and China inspired the "Yellow Peril" scare initiated by Kaiser Wilhelm in 1895, but this conjured up hordes of immigrants, not an insider's plot. The notion of Japan, Inc., a hierarchical Japanese entity that is undermining the West's industrial base, hints at a conspiracy, but it lacks Western agents and dupes, and as Japan's recession continues, this bogey appears to have lost its punch. Otherwise, whole populations are simply ignored, including the Indian, the African, and the

Latin American. When a non-Western party does get into the act, it does so affiliated to Jews or a secret society. The Nazis saw hundreds of millions of Chinese as mere accessories to Jewish efforts to strengthen the Red Army. A Japanese author explains how Taiwan and South Africa become conspirators by joining Israel's effort at world hegemony through economic domination, arms sales, and atomic weaponry. As a rule, then, the excluded 94 percent can become a serious conspirator only by joining with one of the 6 percent, and preferably with Jews.

Why are conspirators limited to Jews, Israel, Freemasons, Britons, and Americans? Perhaps because they share two outstanding characteristics: modernity and idealism.

MODERNITY. In the early nineteenth century, the Jew—urban, urbane, and liberal—came to symbolize modernity itself. For example, in a July 1818 letter, a German military man ascribed the industrial revolution to "Jewish mischief."[97] Late in the century, reactionaries described the liberal program of democracy, rule of law, freedom of speech, and even universal education as the "Judaization" of Europe. The predations of capitalism ("money is the true master of everything") were blamed squarely on the Jews. The famous names of antisemitism dwelled on this subject. Such luminaries as the composer Richard Wagner and the historian Heinrich von Treitschke associated Judaism with modernity. The influential Protestant clergyman Adolf Stoecker presented Jews as the motor force of the changes he feared and despised: "all Germany's troubles come from the Jews" summed up the position he became famous for.[98] Wilhelm Marr, the activist who coined the term *antisemitism*, expressed the same sentiment more melodramatically: *"No triumphant leader of ancient or modern times can boast of greater spiritual or cultural-historical success than the least haggler [Schacherjude] peddling ribbons from his street-corner cart. In fact, without striking a blow, Jewry—politically persecuted through the centuries—has today become Germany's sociopolitical dictator."*[99]

Similar thinking existed outside Germany. In Great Britain, the distinguished novelist G. K. Chesterton dubbed Jews the agents of a "regrettable modernity."[100] In the United States, Ernest Elmhurst (real name: Hermann Fleischkopf) declared that "Democracy is Jewish. Democracy is nothing but the political system of the internationalist Jewish bankers. Baruch, Brandeis, Rabbi Wise, Lehman, Frankfurter—all Jews and all of them for Democracy. That proves Democracy is Jewish."[101] While Jews still fill this role (the Russian communist leader Gennady Zyuganov blames the Industrial Revolution on them), Israel now more often takes the blame; the Middle East's only mature democracy has a per capita income comparable to Britain's. These facts further inspire those wild forms of anti-Zionism in which Jews become responsible for any and all the consequences of modernity.

The strange phenomenon of antisemitism without Jews vividly demonstrates the utility of Jews as symbol and scapegoat. Vehement anti-semitic tracts often come out of places where no Jews live, such as certain rural regions of France or in several Arab countries. One influential anti-semite, Léon Meurin, wrote his major works while serving as archbishop on the remote Indian Ocean island of Mauritius. A Russian counterpart, the monk Iliodor, published antisemitic newspapers from his monastery but admitted never having met a Jew, and the same went for nearly all the other pre-1917 Russian antisemites. Idaho and Montana, recent hotbeds of antisemitism in the United States, are states with among the fewest Jews in the country. Spain produced a bounty of antisemites, though no known Jews had lived in that country for four centuries. But the purest form of "Jewish" being synonymous with modernity exists in Japan, a country with no indigenous Jewish community but which has twice in this century engaged in widespread and visible antisemitic campaigns.

Like Jews, Freemasons tend to be among the most successful members of society. To him who hates modernity, they serve as its plausible motor engine. In the United States, Antimasons found that "Freemasonry embodied currents that were changing their country beyond recognition. . . . As an institution that served an emerging industrial society, Freemasonry understandably evoked suspicion among those not yet rec-onciled to the new system."[102] On a far more massive scale, the United Kingdom and United States fill the same role. In its time, each has been the world's most powerful state and the symbol of capitalist wealth. Beyond symbolism, these states have had a highly disruptive impact on societies around the world. It is sometimes hard for citizens of the most advanced states to understand how deeply their modernity affects others. Their industrial exports render manufacturers around the world obsolete and bankrupt, their cultural exports bring alien and most unwelcome val-ues, and their political ideals divide populations.

More than any others, Jews, Freemasons, and Anglo-Saxons symbolize the achievements and hopes of modern life. Accordingly, their actions hold a strange fascination for those distressed by political ideologies, eco-nomic disruption, and cultural changes. In contrast, how can Muslims,

Indians, and Africans make plausible conspirators? Those are the laggards of modern life, not its initiators.

IDEALISM. Ironically, high ideals seem to make a people or state into a special target of conspiracism. The profound impact of Jews on world history was achieved not by armies but by an array of moral precepts that, through Judaism's daughter religions of Christianity and Islam, won the allegiance of fully half the world's population. Focused as they are on the malign, conspiracy theorists insist on interpreting such wide influence as a lunge for power.

Consistent with this outlook, they look at a state based on ideas, not kinship, as the perpetrator of a conspiracy. The more seriously a state lives up to an ideal, the more it catches the attention of conspiracy theorists. Thus do the United States, revolutionary France, and Israel make for more plausible conspirators than the Soviet Union, Nazi Germany, Pakistan, or the Islamic Republic of Iran. So little are the latter associated with morality that their failures excite scant interest. The United Kingdom does not exactly fit the category of idea-based states, but its long evolution toward constitutional democracy makes it an honorary member of this small club.

Of all these open and democratic governments, the American stands out by virtue of its ambitions, successes, longevity, and consequence. Perversely, these features also turn it into the conspiracy theorist's ultimate enemy, and it is ascribed the most thrillingly evil exploits. America as a shining city—an exemplar to the rest of the world—makes the notion that the U.S. government is engaged in a plot particularly outrageous, and thus all the more alluring to conspiracy theorists. The idealism intrinsic to the American experiment has its underside in paranoid fantasies about the U.S. government. Just as antisemitism is a distorted testimony to the achievements of Jews, so can Americans take oblique satisfaction that their government stands out as the worst secret society danger.

EIGHT

RIGHT-WING
NUTS,
LEFTIST
SOPHISTICATES

On 27 February 1933, just weeks after Hitler came to power, a fire blazed at the German parliament building in Berlin, the Reichstag, burning down part of it. Subsequent inquiry found the facts of the case to be simple. One person, a young Dutchman who had once belonged to the Dutch Communist party, set the fire on his own in the hopes of spurring a popular uprising against the Nazi regime.[1] But then each of the two leading totalitarian governments seized on this nonconspiratorial event and spun an elaborated conspiracy theory to suit its purposes. The Nazis presented the fire as part of a massive communist conspiracy and used it as a pretext to arrest German communists and destroy their party. The Soviets put out the story[2] that the arsonist was actually a member of the Dutch Fascist party who set the fire at the Nazi behest. From the perspective of over six decades later, it is noteworthy that while the Nazi explanation was long ago completely discredited, Soviet disinformation yet lives on and continues to be purveyed both in popular culture[3] and by reputable sources.[4] Likewise, the Right's claim that Jewish money funded the Russian Revolution has disappeared, while the Left's even more preposterous claim, that Jews helped fund Hitler's rise, remains in currency.

This points to two oft-repeated patterns: Right and Left share a deep-set conspiracism, yet conventional opinion blames the Right far more than the Left. Here we look at the reasons for these patterns and assess their implications.

THE EXTREMES CONVERGE

[V]iews that have long been shared by both the far right and the far left . . . in recent years have come together in a weird meeting of the minds, to become one, and to permeate the mainstream of American politics and popular culture. You could call it fusion paranoia.
MICHAEL KELLY[5]

Right and Left engage in similar forms of conspiracism because they share much with each other—a temperament of hatred, a tendency toward violence, a suspiciousness that encourages conspiracism—and little with the political center. As a mentality rather than a specific set of policies, conspiracism can serve any political position or ideology. It offers the means to any end, so long as it is extremist. "Fusion paranoia" is nothing new but has long made it easy for individuals to move from one extreme to the other (the rightist antisemite Wilhelm Marr began his career on the Left; many German communists joined the Nazi party after 1933), to share ideas, and occasionally to cooperate.

To adapt conspiracy theories from Right to Left requires minimal changes. The name of one enemy can simply take the place of another, altering the ideological direction but not the mentality. Replace the Right's bogeys (Illuminati, the Rothschild family, Trotsky) with those of the Left (Jesuits, the Rothschilds, Disraeli), and conspiracism becomes ambidextrous. Politically versatile, it lends itself to every agenda. Indeed, as the Rothschild example suggests, they even agree on some specifics. Antisemitism is so similar at the two extremes that one knowledgeable observer discerns "a monolithic consensus in which it has become difficult if not impossible to distinguish left from right.[6] As though to prove this point, the Communist party's candidate for president of Russia in the July 1996 elections, Gennady Zyuganov, not only borrowed Nazi ideas in his book, *Beyond the Horizon*,[7] but even plagiarized from Hitler's *Mein Kampf*. The American far Right and Left disagree on nearly every issue except the Jewish threat. Agreeing on so much leads them to commend each other's writings and even to copy from the other.

Left and Right also agree on some secret society issues; for example, both see Washington as controlled by international financial interests. Rightist militias have adopted leftist ideas of the 1960s about a U.S. government conspiracy; the Militia of Montana sounds eerily like the Weather Underground or the Symbionese Liberation Front when it rages about the FBI as a "fascist" institution. The militiamen also draw on the Left's tactics to finance their efforts: robbing banks, counterfeiting currency, and passing bad checks. When sentenced to prison, they make remarks like, "I'm just another innocent person caught up in the tyrannical legal system. Power to the people. Up with the revolution."[8]

White and black racists agree on much too. Both see Jews as central to the importation of slaves from Africa: the former sees it as a plot to weaken the white race, the latter as a plot to kill off all blacks in "the greatest criminal endeavor ever undertaken against an entire race of people."[9] Both racist groups concur that the Jewish Holocaust never took place; that Jewish families own the Federal Reserve Board, permitting them to appropriate billions of dollars a year; and that the Internal Revenue Service serves as their collection agency. Racists concur as well on secret society issues. In the aftermath of war with Iraq in early 1991, the Nation of Islam articulated fears that President Bush had manufactured a confrontation in the Middle East to justify suspending the Constitution. Then, having acquired "very close to total, unfettered dictatorial power," it suspected he would round up and transfer to "assembly centers or relocation camps" more than 21 million American blacks.[10] White supremacists had the same worry, but about themselves: the U.S. government had plans to establish concentration camps along the Nazi model; "Christian fundamentalists will be the first to go. . . . Just like the Jews were the last time."[11]

Such agreement helps explain an unpredictable pattern of enmity and alliance. The Soviet-Nazi case provides the paradigm, with its pattern of public execration mixed with silent cooperation, followed by public friendship, betrayal, and barbarous warfare. On a lesser scale, white and black racists in America sometimes join in tactical alliances to fight conspiracies. In June 1961, the American Nazi party's leader, George Lincoln Rockwell, saluted Elijah Muhammad as "the Adolf Hitler of the black man."[12] Farrakhan since 1984 has had connections with elements of the white supremacist Right. For example, Thomas Metzger, a Ku Klux Klan leader in California, has shared information with the Nation of Islam and may even have contributed money to it. He supported it because, he explained in October 1985, "America is like a rotting carcass. The Jews are living off the carcass like the parasites they are. Farrakhan understands this."[13] Farrakhan also joined forces with Lyndon LaRouche to combat their mutual nemesis, the Anti-Defamation League of B'nai B'rith, and "the secret government" it supposedly forms a part of.

On the Right, antisemitism is inevitable, to the point that even groups basically uninterested in this ideology (like the John Birch Society) find themselves attracting its adherents; antisemitism is inherent to the rightist Weltanshauung. Attacks on Freemasons and Washington are optional. Conversely, the Left must have a conspiracy theory about bankers and arms merchants; it can pay attention to Jews or not. Consistent with this difference, on reaching power the Right directs its attention more to Jews; the Left emphasizes anti-imperialism.

Often the contrast is a matter of emphasis; Right and Left agree on the categories of conspirators and disagree only on who is ultimately responsible. For example, the Right tends to see imperialism as a tool of Jews, and the Left sees the reverse, as the case of Israel illustrates. The Right portrays Israel as part of a Jewish world plot. Adolf Hitler in the mid-1920s explained that Zionists "do not think at all of establishing a Jewish state in Palestine to live in it someday; rather, they want a central organization for their international world cheating."[14] In its current version, this view has Israel giving orders to the U.S. government. In contrast, the Left sees Zionism as a cover for imperialist ambitions. As early as July 1919, a Soviet document from the Ukraine called Zionism "one of the branches of the imperialist counter-revolution."[15] Today this attitude has Israel serving as a Western agent to control Middle Eastern oil or Arab nationalism or Islam.

FOCUS ON THE RIGHT

Conspiracies unfold—often enough, not the ones intended. And then history zigs when you might have expected it to zag.
TODD GITLIN[16]

The evidence in this study should establish that over the past two centuries, the Left has promoted conspiracism no less than the Right. Lenin more than matched his rightist counterpart, Rachkovsky. Stalin's conspiracy theories had even more lethal consequences than Hitler's. Around the world, a leftist conspiracy theorist exists for every rightist. For Tojo of Japan there is Mao of China. For Khomeini of Iran, Abdel Nasser of Egypt. In France, Le Pen on the Right is matched by Marchais on the Left. In Russia, Zhirinovsky by Zyuganov.

So much for reality. The common perception tends to focus predominantly on the Right as a source of conspiracism. Journalism and scholarship see fascistic movements around the globe, culminating in the Nazis, and in the United States such organizations as the Ku Klux Klan, the John Birch Society, and the militia movement; they hardly see the leftist equivalents. Thus does Richard Levy, an accomplished analyst of antisemitism, write that "antisemitism as a movement found its home on the right side of the political spectrum, among Christian conservatives, extreme nationalists, and violence-prone reactionaries. Radical democrats and socialists might harbor and give voice to many anti-Jewish prejudices, but rarely did they become antisemites."[17] Walter Laqueur notes in his study of Russian reactionaries that "a firm belief in imaginary conspiracies . . . has been an essential part of the mental makeup of the extreme right" throughout the twentieth century.[18] Michael Lerner, the author of a book on leftist antisemitism, states: "The main danger to the Jewish people is *not* now, nor has it ever been, from the Left. The Right is always the main threat." For him, "Leftists reflect and imbibe the deep anti-Semitism of the larger world";[19] they have, in other words, no responsibility for fomenting this hatred. An author on antisemitism on the European Right finds that conspiracism has an intellectually central role only for the Right.[20]

So too with the fear of secret societies, where scholars again hardly see the Left. Consider the American case. In his renowned 1964 essay, "The Paranoid Style in American Politics," Richard Hofstadter offered a sketch of conspiracist thinking that located this pathology uniquely on the conservative side. The problem, he declares, "is most evident on the extreme right wing . . . particularly in the Goldwater movement,"[21] and every example he offers, including those from the eighteenth century, is indeed on the Right. In their excellent study on the "politics of unreason," Seymour Martin Lipset and Earl Raab point in their subtitle to an exclusive focus on "right-wing extremism in America."[22] George Johnson's survey of "conspiracy theories and paranoia in American politics" finds only "right-wing politics" conducive to conspiracism.[23] Beyond these explicit statements, virtually the entire body of scholarship devoted to American conspiracy theories concentrates on its rightist manifestations. When doubt exists how to classify a conspiracy theorist, as in the case of Lyndon LaRouche, scholars deemphasize his leftist qualities in favor of dwelling on his role in building a "new American fascism."[24]

What explains this overemphasis on the Right while the Left gets a free pass? The discrepancy results from several differences: conspiracism on the Left has more convincing arguments, those arguments are put forward by more sophisticated spokesmen, leftist conspiracism emerged later, and it collapsed more gently (1989–91 versus 1945). In addition, analysts themselves tend to be liberal, and so more sympathetic to the Left.

• The Left has better credentials. With uncommon exceptions,[25] conspiracy theorists on the Right consist of skinheads, neo-Nazis, and other yahoos who express vicious ideas about Jews and batty ones about secret societies. Most of them suffer from a lack of qualifications; many have little education and work at menial occupations. Even leaders fit this profile: Hitler was a failed painter, Farrakhan a would-be nightclub entertainer, "Mark of Michigan" (a prominent conspiracist voice on short-wave radio and leader of the so-called United States Militia at Large) works as a janitor. Yet these individuals declaim on history, theology, finance, and other complex subjects about which they understand little. Even those with weightier credentials (a chemist, a priest) rarely have first-hand knowledge of their chosen subjects; they tend to live in remote places and have few connections to major institutions. In all earnestness, right-wing authors cite as sources the National Enquirer,[26] a grocery-store tabloid, and other publications with no pretensions to accuracy. They might find secret information in numerology, ancient documents, and even in used office machinery.[27]

In contrast, leading leftists boast impeccable educational credentials and sometimes direct work experience. This imbues them with a prestige and credibility inaccessible to most of their rightist counterparts. That Pierre Salinger was press secretary for Presidents Kennedy and Johnson, and then a chief foreign correspondent for ABC-News who won all of America's top television news awards, gave weight to his various conspiracy theories (about the U.S. government's trapping Saddam Husayn[28] or a missile's bringing down TWA flight 800). Gary Sick reached the rank of captain in the U.S. navy, served on the National Security Council staff in the White House, worked at the Ford Foundation, chaired a division of Human Rights Watch, and did research at Columbia University—all of which ensured that his allegations challenging the legitimacy of Ronald Reagan's election became a serious issue in American politics.

Noam Chomsky forwards a conspiracy theory that blames the U.S. government for virtually every ill around the world, including environmental pollution, militarism, economic poverty, spiritual alienation, and the drug scourge. It manipulates the mainstream media (to divert the revolutionary potential of workers), sponsors academic postmodernism (to bewilder the uninitiated), and encourages professional sports (to distract attention from serious issues). Behind the U.S. government stand the corporate giants, especially the sinister arms merchants, responsible for duping the public with the cold war fantasy. This barrage of harebrained ideas springs not from the mind of some ill-educated dreamer but from a leading scholar whose work has transformed the field of linguistics. *The New York Times* calls Chomsky "arguably the most important intellectual alive." His biographer even calls him "one of the century's most important figures."[29] Chomsky's undoubted accomplishments imbue his political writings with a great credibility. And a number of fellow left-wing conspiracy theorists have no less distinguished résumés, including Ramsey Clark, a former attorney general of the United States, and the late Allen Ginsberg, one of America's most renowned poets.

• The Left's presentation is sophisticated. Written materials from the Right are characteristically vulgar. Poorly organized, with factual errors, misspellings, and grammatical mistakes, they sport an overabundance of capitalized words, bold letters, and exclamation points. The materials usually come from unknown presses in obscure towns. One published tract has "* * * * TOP SECRET * * * *" as a running foot on every page, making it look a schoolchild's effort. In contrast, conspiracy theorists on the Left offer sophisticated and elegant arguments that enjoy the imprimatur of prestigious presses. A right-wing conspiratorial antisemite cranks out crude tracts with tiny circulation; his leftist equivalent, a writer like Gore Vidal, produces best-sellers. The Right distributes homemade videos; the Left has Oliver Stone making Hollywood feature films that win top awards.

• The Right's substance is risible. Its writings contain obvious self-contradictions as well as errors of fact. Even someone as accomplished as Pat Robertson (son of a U.S. senator, graduate of Harvard Law School) presents a completely self-contradictory picture about the nature of the

New World Order, its ultimate sponsors, and their motivation. The Right bandies about old and discredited antisemitic tropes, and its secret society fears are too outlandish for an intelligent and balanced person to take seriously. In the 1950s, the National Federation of Christian Laymen portrayed fluorine as "the devil's poison" and considered its addition to drinking water (to prevent tooth decay) "one of the most dastardly plots ever attempted against the human race."[30] In the 1960s, the Christian Crusade portrayed the Beatles as a plot to retard America's youth. In the 1970s, the Liberty Lobby responded with horror to the metric system, a form of foreign subversion. In the 1980s, some fundamentalist Christians saw the bar-lined Universal Product Code (the stripes on grocery store and other manufactured items) as literally satanic.[31] In the 1990s, "patriot" groups found proof of imminent foreign invasion on the back of a Kix cereal box and worried about health food stores fronting for the dangerous New Age movement.

So preposterous are these fears that even normally straitlaced government officials feel entitled to ridicule them. The chief of the FBI's counterterrorism section, John P. O'Neill, explains how his agents respond to Americans worried about a United Nations-led invasion: "We sit on the front porch with them and drink iced tea out of Mason jars with them and try to let them know that if they see Belgian paratroopers falling out of the sky with blue [i.e., U.N.] bonnets on top of their heads, we ask they call the FBI first and let us take the first crack at them."[32] Boutros Boutros-Ghali, the dignified U.N. secretary-general, satirized this same fear in September 1996, on return from his summer break: "It's great to be back from vacation. Frankly I get bored on vacation. It's much more fun to be at work here, blocking reform, flying my black helicopters, imposing global taxes."[33]

• The Left is convincing. Compare Nazi and communist writings. The former derive from a mishmash of pseudoscience and fanaticism; they are vicious and obviously wrong. The latter evolved out of a tradition of high-powered political theory that called on the noblest of sentiments. The first trips over inarticulate and inconsistent schemes, while the second explains in fluent tones and articulate words. The former insists on implausible connections; the latter repackages an indisputable reality. Fascism rejects Western civilization; Leninism claims to improve it. The Right wears its hate overtly, taking pleasure in shocking polite society. Its ideology consists mainly of celebrating violence, exalting in bloodlines, extreme nationalism, and religious triumphalism. The Left offers densely reasoned economic analyses and presents an idealistic vision. The one presents a face contorted with malice; the second offers a smile and a hope. It took the historical experience of Leninism in practice to show that it could be as murderous and destructive as the Nazis.

Consider this parallel: on the Right, Louis Farrakhan forwards a bizarre and unconvincing thesis that derives in large part from the Nation of Islam belief that blacks are the original humans and that the white race came into existence when an evil black scientist named Mr. Yacub created them as a means to teach blacks the urgent need for them to return to Islam, the true religion. Farrakhan tells of a black holocaust a hundred times greater than the Jewish one and blames the Jews for much of it. On the Left, the Afrocentric school offers a sophisticated variant of this same general argument, holding that the ancient civilizations of Egypt, Greece, and Palestine were actually peopled by blacks but that whites conspired to appropriate these jewels for themselves. Jesus was an "African revolutionary," and whites "stole" Christianity from the Egyptians. Afrocentric ideas remain controversial, to be sure, but do not inspire the anxiety and pressure of Farrakhen's antisemitic ones.

When it comes to American classrooms, media coverage, or foundation grants, rightist conspiracy theories are analytically dissected so that students and the public can understand their falsity and not fall prey to them. In contrast, leftist notions are often presented as truth. Consider again the two conspiracist variants of black history. The Nation of Islam's vulgar antisemitism makes it nearly universally condemned as a topic for classroom study. Only a handful of professors teach it, and they are almost universally reviled as a result.[34] In contrast, a great many professors at leading universities teach Afrocentrism, whole doctoral programs are premised on its ideas, and major university presses publish books making these arguments.[35] Afrocentrism has become so widely accepted that it has reached high schools throughout the United States. Some elementary schools have made it the very core of their curriculum.

• The Left is more subtle. The Right tends to postulate a vast, historical, all-encompassing conspiracy; the Left usually focuses on a less implausible plot. The former relies more on forgeries and other distortions. Most important, the Right screams "conspiracy," while the Left often avoids this loaded word. If the entire Leninist corpus is based on the idea of a plot by business interests, hardly anywhere does it actually mention a conspiracy. While Hitler ranted about conspiracies and made the fight against them the very centerpiece of his political program, Stalin whispered his fears and personally disassociated himself from conspiracism. Further, while Hitler battled obviously fantastical world conspiracies, Stalin took on plots only against his own regime. His claims inspired neither the same skepticism nor revulsion as Hitler's.

The Left remains more subtle today. In *Backlash*, a best-selling feminist analysis, Susan Faludi finds women to be the victims of a "largely insidious" and "powerful counter-assault on women's rights" that has "moved through the culture's secret chambers" and been perpetrated by the government, lawyers, scholars, the media, fashion designers, and Hollywood. The media, for example, "have circulated make-believe data," and high-profile men in trouble use women, especially feminists, as their "all-purpose scapegoats." Faludi presents her argument with polish and elegance; she even states that "The backlash is not a conspiracy."[36] But her basic thesis is no less conspiracist—"the culture's secret chambers"?—than those of the unwashed Right.

Or note the Left's concept of "anticommunism," a phenomenon it blames for a host of ills in the United States. Rather than see the struggle with communism as hatred of an oppressive system and a life-and-death struggle over the human future, it chooses instead to see this as a conspiracy. One author on this subject, Joel Kovel, finds that "Communist-hating is used opportunistically as an instrument to secure power and wealth." In particular, it was a mechanism "to neutralize workers' power" in the United States.[37] Kovel does not use the word *conspiracy* in his analysis, yet it undergirds his entire argument.

A substantial portion of American scholarship is based on this sort of sophisticated conspiracy theory. Latin American studies offers an especially egregious example, for the great majority of scholars on that topic subscribe to a belief in a U.S. conspiracy aiming at hegemony over the continent. For example, Peter Smith's history of U.S. involvement in Latin America not only makes this assumption its premise but baldly dismisses the role of accidents and personality; for him, only the conspiracy counts.[38]

• The Left adopted conspiracism late. By the 1780s, "the skeleton of the conspiracist mythology of the Left, as well as that of the Right, can already by discerned."[39] But it was merely an outline on the Left. Conspiracism first acquired political importance only after the French Revolution, and it had a primarily rightist quality. Fearing change and hating the modern, the Right resisted the French Revolution, and as the revolution grew increasingly radical in its Jacobin phase, landed aristocrats, clergy, and others responded with a furious and no less radical response, one element of which was conspiracism. Reactionaries like Robison, Barruel, and Starck found in secret society conspiracism a means to fight the revolutionaries on equal terms. Then the disruptive effects of capitalism and the emancipation of the Jews ensured that successor generations on the Right would continue to depend on conspiracy theories.

The Left was rarely in power (other than in France in the 1790s), but it had great ambitions, so it engaged in plots through the nineteenth century (far more than it worried about them). This situation changed with the Bolshevik seizure of power in 1917. Control of a powerful state made the Left no less paranoid than the Right. Bolsheviks too needed a way to fend off bewildering change, and they too turned to conspiracism. World War II left the Right in shambles but increased the Left's power. The Soviet propaganda apparatus then amplified this conspiracism to a worldwide audience. Throughout the cold war, the communist states were the main purveyor of conspiracism. Not only did Marxist-Leninist politicians, educators, intellectuals, artists, and journalists pick up the latest conspiracy theory from Moscow, but so did seemingly independent periodicals (such as the weekly *Link* in India), which in reality were tools of Moscow's disinformation. Further, more than a few Western fellow travelers endorsed the Soviet line, thereby giving communist calumnies much-needed credibility. As a result, Moscow's line reverberated in the press, in the universities, and in the arts.

• The Soviet Union appeared less bad than the Third Reich. The Nazis rose and fell in spectacular fashion; the communist trajectory was a more gentle one. The Third Reich lasted only twelve years and ended in a blaze of gun smoke and fire; the Soviet Union endured for three-quarters of a century and expired with a whimper. These differences have important consequences. While the results of Nazi conspiracism are the subjects of innumerable studies and artistic works, the comparable Soviet actions remain relatively obscure. Auschwitz, Birkenau, and the other death camps are known by name, but who knows their Soviet equivalents? German archives were captured in a fell swoop. Soviet ones are slowly unveiled.

The same distinction applies to the two dictators. Hitler left behind a far more terrible reputation than Stalin. One ranted; the other calculated. Hitler made no discernable attempt to disguise his wickedness. In contrast, Stalin hid evil with such diligence and success that his crimes became known only three years after his death and were then widely received with shock. Because the facts about Stalin came out in so disjointed a way, his crimes to this day lack the notoriety of Hitler's murder-ousness. Hitler so discredited himself that to find any virtues in him implies a kind of insanity. Not so Stalin. If Hitler's apologists are beyond the pale, Stalin's remain within it.

• Analysts sympathize more with the Left. The liberal orientation of most scholars and journalists means that they treat comparable phenomenon in different ways. They do not hide the Left's turpitude, but they present it less harshly, in isolation, and usually as the idiosyncrasies of an individual rather than faults intrinsic to the system. Leninism would have been more humane if only Stalin had not hijacked the revolution. The Cuban revo-lution might have succeeded if not for U.S. enmity. Also, writers look for con-spiracism overwhelmingly on the Right: Soviet antisemitism and left-wing anti-imperialism not fitting this stereotype, they get off more easily. Leftist paranoia about Washington not fitting the pattern, it does not get nearly as much objectified, vilified, and ridiculed as that of the Right.

In the end, how do the scales tip? Right and Left conspiracism have both had great success in this century, but which one had more of an impact?

When it comes to anti-secret society and anti-imperialist phobias, there is no contest. This has always been the Left's core outlook. In the realm of antisemitism, the Right predominated until 1945, but the Left then took over. To be sure, the long reach of antisemitism owes much to the Right, as Juan Perón in Argentina and Japan in the 1980s both reflect. But Jew-hatred of the past half-century owes more to the Soviet state, which lasted for so long and established powerful networks of influ-ence. As "the world's largest exporter of anti-Jewish hate materials,"[40] especially during the period 1967 through 1991, it spread anti-Zionism to nearly all the Communist states, the international Left, and much of the Third World, reactionary as well as progressive. Thanks to the Soviet push, a wide range of individuals and institutions accepted antisemitic notions and fulminated against Zionism:

> Anti-Zionism has become the great bazaar [wrote Robert Wistrich in 1978] in which Soviet and Chinese Communists, Arab and Third World Marxists, Trotskyists, anarchists and Cas-troists along with feudal sheiks, conservative Islamic rulers, oil companies and capitalist interests in the West (not to speak of fascist fringe-groups) can find common ground in their hatred of the Jewish State.[41]

One informed observer notes the irreparable damage done by Moscow's campaign: "The Soviet-produced anti-Semitic and anti-Zionist propaganda has now penetrated much of the globe; its baleful effects cannot be undone."[42] Looking back on the two most powerful totalitarian states of Europe, a division of labor emerges: Hitler deepened antisemitism to kill millions; the Soviets so extended its reach that the ideology has become nearly universal. Further, antisemitism today flourishes in the former Soviet Union, but not in Germany. The worldwide appeal of antisemitism today reflects Soviet influence more than Nazi.

More generally, the Left has a more insidious presence and greater reach. The Right's curious reluctance to blame states means that much of the time it engages in an inconsequential fret against such nonstate actors as Jews, Freemasons, the Council on Foreign Relations, European bankers, and the United Nations. The Left has more sensibly focused primarily on the governments of powerful states, especially the British and American. These different approaches lead to dramatically different institutional results: the Right built a number of feeble institutions (such as the Antimasonic party, limited to a few years and a few American states) or transient ones (the Nazi party); the Left built up communist parties around the world, many of which came to power and stayed there for decades.

The sophistication of the Left enables it to exploit conspiracism more than does the Right. A worldly, well-educated analyst does not fall prey to conspiracist demons with the same sincerity as does a janitor. Yahoos on the Right appear almost universally heartfelt in their fears of Jews and Freemasons; leftist sophisticates lack that same veracity. Rather, they seemingly spread conspiracy theories as a means to further their political agenda; in case after case, conspiracism serves their goals. On the grandest scale, if Hitler represents conspiracism gone mad, Stalin stands for something altogether craftier. The Nazi state held conspiratorial antisemitism to be its highest truth and singlemindedly pursued it, but the Soviet state used anti-imperialism more instrumentally, retaining an ability to turn it on and off as circumstances warranted. If Nazis were the creatures of conspiracism, Soviets were its masters.

The same difference holds in the American context, notably the Left's use of conspiracism in the Kennedy assassination, the October Surprise, and the O. J. Simpson trial. The Left forwards conspiracy theories that conveniently explain how two of the previous four Democratic presidents (John F. Kennedy and Jimmy Carter) left office through plots most foul. The Kennedy case is remarkable for its gumption given that the main figure, Lee Harvey Oswald, was an extreme leftist who moved to the Soviet Union, renounced his American citizenship, participated in a pro-Castro group (the Fair Play for Cuba Committee), and nearly assassinated General Edwin Walker, a well-known right-wing figure. Yet attention shifted away from Oswald soon after the Kennedy murder, thanks to the work of a network of leftist activists (e.g., Jim Garrison) and book authors both famous (Edward Jay Epstein, Mark Lane)[43] and obscure (Thomas Buchanan, Joachim Joesten, Sylvia Meagher, Harold Weisberg).[44]

These "assassinologists" took two tacks. One turned Oswald into an extreme rightist ("Oswald would have been more at home with *Mein Kampf* than *Das Kapital*")[45] and his life into an elaborate charade (Fair Play for Cuba was seen as a front for American intelligence). The other tack turned Oswald into a minor figure by focusing attention instead on a grand conspiracy in which he was but a minor cog. Oswald's politics, motives, and connections to Soviet intelligence nearly disappeared, replaced by topics that pointed to others involved in the murder. Assassination buffs raised questions about the number of guns that went off (up to sixteen), the number of shots, their trajectories, and the number of bullets that hit Kennedy. In the process, they fingered some thirty gunmen as Oswald's accomplices. This profusion of accomplices focused attention away from Oswald and onto the sponsors of this huge effort. Prominent suspects included the CIA (because Kennedy planned to shut it down), anti-Castro Cubans (due to the failure of the Bay of Pigs invasion), White Russians (angry about improved relations with the Soviet Union), the mafia (to stop Robert Kennedy's investigations into organized crime), the FBI (Hoover feared being forced out of office), the military-industrial complex (which hated the Nuclear Test-Ban Treaty), the generals (intent to stop a pullout of Vietnam), Texas oil millionaires (to end talk about canceling the oil depletion allowance), international bankers (who disliked current monetary policies), and Lyndon Johnson (who feared being dropped from the ticket in 1964). To this list, black Americans added the idea, still alive a generation later, of the Ku Klux Klan or other white supremacists killing Kennedy because of his civil rights stance. As controversy swirled about the precise identity of the right-wing conspirators, the numbers involved steadily increased ("their meetings would have had to held in Madison Square Garden"),[46] and Oswald's role faded. Some books almost ignored his existence; others turned him into a scapegoat. Thanks to the combined efforts of leftist writers, Gerald Posner noted in 1993, "The debate is no longer whether

JFK was killed by Lee Oswald acting alone or as part of a conspiracy—it is instead, which conspiracy is correct?"[47]

This orgy of speculation appears all the more artificial when seen against the background of other recent American assassinations that did not spur conspiracism. Robert F. Kennedy was killed in June 1968 by Sirhan Bishara Sirhan, a Jerusalem-born Palestinian who explicitly portrayed his act as a protest against Kennedy's pro-Israeli views. By that date, Yasir Arafat's Al-Fatah had already established an international reputation for terrorism, so Sirhan might well have been thought part of a conspiracy, but he was not. Americans saw him in isolation, not connected to an organized group, much less to a concerted campaign of intimidation.[48]

Similarly, John W. Hinckley, Jr.'s, attempted assassination of Ronald Reagan in 1981 prompted little speculation, though the videotape of the shooting incident has unexplained flashes of light, and presidential guards initially looked the wrong way for the gun—possible indications of more than one assassin. More interesting yet, Hinckley's father was reported to be a friend of Vice President George Bush, who would have been the direct beneficiary of Reagan's death. Most remarkable, John Hinckley's brother Scott was scheduled to have dinner with Bush's son Neil on the very evening of the shooting. Yet these connections cast no suspicions on the vice president. The silence surrounding the RFK and Reagan episodes points to the exceptional, and possibly manufactured, nature of the speculation surrounding the JFK assassination.

The October Surprise theory claims that Ronald Reagan won the presidency in 1980 by striking a deal with the Iranian mullahs: they would keep American hostages in Iran until after the U.S. election, thereby ruining Jimmy Carter's electoral chances. Lyndon LaRouche made up the theory, and a network of leftists—Hodding Carter, Seymour Hersh, Christopher Hitchens, Robert Parry, Gary Sick, Craig Unger, plus a substantial supporting cast—then promoted it. Newspapers gave over their opinion pages to this subject, television shows devoted large chunks of time to it, and national weeklies put it on their covers. So widespread had the allegation become by January 1992 that a poll showed 55 percent of Americans believing these allegations to be true and just 34 percent finding them false.[49] Jimmy Carter called for an investigation, and both houses of Congress (as well as several investigative journalists) did his bidding. All found the claims to be utterly without merit, and the issue died away.

Republicans whose ascent cannot be tarred with a specific conspiracy get accused by innuendo. George Bush is a case in point. The Left portrayed him as uniting more secret society associations than anyone else: Skull and Bonesman at Yale, Texas "oil boss," member of the Council on Foreign Relations and Trilateral Commission, head of the CIA, sometime associate of the Iran/*Contra* enterprise. One author called him "an embodiment of conspiracy" and even the greatest conspirator of the past two centuries.[50]

The O. J. Simpson trial offers another example of the Left's using conspiracism as a political tool. To escape the state's watertight evidence that he had murdered his ex-wife and her friend, Simpson's finest-money-could-buy legal team relied on a conspiracy theory that the Los Angeles Police Department, for reasons of racial animosity, entrapped Simpson, and then constructed a vast conspiracy to pin the blame on him. The defense lawyers made this argument so convincingly that Simpson won his acquittal.

Finally, liberals spin conspiracy theories in an effort to delegitimate conservatives. Two more American examples show how this works. Michael Lind, an editor at the *New Yorker*, portrays a handful of leaders engaged in a "behind-the-scenes coordination of the intellectual right" that suppresses dissent and debate. They do so, he suggests, by relying on methods that derive from Stalin:

> The modern conservative brain trust originated in a scheme hatched in the 1970s by William E. Simon, Irving Kristol, and others. . . . [T]he conservative intellectual network set up in the 1970s and persisting today [1996] bears a striking resemblance to the CIA-orchestrated network of cultural fronts in the United States and Europe of the early years of the cold war. . . . The CIA, in turn, learned these techniques from the front organizations of the Soviet Union and the pro-Soviet communist parties. . . . American conservatism, then, is a countercommunism that replicates, down to rather precise details of organization and theory, the communism that it opposes. . . . [It degenerated] into a style of politics as conspiratorial and authoritarian as the original threat.

Lind, a renegade conservative, purports to reveal how the Leninist machinery worked; for example, the "party line tended to be adopted at periodic 'conservative summits,' private meetings once a year or so." This conspiracy worked: after several decades of coordination by foundations and well-placed fixers, "there is no longer an independent conservative intellectual movement in the United States."[51] Outside of conservative publications, Lind's strange ideas went unremarked.

Even the Clinton administration promoted a conspiracy theory about conservatives. In January 1997 the Office of the White House Counsel released a 331-page document bearing an opaque title, "Communications Stream of Conspiracy Commerce." In it, anonymous White House aides propose and document the existence of a "media food chain," which they explain as

> the system by which right-wing activists feed conspiracy theories and innuendo from the fringes into the mainstream media. The "food chain" starts with activists such as Willie Horton creator Floyd Brown, Sheffield Nelson and Larry Nichols. These activists feed the partisan conservative press, publications such as the *American Spectator*, the *Washington Times* and the editorial page of the *Wall Street Journal*. The mainstream press then picks up on these reports.

But this time, the conspiracy theorists went too far; with the exception of the leftist press, the claim that anonymous Internet authors drove the news met with universal disdain.

To conclude, we survey the development of conspiracism, consider what harm it has done, and speculate about the possible future dangers of this way of thinking.

NINE

CONSPIRACISM'S

COSTS

Conspiracism is a story in six acts. Suspicions about Jewish and secret society conspiracies emerged during the Crusades. The Enlightenment period saw petty conspiracy theories become a common tool of interpretation. The French Revolution raised the stakes, stimulating conspiracy theories about enemies who seek world hegemony. Through the nineteenth century, these ideas acquired greater scope and depth, finding their classic expression in Russia in the 1890s. The world wars saw such widespread acceptance of the paranoid style that conspiracy theorists seized power in several major countries and came close to global hegemony in 1940–41. In the next half-century, conspiracism declined in the West while gaining importance in other parts of the world. Summed up, conspiracy theories grew steadily in importance over a period of nearly two centuries, culminating with the years around 1940, and then they retreated.

This schema has several implications. First, conspiracism is closely connected to the great events of European history since 1750, and these mark its key turning points. The paranoid style became serious with the French Revolution, came to power after World War I, peaked with World War II, then declined with the cold war.

Second, what began as the phobias of marginal figures became forces that affected vast populations. As Norman Cohn observes, "an antisemitic myth originally concocted by a few eccentric priests in reaction against the French Revolution became in the 1930s a device by which a despotic government could consolidate its hold over a great European nation"[1] Similarly, the fear of secret societies that began its existence as an alarmed but doomed reaction to 1789 eventually came to power in 1917. In the next three decades, conspiratorial antisemitism and Marxism-Leninism moved the world and almost ruled it. It is not hard to imagine some alterations to the history of the period 1929 through 1945 that would have found the totalitarians on top. Hitler in November 1940 proposed to Molotov a division of the world between the German, Soviet, Japanese, and Italian dictators; at other times he mused about keeping Stalin on as his *Gauleiter* in Russia. After the war's end, Stalin's daughter reports, her father would mutter, "Ech, together with the Germans we would have been invincible!"[2] The world was not far away from a conspiracist hegemony. But that was not to be. Instead, the great totalitarian projects collapsed, one after the other: 1945 in Germany, 1976 in China, and 1991 in Russia. With the weakening of totalitarianism, conspiracism receded.

Third, at key turning points, Right and Left have absorbed ideas from the other. The Left initially learned conspiracism from the Right and learned it so well that by 1945 it took over the conspiracist baton from the Right and has since taught conspiracism back to the Right. Indeed, Leftist conspiracism dominated the world scene after 1945, losing its predominance only with the start of the Soviet collapse. Accordingly, the years since 1985 have seen Rightist conspiracism loom larger than previously was the case.

Finally, in assessing the impact of conspiracism, it helps to distinguish between intellectual and operational influence, for they do not necessarily go together. The paranoid style can have wide appeal without affecting the policies of state, or it can rule without popular support. The fear of secret societies had a serious claim on the thinking of the West's powerful (including politicians, religious leaders, journalists, academics), starting with the French Revolution in about 1789 and ending with Khrushchev's speech in 1956 revealing Stalin's crimes. Separately, this fear had operational importance during a briefer period, the life of the Soviet Union (1917–91). For conspiratorial antisemitism, the fear became intellectually significant in the 1870s and remained a factor until the collapse of the Third Reich in 1945, reviving somewhat in recent years. It acquired an operational role in Russia at the end of the nineteenth century and remained powerful until the Soviet collapse in 1991.

Thus did the antisemitic and anti-imperialist fears follow different trajectories. The fear of Jews disappeared with Hitler's defeat in World War II, then grew in prominence as the Nazi interlude receded. Anti-imperialists remained prominent for decades longer, fading only with the Soviet decline. In temporal terms, imperialists were more prominent in 1970, Jews in 1995. These patterns lead to two observations: Germany's experience, though very intense, came and went; Russia alone virtually defines the operational importance of both myths. And the secret society myth lasted longer, but the antisemitic one did proportionally far more damage far more quickly.

CONSPIRACISM'S COSTS

He who fights with monsters must take care lest he become a monster.
FRIEDRICH NIETZSCHE, BEYOND GOOD AND EVIL (1886)

Conspiracism has had a profound impact on European and world history. Already in the eighteenth century the secret society myth contributed to the American colonists' decision to break away from Great Britain and added to the intensity and enmity of the French Revolution, while antisemitism spurred pogroms in the period 1850 through 1920. But conspiracism achieved its potential only in the middle of this century, when it added malice and ruthlessness to the greatest of internal upheavals, the most deadly wars, and some of the greatest calamities of the human experience. Even in the last half-century it continues to poison public life, especially in select non-Western regions. Conspiracism has inflicted a number of wounds.

A POISONED DISCOURSE. Conspiracism encourages a vortex of illusion and superstition. Like paranoia, it "is the watery plaster that seals over the gaping cracks in unsound reasoning."[3] By reducing complex developments to a plot, it obstructs an understanding of historical forces. It shifts blame for all ills to outsiders ("We didn't lose; they cheated"), preventing an accurate assessment of causes and thereby prolonging problems. It causes people to fear and hate what does not harm them, while not fearing or hating what does harm them. It directs them to waste their attention on the irrelevant and ignore the significant.

ADVERSARY CULTURE AND SELF-HATRED. Revealingly, the only three countries with a substantial body of opinion that suspects and hates its own government—Great Britain, the United States, Israel—are precisely the three most targeted by conspiracism. "We actually fear our government more than the drug cartels and the Mafia," says one American militiaman, voicing a near-universal view in his circles.[4] Prominent figures of the adversary culture such as Alexander Cockburn from Britain, Noam Chomsky in the United States, and Israel Shahak in Israel find that behind almost any evil lies their own government, engaged in a conspiracy. Indeed, it is the internal adversary culture (and not foreign enemies) that develops most of the conspiracist ideas; revealingly, two-thirds of a major study on anti-Americanism deals with Americans and only one-third with foreigners.[5] Americans devise the key notions (such as "dollar diplomacy"), which foreigners then pick up and adapt to suit other circumstances and ideologies.

The same applies to the one ethnic group subjected to conspiracism, the Jews. To what other people does the adjective *self-hating* apply? Some Jews have reached the point that they band together in organizations whose exclusive purpose is to reject Judaism (e.g., Jews for Jesus) or Zionism (American Council for Judaism). Conspiracism also helps account for bourgeois self-hatred; communists of middle-class or privileged backgrounds burn with a more intense hatred toward their own than do those of worker families, again reflecting the absorption of conspiracist ideas.

REAL CONSPIRACIES. A terrible irony dwells at the heart of conspiracism: though inspired by a powerful urge to combat conspiracies and reduce their numbers, it has the actual effect of doing precisely the opposite—increasing the number of conspiracies. This subtle and intricate topic requires a study of its own; here I offer some examples concerning the two men who most consequentially advocated conspiracy theories and engaged in conspiracies, Vladimir Lenin and Adolf Hitler.

Lenin portrayed "monopoly capitalists" in his writings as a disciplined group that imposed its wishes on all others by clandestinely taking control of the state. If this worked so well for capitalists, why not for socialists too? Lenin not only endorsed conspiratorial tactics for the vanguard party but in 1902 even publicly boasted of them:

In form such a strong revolutionary organisation in an autocratic country may also be described as a "conspiratorial" organisation. . . . Secrecy is such a necessary condition for this kind of organisation that all the other conditions (number and selection of members, functions, etc.) must be made to conform to it. It would be extremely naïve indeed, therefore, to fear the charge that we Social-Democrats desire to create a conspiratorial organisation. Such a charge should be flattering.[6]

Faithful to this early vision, Lenin organized his party as a small, secretive, and hierarchical structure "grouped round a band of conspirators who were all linked by personal allegiance to their chieftain, Lenin."[7] It worked. David Annan calls the Bolsheviks "the most successful national secret society of all time" and explains how they cobbled together the practices of earlier groups: "The history of the Bolshevik movement, indeed, is a history of *Russian* conspirators, who imitated the Blanquists in their small, close-knit brand of trained revolutionaries, the Carbonari in their appeal to officers in the armed forces, the Irish rebels in their exploitation of agrarian disaffection, and the Paris Communes in their use of the urban mob."[8] On reaching power, Lenin continued to think and act as a conspirator, now affecting the lives of millions: "even as dictator of Russia, Lenin did not shed the habits acquired in the prerevolutionary underground, to judge by the frequency with which the words *secret, conspiratorial,* and *clandestine* appear in his confidential communications."[9]

Lenin then used this alleged capitalists' conspiracy for his own purposes. To battle the capitalists who "would stop at no crime in order to wreck our peaceful work," he founded the Cheka (later known as the KGB) to serve as a "devastating weapon against countless conspiracies and countless attempts against Soviet power by people who are infinitely stronger than us."[10] By asserting a ubiquitous conspiracy, in other words, he also laid the ground for a totalitarian police state.

Adolf Hitler conspired his way to power, guided by the methods of his many enemies.[11] From the Jesuits, he adopted the structure of command, which he applied to the SS force; thus would Hitler refer to the SS leader, Heinrich Himmler, as "my Ignatius."[12] From the Freemasons he took the hierarchical order. From his main enemy, the Jews, he took the alleged plan for world domination as set out in the *Protocols*. Hitler candidly acknowledged that he "learned enormously" from it and declared that "we would have to imitate it, in our own way, of course."[13] Imitate it he did: the list of similarities between *The Protocols* and Hitler's actions is a long one. His speeches closely tracked its contents[14] and he was a "pupil of the Elders" in the sense that he adopted methods from the *Protocols*, to the point that his vision of a Jewish-run world and the reality of Nazi society contain stunning resemblances. Herman Bernstein, an early debunker of *The Protocols*, explains that

> the Nazi dictator has apparently appropriated the Machiavellian ideas contained in the "Protocols" and the "Dialogues in Hell,"[15] and has been translating them into actuality. While accusing the Jews of scheming for world domination and pointing to the forged "Protocols" as proof of the imaginary Jewish conspiracy, the Nazi Leader has followed the "Protocols" in many respects, building his dictatorship upon the diabolic theories of these documents.

Bernstein then points to five such diabolic theories: fomenting disorder, dictatorship, use of mobs, shows of force, and press controls.[16] Other themes include adulation of the leader, might before right, and disdain for democracy. Hitler's global ambitions echoed those of the putative Elders; like them, he had no respect for laws; he controlled a whole country as a grand master rules his novices; he relied simultaneously on the big lie and on secrecy; and his organization maintained the trappings of a clandestine society (initiation rites, elaborate hierarchies, mistrust of outsiders) and a secret agenda even as it had a public face. The Nazi party resembled a religious cult more than a normal political party, and so in some fashion it paralleled Judaism. Nazis fully adhered to the *Protocols'* declaration that "to attain a serious end it behooves us not to stop at any means or to count the victims sacrificed for the sake of that end."[17] In words meant to arouse anger, the *Protocols* announce that "Everything that benefits the Jewish people is morally right and sacred"; the Nazis echo this with, "Right is what is good for the German people."

Beyond these specifics, Nazis closely emulated the putative Jewish conspiracy in *The Protocols* because it showed how to finesse one's limited objective circumstances and achieve world conquest through organizational skills alone, a goal of obvious interest to them. The wide appeal of *The Protocols* among Germans may have had to do not just with antisemitism but with a fascination in learning from the Jews how to extend

German power. As Hannah Arendt writes, "the delusion of an already existing Jewish world domination formed the basis for the illusion of future German world domination.... The Nazis *acted* as though the world were dominated by the Jews and needed a counterconspiracy to defend itself."[18] Norman Cohn, who more than anyone else has shown the *Protocols'* impact, is emphatic on the connection between the *Protocols* and Hitler's career:

> The ruthless struggle of a band of conspirators to achieve world-domination—a world-empire based on a small but highly organized and regimented people—utter contempt for humanity at large—a glorying in destruction and mass misery—all these things are to be found in the *Protocols*, and they were of the very essence of the Nazi régime. To put it with all due caution: in this preposterous fabrication from the days of the Russian pogroms Hitler heard the call of a kindred spirit, and he responded to it with all his being.[19]

Thus does conspiracy theory lead to conspiracy. Like Lenin and Hitler, many other real-life conspirators are also individuals and organizations who see conspiracies everywhere, base their political outlook on the importance of conspiratorial enemies, and devote themselves to combating this menace. Just as life sometimes imitates art, so do actual conspiracies imitate the crazed ideas of conspiracism. The distance from accusing others to undertaking one's own conspiracy is startlingly short. On reflection, this paradox is not terribly surprising. Someone convinced about the utility of plots is himself highly likely to take up this method of organization. Certain that plots take place all about you, and to great effect, you are prone to adopt precisely this same method. Thus do opponents of the hidden hand take on the very characteristics they most fear.

VIOLENCE. Conspiracism exacerbates political conflicts by inducing hostility to the other, whether a minority or foreign group. Violence often results, as recent incidents in the United States demonstrate. Imagining Freemasons to be an anti-Catholic group intent on taking over the world, John Salvi struck his blow for the Church by killing two people at Boston-area abortion clinics in December 1994. Seven members of the self-styled West Virginia Mountaineer Militia were arrested in October 1996 and accused of planning to blow up the national fingerprint center, the FBI's Criminal Justice Services Facility. As one militia member explained to undercover agents, this building was a key target because it was believed to serve as a command center for the New World Order.

A conspiracist tract, *The Turner Diaries*, has been associated with many acts of violence, including a 1983 near-bombing in Oklahoma City; a 1984 armored car holdup in California, netting $3.6 million; the 1984 murder of Alan Berg, a Jewish talk-show host in Denver; the Aryan Republican Army's robbing of twenty-two midwestern banks in 1994–95; and the 1995 bombing of the Federal building in Oklahoma City, killing 168. The connection appears particularly tight in the last case, where the operation closely followed the novel in a number of details, including the kind of explosive and the time of day. The convicted lead perpetrator, Timothy J. McVeigh, held *The Turner Diaries* in awe; as one account puts it, he "preached about the book as if it was a survivalist's bible."[20]

A number of black organizations (including the Nation of Islam and the Student Non-Violent Coordinating Committee) exude conspiratorial antisemitism. On occasion, their hateful sentiments spill over into violent action. Roland J. Smith, Jr., a lifelong believer in the hidden hand ("Everything to him was a conspiracy against black people"), regularly demonstrated outside a Jewish-owned store in Harlem where Al Sharpton and other black leaders inveighed against the "bloodsucking Jews" and their conspiracy to emasculate black power. At a certain point, shouting antisemitic remarks no longer sufficed for Smith. In December 1995, he took action by setting fire to the store, killing seven employees and himself.[21]

EXTREMISM. Every hate group has a conspiracy theory at the heart of its thinking. In general, the more conspiracy theories appeal, the less healthy the body politic is. As both a cause and a consequence of political extremism, conspiracism discourages moderation and strengthens extremism. For example, a specialist on the militiamen reflects, "if one can generalize about the picture of the world these people have, it's America being ruled as a country by an evil conspiracy."[22] This fits a larger pattern, noted by the philosopher Karl Popper: "The adoption of the conspiracy theory can hardly be avoided by those who believe that they know how to make heaven on earth. The only explanation for their failure to produce this heaven is the malevolence of the devil who has a vested interest in hell."[23] As a consequence, the further out a person stands to the Right and Left, the more consistently he relies on conspiracy theories and the more profoundly do they shape his worldview. "For the lunatic fringe . . . a conspiracy theory was absolutely crucial; one cannot understand fringe thinking without it."[24]

TOTALITARIANISM. Conspiracism implies totalitarianism, for it fosters a sense of emergency that can be confronted only through strong rule. It thus "leads directly towards dictatorship championed as democracy."[25] For example, Hitler explicitly called for a dictatorship to deal with the plots swirling around Germany. As David Pryce-Jones observes, absolute rule is "the final fulfillment of conspiracy, a gigantic plot of one man against everyone else."[26] Totalitarian movements have been the main carriers of conspiracy theories; not coincidentally, the two peaked together in the period 1930 through 1945. Conversely, the repudiation of conspiracism means a return to more normal politics. On 3 April 1953, shortly after Stalin's death, Beria's ministry issued a communiqué that the doctors had been "unlawfully arrested," an admission that meant the disavowal of Stalin's reign of capricious terror and the end of the one-man rule. In the words of a historian, this "official statement disavowing the Doctors' Plot marked a watershed of Soviet history"[27] and began the process that ultimately led to the dissolution of the Kremlin dictatorship nearly four decades later.

WARS. Conspiracy theories very often provide a reason, truly believed or conveniently manufactured, for an aggressor to take up arms. When Hitler invaded Poland, he did so on the pretext that Polish soldiers had attacked a German radio station—an attack that the Nazis themselves had faked. The Arab military buildup in 1967 followed on conspiracy theories about American attempts to overthrow Gamal Abdel Nasser. Saddam Husayn told of a Kuwaiti conspiracy to undermine the Iraqi economy by lowering the price of oil. "All wars start with Conspiracy Theories put out by the various governments, proving to the satisfaction of their citizens, at least for a while, that all the trouble was caused deliberately by the other side."[28]

Conspiracism also creates a bellicose climate that primes populations for war and can create an illusion of strength conducive to war. Certainty that Germany lost World War I because of a conspiracy by its leaders— and not because of American entry into the war—prompted Hitler blithely to declare war on the United States in 1941. To ascertain the general role of conspiracism in World War II requires only a simple mental exercise. Imagine that the leading conspiracy theorists worried not about the Jews and Great Britain but about the Vatican and Moscow. Hitlerism and Leninism would have been different from top to bottom; the war could not have taken place in anything like its actual shape.

MASS MURDER. Conspiracy theories have a key role in developing murderous instincts, whether in every step of preparing and carrying out mass murder (as in the Nazi slaughter of Jews, Slavs, and others) or only indirectly present (as in the Japanese murderousness during World War II). Conspiracism deprives the accused of their humanity and makes them vulnerable to elimination as though an unwanted pest. The killing fields begin by turning citizens into saboteurs, counterrevolutionaries, and spies, and then go on to make them into vermin, dogs, bacteria, or just "garbage." No other set of ideas so thoroughly transforms neighbors into enemies worthy only of extermination. Without such a view of victims, it is difficult to incite cadres to carry out atrocity after atrocity. This was the case in Stalin's starving the Ukrainians, murdering the *kulaks*, and purging the Trotskyite saboteurs; in Mao's consolidation of power, antirightist campaign, Great Leap Forward, and the Cultural Revolution; in the Khmer Rouge efforts at purification; and in Saddam Husayn's *Anfal* campaign against the Kurds of Iraq. In part, Slobodan Milosevic spurred Serbian "ethnic cleansing" by telling of a Muslim plot to capture Serbian women and place them in harems. Thus conspiracism, in its most debased form, becomes the vital accomplice of genocide.

No other people has been subjected to such conspiratorial suspicion as much as Jews,[29] nor has any other experienced such terrible consequences. Conspiratorial antisemitism helped spawn physical violence against Jews, violence that increased in intensity over time; fear of Jewish conspiracy turned hatred of Jews into a way of life and occasional persecution into genocide. It began with spontaneous mobs, such as those inspired by the crusading fervor of 1096; moved on to semiofficial pogroms, as in Russia of the late nineteenth century; then to organized assaults, as in the White Army outrages of 1918–20; and culminated in the Nazis' machinery of death.

Antisemitism, it is important to note, also harms non-Jews. Hitler saw other races (especially Slavs) as subject to Jewish influence and so engaged in genocide against them; others too, such as Gypsies and the disabled, fell into the maw of his extermination industry. Japanese antisemitism may seem like a harmless fantasy, but it too has had tragic consequences. The cult group Aum Shinri Kyo published a crude antisemitic tract in January 1995 in which it presented Japan's entire postwar history in terms of Jewish domination of the country. To fight this monstrous power, Aum Shinri Kyo announced that it "formally declares war on the 'world shadow government' that murders untold numbers of people."[30] Just two months later, when the group launched a poison gas attack, it picked the subway in Tokyo because it saw the capital city as the "Jewish" heart of the country. Due to logistical mistakes, many thousands were only injured, and not killed, but it could easily have been otherwise.

On the secret society side, conspiracism inspires a bellicosity that has consequences no less terrible. The portrayal of foreign states as fiendishly grasping for power provided the raw materials to foment a new kind of hatred. When the revolutionary French government under Robespierre spread stories in the 1790s about Britain's causing all the country's problems, the result was a surge of emotion that led to a profound change in the nature of international politics, as the historian H. D. Schmidt explains:

> For the first time the seed of national hatred was methodically sown by a government. The crop of hatred and national prejudice was infinitely larger than anything Robespierre and his colleagues could have imagined. The anti-British propaganda initiated by Robespierre and perfected by Napoleon survived its instigators by a hundred and fifty years, affecting the thought of leading European statesmen, who were often unaware of what had been the actual source that had poisoned their minds.[31]

These hatreds culminated in Stalin's demonization of Great Britain, and although he did not directly confront this enemy, he did turn the full force of Soviet power against Britain's alleged Russian agents (starting with Leon Trotsky and ending with hapless peasants). Similar myths of British and American conspiracy led to tragedies of comparable magnitude in other communist-ruled countries, but perhaps nowhere else so relentlessly as in Cambodia under the Khmer Rouge, where the slightest connection to the West—knowledge of the English or French language, possession of books in those languages, education beyond the seventh grade, or even eyeglasses—could be the cause for murder. In their monstrous ambition to break Cambodian connections to the outside world, the Khmer Rouge began a program of killing all but 1 million of their country's 7 million inhabitants; they reached about 2.4 million before being ousted from power.

The conspiracist mentality appears to have special importance when governments set out to commit democide, mass murder outside the context of warfare. Indeed, an analyst estimates the victims of democide to be "several times greater than the number killed in all of this century's wars"[32] and calculates the dead at 62 million in the Soviet Union, 35 million killed by the Chinese Communists, 21 million by the Nazis, 10 million by the Chinese nationalists, and 6 million by the Japanese militarists. Looking at the deaths carried out by just the top governmental killers in the twentieth century, he estimates they took 169 million lives.[33]

HOW MUCH TO WORRY?

Practical men who believe themselves to be quite exempt from any intellectual influences, are usually the slaves of some defunct economist. Madmen in authority, who hear voices in the air, are distilling their frenzy from some academic scribbler of a few years back.
JOHN MAYNARD KEYNES, THE GENERAL THEORY OF EMPLOYMENT, INTEREST AND MONEY (1936)

What does the history of conspiracism suggest for the future? Less or more trouble ahead? In the West, it appears that the marginalization of recent decades is permanent, so that conspiracy theories will not again acquire operational significance. But in Russia, the Middle East, and beyond, they remain a force, and so a matter the outside world must deal with.

Two contending interpretations exist about the United States, pessimistic and optimistic. The pessimistic version sees conspiracy theories on the rise and worries about the consequences. In 1967 the eminent American historian Henry Steele Commager observed that "there has come up in recent years . . . something called a conspiracy psychology. . . . We are on the road to a paranoid explanation of things."[34] More recently, Clarence Page, a syndicated columnist, concurs: "There's a lot more talk of conspiracy than there used to be."[35] Charles Paul Freund of *The Washington Post* concludes: "It is a powerful force, the belief in conspiracy, and threatening to grow more so"; he finds this "a potentially troubling phenomenon."[36]

Pessimists also note the increasing legitimacy of conspiracism as a form of political discourse. Serious presidential aspirants talk in these terms, as do many black leaders and not a few academics and journalists. Even incumbent politicians, who must keep the electorate in mind, indulge in conspiracism. Thus, Representative Helen Chenoweth (Republican of Idaho) makes statements about a one-world government and warns an undersecretary of agriculture that unless black helicopters stop flying, she will be his "worst nightmare." Charles Duke, a Republican state senator in Colorado, raises the issue of microchips implanted in American babies to control their behavior as adults.

One analyst, Michael Barkun, noted in 1996 that "the gap between the worldview of conspiratorialists and the mainstream appeared virtually unbridgeable as little as five years ago. Beliefs once consigned to the outermost fringes of American political and religious life now seem less isolated and stigmatizing than they once did." He points to two particularly important bridges across that gap: Pat Robertson, whose media empire incorporates conspiracism, and the militias, which espouse ostensibly mainstream values but introduce novices to a whole separate communications network and world outlook. Barkun acknowledges that "there is as yet no evidence that [the militias] have secured even the beginnings of a mass following," but he clearly sees this as a real possibility.[37]

The optimistic view sees the paranoid style having become just another form of diversion in the United States, a country where information overflows anyone's capacity or attention span. Millions read books by Pat Robertson, listen to songs by Ice T., or watch Oliver Stone's movies, all of which have deeply unsettling implications about the existing order. They might accept the conspiracist interpretations of Kennedy's death or Reagan's election, and perhaps believe in a UFO cover-up. Yet the great majority of audiences and electorates seem curiously unaffected by the conspiracy theories that swirl around them. With the exception of small numbers of militiamen, black Muslims, and others at the edges, conspiracy theories seem not to have much of an impact. The drumbeat of contending ideas, some sane, some not, is so intense in a media-saturated culture that their messages, the columnist Charles Krauthammer explains,

> raise an eyebrow, but never a fist. A politics so trivialized is conducive to neither great decision making nor decisive leadership. But it is also nicely immunized from the worst of political pathologies. In the end, Oliver Stone—like David Duke and Louis Farrakhan and the rest of America's dealers in paranoia—is just another entertainment, another day at the movies. The shallowness of our political culture has a saving grace.[38]

Returning to the terminology used at the beginning of this book, pessimists focus on the potential of the disaffected, and optimists stress the frivolity of the suspicious. One sees anger and danger, the other vacuity and stupidity.

I am more inclined to the optimistic view, at least in regard to North America and Western Europe. Serious conspiracism in those regions belongs more to the past than the future. It no longer drives the actions of governments or other major institutions. In the final analysis, a Chenoweth or Farrakhan has limited importance. Further, though it may not often seem so, societies do learn from their mistakes, and this century witnessed some big ones to learn from. The age of dictators seems to have inoculated the West from again handing over power to leaders enthralled by conspiracy theories. "Society's intellectual antibodies are respond-ing."[39] The impulse that prompted large and sophisticated populations to place their fate in the hands of ruthless conspiracy theorists does seem to have passed. As the political mainstream returns to a less fevered outlook, the paranoid style finds a place approximating what it had in the Enlight-enment: a widespread presence without being capable of changing the course of history. Chenoweth accuses and Farrakhan raves, but neither moves history.

The maturation of democracy also has much to do with this whole-some development; conspiracism bedevils countries in transition to democracy (the young United States, the Weimar Republic, post-Soviet Russia), but it has a far lesser role where democracy is fully established—meaning not just where voting for politicians is routine but where the other facets of civil society are in place, such as the rule of law, freedom of speech,˙ and minority rights. Shaking off conspiracism after two centuries of its increased importance marks an important, perhaps a historic, trans-formation in public life of the West.

This return to common sense is most striking in North America and Western Europe, less so in Eastern Europe and the Soviet Union. In nearly all of the former Soviet bloc, the conspiracism that regimes spon-sored in earlier decades now wins votes. Still, there are signs for optimism there too, as those societies find their way back from the harrowing expe-rience of Leninist rule. Stalin dominated his era and very nearly the world; Gennady Zyuganov had to run for office and lost. The much-expected outbreak of antisemitic violence did not take place in Russia. Freemasonry is returning to Eastern Europe and the former Soviet Union.[40] The pervasive conspiracism of earlier times appears to be in retreat. Explaining the unseasonably warm weather in December 1996, a Russian storeowner noted that "In the old days we would have thought the C.I.A. did it," but himself dismissed this explanation.[41] Some Russians are making a vigorous effort to slough off the old conspiracist mentality. Though it is not an easy task, level-headed analysts and explicit arguments to establish that not everything that happens has been planned[42] are eventually likely to prevail.

Things are less hopeful in other parts of the world, where the conspiracist import has become fully indigenous and appears to have settled in. Although it is hard to generalize about many regions in all their diversity, the major improvement in the West's public discourse holds two implications for the rest of the world. On the positive side, it suggests that those regions under the sway of conspiracism can look forward to its eventually passing. This is not a permanent affliction; there is an end. Bitter experience does teach individuals, organizations, and societies that conspiracy theories are the wrong way to deal with problems.

Less positive is the message that conspiracism can grow for centuries, hold sway for decades, and contribute to immense tragedies along the way. The toll of conspiracism in the West, in lives lost and otherwise harmed, far exceeds what any non-Western region has yet suffered. Must the Philippines, India, Iran, and Haiti go through a destruction comparable to that experienced in the West before their peoples can exorcise the conspiracist demons? Sound logic and superior leadership do not of their own appear sufficient to make the paranoid style fade away; more profound changes need to take place, so that this outlook no longer serves a function. That usually requires a thorough reevaluation of self, plus fundamental changes in thinking processes and social perception. As in Europe, it might take disasters to achieve this. With luck, it will not.

BENIGN ANTISEMITISM

I have asked many people in position—in England and elsewhere—why England has capitulated to the Zionists, and none of them has been able to give me a straight answer. It is not money. But what is it?
—A British general serving in Palestine (1920)[1]

The myth of Jewish power and world conspiracy in most cases wreaked destruction on Jews—but not always. Curiously, it also had some positive consequences for them. In these incidences, fear of Jews led antisemites to treat Jews with a caution that redounded to the latter's benefit. Notable cases include the British decision to issue the Balfour Declaration in 1917, various Arab leaders' interest in winning Great Power favor, Stalin's support for the nascent Israel, and the confused Japanese treatment of Jews during World War II.[2]

From its inception, Zionism has won the backhanded support of antisemites, who saw in it a means to reduce or even remove Jews from their presence. In 1878, a prominent Hungarian antisemite urged Jews to take power in the distant expanses of the East: "[N]ow is time for a people as progressive, educated, and of great intellectual competence as the Jewish to take a leadership role in the Orient." He then called on Jews "to realize the regeneration of the Muhammadan empire."[3] A German counterpart went further, admonishing the Jews, "Conquer Asia, your homeland, like you conquered US."[4]

The same ideas recurred all over the world. Katsuisa Sakai, a Christian minister, published three *Protocols*-inspired tracts in 1924, warning Japanese that the Jewish conspiracy would soon extend to Japan "and even encroach on the Imperial family itself."[5] At the same time, Sakai enthusiastically supported Jewish nationalism: "The rebuilding of Zion is not merely the ambition of the Jews but a mission from God. Their movement is thus not an invasion but a revival. They should attack proudly, their flag unfurled!"[6] So stalwart a Zionist did Sakai consider himself that he used this credential to petition (without success) for a loan from a Zionist organization in England.

British overestimation of Jewish power in the United States and Russia had a central role in the decision to issue the Balfour Declaration in November 1917. The story begins in July 1908, when the Young Turks (formally, the Committee of Union and Progress) took effective power in the Ottoman Empire. Although the Young Turks consisted primarily of Turkish-speaking, Muslim military officers, the British ambassador in Istanbul, Gerard Lowther, saw them as mainly Jewish in inspiration and leadership. This overestimation of Jewish power struck many Europeans as plausible and was widely accepted (some added a Masonic influence). In antisemitic eyes, then, Jews controlled one great power leading up to and during World War I.

This event did much to strengthen belief in Jewish power. As early as 1910, Ambassador Lowther raised the prospect of Zionists' helping the German government of Kaiser Wilhelm II to achieve its expansionist goals. When the world war came four years later, the Germans did indeed try to win the Zionists' favor, for Berlin also overestimated their power and thought that by winning Jewish favor they could influence a group of key Americans. Specifically, the Germans intervened with their Ottoman ally to reduce his hostility to the Zionists in Palestine and provided many other services (including German diplomatic travel documents made available to a Zionist leader).

But all this was merely preliminary skirmishing. By 1915, stalemate had descended on the Western Front, with British (as well as French and German) soldiers going off to their deaths by the hundreds of thousands, and to no avail. To extricate themselves from this impasse, diplomats in London desperately sought new allies, including both Zionists and Arabs. The Arabs' location and numbers gave them obvious leverage. The case of the Jews is more subtle and reflects the prevailing overestimation of their power. To win Jewish favor, David Lloyd George (the future prime minister) as early as 1915 looked favorably on a Zionist state in Palestine. A Foreign Office cable dated 11 March 1916 suggested that the side that favored Jewish settlement in Palestine might appeal "to a large and powerful section of the Jewish community throughout the world." This being the case, "the Zionist idea has the most far-reaching political possibilities." Were the Entente Powers to support Zionism, the author raised the danger that they would win to their cause "the Jewish forces in America, the East and elsewhere."[7] Were the British to preempt, they could benefit from these same forces.

Seven days later, Mark Sykes, a key British official, gave his total support to this approach: "To my mind the Zionists are now the key of the situation—the problem is how are they to be satisfied." What exactly could Zionists do for the British war effort? Sykes enumerated: "[I]f the Zionists think the proposal good enough they will want us to win—If they [want] us to win they will do their best which means they will (A) calm their activities in Russia, (B) pessimise in Germany (C) stimulate in France England & Italy (D) enthuse in U.S.A."[8] As the war proceeded, other influential British politicians (Lloyd George, Lord Milner, Herbert Samuel) joined Sykes in arguing that a pro-Zionist stance could have a critical impact on public opinion in the United States and Russia.

This awe of Jewish power had an importance that far transcended the politics of the moment, leading as it did to the Balfour Declaration in November 1917, a statement that announced the British government's favoring "the establishment in Palestine of a national home for the Jewish people." Foreign Secretary Balfour argued (during the War Cabinet meeting at which the declaration was adopted) that its passage would allow the British government "to carry on extremely useful propaganda both in Russia and America."[9] Other observers took this idea to extremes. Noting that Lenin seized power just five days after the Balfour Declaration was issued, one member of the Intelligence Directorate at the War Office speculated that "it is even possible that, had the Declaration come sooner, the course of the [Russian] Revolution might have been affected."[10]

These exaggerated visions of Jewish power had the effect of placing the British Empire on the side of Zionism, however fleetingly, and thereby enormously boosting the Jewish national movement at a critical moment.

After World War I ended, some Arab leaders followed the British and German lead in trying to win favor with the all-powerful Jews. King

Faysal of Syria made some calculatedly friendly moves toward the Zionists, culminating in a secret agreement with Chaim Weizmann in January 1919. In large part, Faysal signed this accord because of an exaggerated sense of Jewish power, as Moshe Ma'oz explains:

> Apparently, he believed that the Zionists, in addition to representing a potential economic asset to Syria, possessed great influence with the world's major power, Great Britain (from whom they had already gained the Balfour Declaration). Since the Zionist movement also carried some weight in the United States (which was involved in the post-war peace conference), it could, in Faysal's thinking, help him achieve his grand aim, namely, Arab independence under his leadership, backed by Britain and recognized by the international community. To realize this goal and to nullify France's claim to control Syria, Faysal conditionally agreed to the creation of the Jewish national home in Palestine.[11]

Note the progression here: first the British issued the Balfour Declaration, believing Jews to be influential in the United States; a year later, an Arab king reached an agreement with the Zionists in good part because the Balfour Declaration showed Jewish influence over London!

Nearly twenty years later, Syrian and Lebanese leaders met with Chaim Weizmann and other Zionists, again as a way to curry favor. This time they did so with an eye not to London but to Paris, where the Jewish and pro-Zionist Léon Blum had become prime minister in June 1936. Weizmann reported that Syria's Prime Minister Jamil Mardam had offered "to tell the Arabs in Palestine to lay off, if we would help them in Syria; the assumption being, apparently, that we had Blum in our pockets."[12] Likewise, an Israeli source reported that the Sunni leader (and later independent Lebanon's first prime minister) Riyad as-Sulh was prepared, "if Syria achieved independence," to "do all that was possible to try and ease the situation in Palestine," in return for Jewish economic and organizational assistance.[13]

In recent years, Israel's reputed clout in Washington has won it the amity of weak states around the world interested in improving relations with the U.S. government, to the point that Israeli leaders sent word to their embassies to cut down on the influx of high-level visitors. More remarkably, operating on the basis of an inflated idea of Israel's utility as a door to the United States, anti-Zionist states seek Israel out. Iran accepted the Israeli initiative that led to the Iran/*Contra* scandal for this reason; then Iraq and Libya initiated diplomatic contacts with Israel. This led to an odd situation in which the U.S. government rapped Israel's knuckles for contacts with Arab states. In August 1993, it reportedly delivered a "stern" warning to Jerusalem "to stop its efforts to establish contacts with Libya."[14] A year later, Washington admonished Jerusalem for its diplomacy with Iraq. Reviewing these strange developments, the Israeli commentator Yo'el Marcus concluded that these Arab leaders have a "mystical belief . . . in the veracity of the *Protocols of the Elders of Zion*. . . . Never has such a groundless anti-Semitic document done us [Israelis] such service as this document. . . . Small wonder that it is difficult to walk around in this country without bumping into some minister, prince, king, prime minister, et al., who are visiting us with an unconcealed hope that we open doors for them in America."[15]

Soviet support for Zionism in 1947–48 had a very different quality: not to win the favor of a great power but to harm its interests. Faced with London's efforts to exclude the Soviet Union from the Middle East, Stalin reacted by seeking out and supporting the most powerful force in the area in the hopes of turning it into an anti-imperialist ally. He and his aides did not see the Arab leaders filling this role, having deemed them as nothing but weaklings and lackeys of the imperialist powers. In the colorful wording of one Soviet official, "There will be revolutionary developments in the Hawaiian Islands before anything will move in the Arab East."[16] In contrast, Stalin apparently believed in a Jewish power so vast that, in league with the British, it would overwhelm Soviet efforts. To prevent this, he did his best to separate the Zionists from London. And so, for one year's duration, the Soviet Union became the prime supporter of Zionist aspirations to found a sovereign Jewish state, forwarding its cause diplomatically and militarily at its moment of supreme need.

Thus was the establishment of the state of Israel, from the Balfour Declaration to its war of independence, helped by the strange phenomenon of benign antisemitism.

Benign and malign views of Jewish power have co-existed in Japan for nearly a century, leading to confusion so intense it has a near-comic quality. Curiously, both originated in war against Russia. The benign view began when some Jews (notably Jacob Schiff) won financial assistance for Japan in its war of 1904–05 against Russia. The Russians responded to that loss by resorting to a Jewish conspiracy. It was precisely that malign view that they imparted to Japan in 1918–22, as White Russians fought alongside Japanese troops in Siberia. The anti-Bolsheviks widely accepted the *Protocols of the Elders of Zion* as the explanation for the Russian Revolution and convinced their Japanese contacts of its truth.

Profoundly ignorant about Jews but fascinated by this reputedly powerful force and convinced of the reality of a Jewish conspiracy, the leaders of fascist Japan wavered between hostility and friendliness (appealing to Jews, "you should actively support and contribute to the Holy War of Sacred Japan").[17] To win Jewish goodwill, they invited Jews in the late 1930s to settle in the occupied territory of Manchuria, hoping this gesture would inspire the Elders of Zion to use their influence to improve American opinion toward Japanese imperialism.

These contrary views came to a head at a December 1938 cabinet meeting. Hours of debate on the Jewish issue kept the cabinet in session deep into the night, with one side arguing for the malign view coming out of Nazi Germany and the other for the benign view that had some strength in Japan. Advocates of the benign view recalled the war of 1904–05 and hoped in the future for more financial and political help (e.g., to make President Roosevelt look on Japan more kindly). In the end, the latter won ("We cannot afford to alienate the Jews"): Jews would be allowed into Japanese-occupied Manchuria so that they would develop the area and bring favorable publicity to Japan. In deference to Nazi Germany, however, this policy was not publicly declared.[18]

STALIN'S BLIND SPOT

We must remember that we are always
within a hairsbreadth of invasion.
—JOSEPH STALIN, 15 FEBRUARY 1939[1]

Surely we have not deserved that!
—FOREIGN COMMISSAR MOLOTOV,
RESPONDING TO THE GERMAN
DECLARATION OF WAR, 22 JUNE 1941[2]

The most distrustful persons are
often the biggest dupes.
—CARDINAL DE RETZ[3]

T he culmination of conspiracism took place between 1941 and 1945 on the Eastern Front of World War II, where Hitler's and Stalin's armies met in a battle that resulted in large part from what may be the two greatest mistakes in the history of warfare. Hitler erroneously started a two-front war; Stalin did not see what was coming. Stalin's error being closely tied to his fear of conspiracy, I look at it in some depth.

The German-Soviet Non-Aggression Pact of August 1939 (and its secret annexes) had called for a ten-year truce between the two sides. By December 1940, however, Hitler had decided to renege on it and launch a surprise attack against the Soviet Union. Throughout the first half of 1941, Stalin had a great abundance of accurate information about German activities and plans, all of it accurately pointing to Hitler's plans.

The warnings began in January 1941, with a U.S. government alert based on information from Berlin; this was confirmed by further American admonitions, letters from Winston Churchill, and a wide range of

Soviet sources (including embassy sources in Berlin, the brilliant Richard Sorge reporting from Tokyo, and others). By late March, Moscow was steeped in rumors of approaching disaster. In perhaps a unique act of diplomacy, the German ambassador to Moscow on 19 May revealed the date of his government's invasion plan. One defector from the Nazi forces who told of an imminent invasion was ignored; another was summarily executed for spreading disinformation. In all, the Kremlin received one hundred or more separate warnings of a Nazi assault.

Beyond these diverse and authoritative sources, Soviet commanders at the front could see for themselves the massive German preparations. The Nazi assault forces, prepared over a ten-month period, ranged along an 1,800-mile front from the Baltic coast to the Black Sea; the *Ostheer* included 3.2 million men (out of a total German force of 3.8 million), 600,000 trucks and 600,000 horses, 7,000 artillery pieces, 3,350 tanks, and over 2,000 airplanes. In all, "Few nations have been better warned of impending invasion than the Soviet Union in June 1941."[4]

Yet Stalin chose to ignore, in both public and private, all this information.[5] To every alarmed piece of news he had roughly the same reply sent down: "Don't panic. Take it easy. 'The boss' knows all about it." On Saturday evening, 21 June, Soviet military leaders spent a "quite ordinary" evening going to the theater or engaged in other amusements; security offices were nearly empty. Stalin dismissed reports of imminent attack as "panicking to no purpose"[6] and himself may have watched a movie.

Over the years Stalin had taken many steps to win the Nazis' confidence. As the German ambassador in Moscow correctly reported back, "Stalin has set himself the goal of preserving the Soviet Union from a conflict with Germany."[7] Already in 1938, during the Czechoslovak crisis, he seemed eager to show the Nazi leadership that no Soviet forces were moving toward Czechoslovakia. He went out of his way punctiliously to fulfill every commitment made in the non-aggression pact. In 1940, as Nazi forces rolled west, he adopted an anti-French and anti-British line. Soviet intelligence agents in Germany had to work under a uniquely restrictive set of instructions, while Stalin passed on some of the warnings he received (including at least one from Churchill) to the Germans. So complete was Stalin's goodwill that full trains loaded with Soviet goods were entering Nazi-held territory even as the German assault began (and despite the Germans' having stopped making deliveries months before).

In the spring of 1941, Stalin took many steps to demobilize Soviet opinion. Anti-Nazi statements had already ceased entirely, earlier materials were withdrawn from circulation, friendship was publicly declared, and Soviet citizens of German origins were released from incarceration. A public statement on 14 June rejected talk of a German invasion as "clumsy fabrications," then asserted that "the rumors that Germany intends to violate the Pact and attack the Soviet Union are completely groundless, while the recent transfer of German troops, having completed their operations in the Balkans, to the eastern and northern parts of Germany must be assumed to have to do with other motives unconnected to Soviet-German relations."[8] Time and again, Stalin's words, and those of his underlings, emphasized not the reality of over three million hostile soldiers perched on the frontier, but the importance of doing nothing that might "provoke" them. To an assistant Stalin wrote, "Hitler shouldn't get the idea that all we're doing is preparing for war with him."[9] The Soviet populace, battered into taking very seriously everything their superiors told them, understood such statements to mean that war would not take place.

As Nazi forces prepared for an assault, Stalin took specific steps to make his forces vulnerable to them. On one occasion, he countermanded a military commander's orders partially to black out naval bases and airfields, and on another he refused to prepare antiaircraft guns to shoot down German reconnaissance planes overflying Soviet territory. Indeed, when some of those planes had to land, they were repaired and given a full tank of gas for their return journey; in one case, when a border unit downed a German spy plane, killing two, the Soviets apologized to Berlin for the incident and punished the soldiers involved.

So much did Stalin fear falling into a trap that for over eight hours after the German assault had begun in the early hours of 22 June, he still continued to restrict his troops' response, hoping in vain that the attacks were an unsanctioned effort by German generals to provoke war. In keeping with this fear, a military dispatch (issued about 12:30 A.M.) ordered Soviet commanders "not to give way to provocative actions of any kind which might produce major complications."[10] Similarly, the general in charge of the Baltic region gave instructions at about 2:30 A.M. that included the following phrases: "In the case of provocative action by the Germans fire *not* to be opened. In the event of flights by German aircraft over our territory, to make no demonstration and until such time as enemy aircraft undertake military operations, *no fire* to be opened on them. In the event of strong enemy forces undertaking offensive operations, to destroy them."[11] At 7:15 A.M., Stalin agreed to a directive telling the troops to "attack the enemy and destroy him,"[12] but even then, hoping against hope, he restricted the order to Soviet territory and admonished the soldiers not to cross the frontier line; still, in other words, he issued no declaration of war or general mobilization orders.

Only at noon did the Soviet foreign minister declare war. Soviet forces, the German chief of staff recorded in his diary, were "tactically surprised along the entire front."[13] Their unreadiness permitted the Germans to win an immense initial advantage, one that cost the Soviet Union uncounted millions of lives over the next four years.

Conspiracism contributed to Stalin's error in three main ways: by isolating him from the outside world, distracting him with nonexistent plots, and creating in him a weird faith in Hitler.

ISOLATION. Stalin was vulnerable to making a monumental mistake because the purges of previous years had made it impossible for anyone to stand up to him. In Stalin's mind, criticism of him amounted to a conspiracy against him. Anti-Stalin jokes were a form of terrorism, contact with foreigners amounted to espionage, and after-dinner political griping constituted a first step toward his assassination. Stalin had long seen individuals scattered across the huge Soviet expanse as a single and purposeful group who carried out the commands from distant Mexico of his now-dead archenemy Trotsky, receiving his orders via such methods as invisible ink in magazines about movie stars.

Living in morbid fear of a plot, Stalin restricted himself to the Kremlin and his country house, surrounded himself with guards and yes-men, and became disengaged from reality. As Khrushchev explained in his 1956 speech denouncing Stalin, the latter never traveled or spoke with ordinary people. "He knew the country and agriculture only from films. And these films had dressed up and beautified the existing situation in agriculture. Many films so pictured kolkhoz [collective farm] life that the tables were bending from the weight of turkeys and geese. Evidently, Stalin thought that it was actually so."[14] Stalin came to believe in the illusion he had created, becoming captive—perhaps the only one in the country—of his own dream world.

In a sense, he had no choice, for having weeded out anyone with an independent mind and accused them of conspiracies, he was left not just with sycophants who dared not express any opinion ("Yes, Comrade Stalin, of course, Comrade Stalin, you have taken a wise decision, Comrade Stalin") but with mental dwarfs who actually believed in Stalin's wisdom and farsightedness. The system he created permitted him alone to make important decisions. Those who might disagree within the ruling councils, in the media, or in the academy had learned otherwise. "Locked up in the Kremlin, the master of a world which he had created by his own selective killings and which reflected back upon him only those images he had himself ordained, steeped in his own 'genius' and fed on its outpourings, Stalin could rage away dissension and doubt."[15]

In the case of Germany, Stalin created his own dream world by deciding that Hitler, wanting to avoid a two-front war, would not attack him before May 1942. Perhaps counting too much on his own good fortune, Stalin made up his mind, and that was that. He then set about to order the world in accord with his decision. Specifically, he made himself prime minister in May 1941; also, he directed his intelligence aide to file information about German ambitions against Great Britain in the "reliable sources" dossier, whereas those about the Soviet Union were relegated to the "doubtful sources" file. Generally, the "doubtful sources" did not circulate beyond Stalin himself.

CONSPIRACY THEORIES. Building on this susceptibility, Stalin explained away the many warnings coming his way by conjuring up conspiracy theories.

The first theory was a British plot. Remembering Churchill's profoundly anti-Bolshevik sentiments from the 1920s and suspecting him of efforts to provoke a war between the two totalitarian states, Stalin rebuffed the British prime minister's many warnings. Ironically, pilfered documents from the Foreign Office confirmed this mistrust, for Whitehall had a more sanguine interpretation of Nazi intentions, and Stalin saw these as a more authentic reflection of British views than Churchill's letters to him. He suspected the prime minister of trying either to break the Nazi-Soviet Non-Aggression Pact of 1939 or to join with Germany in a war against the Soviet Union. The May 1941 flight of Rudolf Hess to Scotland confirmed his fear of a British conspiracy to join with Hitler against Stalin. Indeed, it got to the point that "Stalin tended to see all warnings of a German attack, whatever their source, as further evidence of a British conspiracy."[16] For example, to predictions from a Soviet intelligence source in Prague of a German attack, he responded with the comment, "English provocation. Investigate! Stalin." Following Stalin's obsession with "provocation," top Soviet officials "saw provocation as an inevitable tool of the unending conspiracy by capitalist powers against the Soviet state. If the U.S.S.R. allowed itself to be provoked on issues chosen by its capitalist opponents, it played into their hands and temporarily lost control of the march of history."[17]

His second theory concerned freelancing German generals. Stalin sometimes expressed fears that the *Wehrmacht* leadership, in defiance of Hitler's wishes and carried away by their extraordinary string of successes between 1939 and 1941, sought to start a war with the U.S.S.R. (In fact, nearly all the generals opposed Operation Barbarossa.) When, just a few hours before the all-out German assault, a deserter informed the Soviets of what lay in store for them, Stalin rejected his warning on the grounds that the German generals had dispatched him "to provoke a conflict."[18] Even after the attack began, Stalin refused to respond with full force, thinking that "this was only a provocative action on the part of several undisciplined sections of the German army, and that our reaction might serve as a reason for the Germans to begin the war."[19]

AWE OF HITLER. On signing the non-aggression accord in 1939, Stalin made two contradictory comments. To the German foreign minister he expressed pious sentiments: "The Soviet government takes the new pact very seriously. I can guarantee on my word of honor that the Soviet Union will not betray her partner."[20] To his underlings he cynically asserted that "it's all a game to see who can fool whom. I know what Hitler's up to. He thinks he's outsmarted me, but actually it's I who have tricked him."[21] It defies reason, but the first remarks describe his actions far better than the second. Stalin, in other words, displayed a unique and inexplicable trust in Hitler.

For once in his life, Stalin lived up to his word and trusted another human being; how strange that he should have chosen Hitler as the beneficiary. (The Soviet term for Hitler's assault, revealingly, came to be known as the "breach of faith," or *verolomstvo*).) Several factors related to conspiracism help explain this choice.

One was respect. At the same time that Stalin excoriated Nazis, he learned conspiratorial tricks from them. For example, Stalin watched Hitler turn on his friends and get rid of them by accusing them of conspiracies against himself. Hitler's June 1934 killing of Ernst Röhm, the Storm Troops commander, on the false grounds that Röhm intended a coup d'état, prompted Stalin's admiration: "Some fellow that Hitler. Knows how to treat his political opponents."[22] Edvard Radzinsky, a biographer of Stalin, concludes that "After Lenin and Trotsky, Hitler was Stalin's third teacher."[23]

Second, it could be that Stalin's many years of conspiracist obsession with Trotsky, supported by a vast police and propaganda apparatus, left him psychologically unprepared for Hitler. The ruler is no less influenced by his own words than the populace—indeed, probably more so—and so turning Trotsky into the devil incarnate perhaps dulled his perception of the real devil incarnate.

Third was his willingness to share power. Stalin's readiness to divide global hegemony with Hitler apparently led him to assume that Hitler would also share power with him. That was not the case. In this sense, Hitler was one step more evil yet than Stalin; he wanted the whole world, to Stalin's accepting just half. Thinking that Hitler would split the loot led Stalin to believe that making it absolutely clear he had no intention of attacking Germany would cause Hitler to leave him alone. He seemed to believe that taking no steps to "provoke" the Germans—even not taking normal precautions to defend Soviet territory—would put Hitler's mind at ease and cause him not to attack (as though Hitler would have allowed some Soviet misbehavior to set off a war he did not intend to fight). To do otherwise would bring on the attack that Stalin so feared, before he had time to rebuild Soviet forces. Ironically, the one time Stalin did not insist on total power was the one time he nearly made a fatal mistake.

Ironically, Stalin never thought of appeasing Churchill and Roosevelt, whom he saw as avaricious and destructive; Hitler, however, he tried to fend off by acting like a lamb. Here the Soviet dictator fell into the conspiracy theorist's most catastrophic mistake: he ascribed Hitler's character to Churchill, as well as the reverse. Thus did "appearances deceive" cause Stalin to kill millions for imaginary reasons but not see a real conspiracy. A host of imagined conspiracies blinded him to the real one.[24]

APPENDIX C

THE INTERNET

*The Internet was one of the major
reasons the militia movement
expanded faster than any hate
group in history.*
—KENNETH STERN[1]

New technologies, including inexpensive radio transmitters and the photocopier, have boosted the fascination with conspiracy theories. Conspiracy theorists, insatiably hunger for materials and irrepressibly seeking ways to express themselves, have taken to these new media with gusto. The Internet in particular, in its several guises—electronic mail, discussion groups, and the World Wide Web—provides a near-perfect vehicle for widely dispersed individuals to make contact with each other, share interests, and access vast amounts of information, all at minimal cost. These are the ideal back channels for those excluded from the mainstream media.

Standard conspiracist themes—antimasonic, antisemitic, anti-imperialist, the John Kennedy assassination, the New World Order—have a conspicuous presence in cyberspace. New issues spread more quickly in weeks than they previously could in years, then echo far more broadly. For example, less than two days after TWA flight 800 crashed just outside New York City in July 1996, a rumor posted on the <rec.aviation.piloting> newsgroup asked, "Did the Navy do it?" and noted "how much evidence there is that it [the plane] was hit by mistake." The idea that the U.S. Navy launched a missile that shot down an American plane, and that large parts of the Federal Government, including the White House, were engaged in a conspiracy to cover up the deed, then found a wide following on the Internet. This suspiciousness prompted journalists on several occasions to ask officials about the possibility of friendly fire, and the heated response ("an outrageous allegation") only confirmed conspiracist doubts. The rocket idea made international headlines when, relying entirely on information from the Internet, Pierre Salinger of ABC News in early November endorsed this conspiracy theory. He was even photographed holding a printout of the version he had downloaded from <http://www.lsoft.com>.[2]

The legitimate press can also make use of this alternate network to spread conspiracism. *The San Jose Mercury News* story connecting crack usage in Los Angeles with the CIA, published in August 1996, would probably have garnered little national attention before the age of the Internet. With computer distribution, however, the *Mercury News* site not only received an extra 200,000 or more hits a day for weeks, but blacks nationally made it a focus of attention: newsgroups picked it up, radio stations read out excerpts, and community groups discussed it. Anyone with a computer could download and print out the three-part series, and many did, to the point that hard copies appeared even in beauty salons.

Sites listed below represent either significant institutions or important views, or they provide access to many other sites (they are, in effect, bibliographies).

Antisemitic Sites[3]

Holocaust denial: <http://www.nizkor.org>.

Radio Islam: <http://abbc.com/islam>. Located in Sweden, promoter of a wide range of antisemitic theses—with an Islamic twist.

Stormfront White Nationalist Resource Page: <http://www.stormfront.org>. The most listings of neo-Nazi sites.

Anti-Secret Society Sites

Antimasonic materials: <http://www.crocker.com>. For Masonic materials, see <http://www.chrysalis.org/masonry/>.

John Birch Society: <http://www.jbs.org>.

John F. Kennedy assassination: <alt.conspiracy.jfk>. Many sites provide old documentation; this one monitors current thinking.

Noam Chomsky is one of the most popular writers on the Internet, with many sites, including:

<http://www.whistler.net/worldtour/homepage/gallery/cmsky001htm>,

<http://www.whistler.net/worldtour/homepage/ejournal/chomsky.htm>,

and <http://www.worldmedia.com/archive/>. MIT Press even put its full-length biography of Chomsky[4] on the Internet, at <http://www-mitpress.mit.edu/chomsky/>.

The Consortium: <http://www.delve.com/consort.html>. Excerpts of a conspiracist publication edited by Robert Parry.

San Jose Mercury News: <http://www.sjmercury.com>. The Story about the CIA's selling drugs in Los Angeles to finance the *contras* in Nicaragua, plus reactions and follow-up.

Sixty Greatest Conspiracies of All Time: <http://www.conspire.com/conspire/>. A somewhat tongue-in-cheek presentation by Jonathan Vankin and John Whalen of many recent conspiracy theories, including Aum Shinri Kyo, Buchanan, Nation of Islam, JFK, Lyndon Larouche, and UFOs. The "Rant-O-Rama" includes documentation, some aural.

UFO coverup: <http://www.conspire.com/conspire/ds/ufochap.html>. Over 300 Web sites deal with aliens.

Both Antisemitic and Anti-Secret Society

Pat Buchanan: <http://www.buchanan.org>. Speeches and other statements, as well as responses from supporters. Provides a search engine.

Lyndon Larouche: <http://www.etext.org/Politics/LaRouche>. Documents and periodicals from him and his supporters, such as transcripts of television and radio broadcasts, a chapter from a book, and excerpts from his periodicals.

Militia of Montana: <http://www.logoplex.com/shops/mom/>.

Nation of Islam: <http://www.noi.org>. The Final Call Online, with speeches by Louis Farrakhan.

Readers who wish to spread conspiracy theories of their own may go to the newsgroup <alt.conspiracy>; it contains discussion groups on practically every topic mentioned in this book.

For relief from these many hate-mongers, the Anti-Defamation League provides original research and documentation, primarily but not exclusively about antisemitic groups, at <http://www.adl.org>.

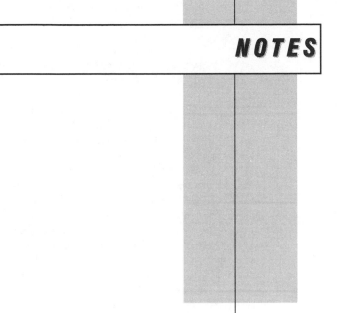

NOTES

True scholars and true believers can be confused (as chapter 3, "Unmasking the Conspiracy Theory," explains). To help keep them apart, the notes provide names of non-conspiracy theorists in normal letters, and names of conspiracy theorists in small capitals. In the case of individuals who wander in and out of conspiracism (Gary Sick, Jonathan Vankin), the lettering changes, reflecting their various outlooks.

To give a sense of the vast literature of conspiracism, the notes provide references to major writings, including some not quoted in the text.

All emphasis in quotations is in the original text.

EPIGRAPH PAGE

American Mercury: 29 August 1799. Quoted in Vernon Stauffer, *New England and the Bavarian Illuminati* (New York: Columbia University Press, 1918), p. 307.

Prince Metternich: Quoted in Hans J. Morgenthau, *Politics Among Nations: The Struggle for Power and Peace,* 5th ed. (New York: Alfred A. Knopf, 1973), p. 527. Alternatively: "I wonder why he did that," quoted in Robert Jervis, *Perception and Misperception in International Politics* (Princeton, N.J.: Princeton University Press, 1976), p. 320.

Joseph Stalin: Quoted in Edward Crankshaw, *Khrushchev Remembers,* trans. and ed. Strobe Talbott (Boston: Little, Brown, 1970), p. 307.

PREFACE

1. Robert Conquest, *The Great Terror: A Reassessment* (New York: Oxford University Press, 1990), p. 65.
2. R. J. Rummel, *Death by Government* (New Brunswick, N.J.: Transaction, 1994), p. 8, estimates that Stalin killed some 43 million of his own subjects, versus 21

million killed by Hitler; Rummel also attributes 38 million murders to Mao, one of Stalin's many adepts.

CHAPTER 1: CONSPIRACY THEORIES EVERYWHERE

1. *The Wall Street Journal*, 13 November 1996; *The New York Times*, 1 December 1996.
2. Richard Grenier, "On the Trail of America's Paranoid Class: Oliver Stone's *JFK*," *The National Interest*, Spring 1992, p. 84.
3. Jonetta Rose Barras, "Race, Crime, and Conspiracies," *The Washington Times*, 11 October 1996.
4. JEWELLE TAYLOR GIBBS (for an explanation of names in small capitals, see p. 203), *Race and Justice: Rodney King and O. J. Simpson in a House Divided* (San Francisco: Jossey-Bass, 1996), pp. 241, 237–38. GIBBS offers a detailed but semi-approving exposition of conspiracism.
5. Patricia A. Turner, *I Heard It Through the Grapevine: Rumor in African-American Culture* (Berkeley: University of California Press, 1993), pp. 82–107, 128–36, looks at these corporate conspiracy theories in detail and notes that all of them share certain characteristics as white-owned companies that advertise little and offer non-essential goods primarily in black neighborhoods. She then lauds the conspiracy theories against these firms as "a sort of self-imposed consumer harness" (p. 98).
6. MALIK ZULU SHABAZZ, speech at Howard University, 23 February 1994.
7. *The Washington Post*, 4 October 1996.
8. *The New York Post*, 4 December 1991.
9. For an example of the advertisement, see *Rolling Stone*, 12 November 1992.
10. *U.S. News & World Report*, 12 March 1990; *Essence*, September 1991.
11. *The New York Times*, 29 October 1990. Among whites, the comparable figures were 5 and 12 percent. Another 1990 survey of black churchgoers in five cities found 34 percent agreed that "the AIDS virus was produced in a germ warfare laboratory," *The Boston Globe*, 2 November 1995.
12. Gary Webb, "Dark Alliance: The Story behind the Crack Explosion," *San Jose Mercury News*, 18–20 August 1996.
13. Roberto Suro and Walter Pincus, "The CIA and Crack: Evidence Is Lacking of Contra-Tied Plot," *The Washington Post*, 4 October 1996.
14. Jesse Katz, "Tracking the Genesis of the Crack Trade," *The Los Angeles Times*, 20 October 1996. This was the first of a three-part series.
15. Tim Golden, "Tale of C.I.A. and Drugs Has Life of Its Own," *The New York Times*, 21 October 1996.
16. Notably, K. L. Billingsley, "Déjà Voo-Doo: The *Mercury News* Dredges up the Christics," *Heterodoxy*, December 1996.
17. *San Jose Mercury News*, 8 September 1996.
18. Ibid., 27 September 1996.
19. Associated Press, 29 September 1996.
20. *The Boston Globe*, 12 November 1996.
21. Quoted in Tucker Carlson, "A Disgraceful Newspaper Exposé and Its Fans," *The Weekly Standard*, 30 September 1996.
22. *San Jose Mercury News*, 6 October 1996.
23. *The Philadelphia Inquirer*, 6 October 1996.
24. For statements at the conference, see "The Other Face of Farrakhan: A Hate-Filled Prelude to the Million Man March," *ADL Fact Finding Report*, October 1995.

25. *The Final Call*, 23 March 1992. Quoted in Mattias Gardell, *In the Name of Elijah Muhammad: Louis Farrakhan and the Nation of Islam* (Durham, N.C.: Duke University Press, 1996), p. 327.

26. Tynetta Muhammad, "$4.4 Billion Dollars Is Not Enough!" *The Final Call*, 17 December 1996. Tynetta Muhammad was one of Elijah Muhammad's mistresses and later became a Nation of Islam theologian.

27. *The Washington Post*, 1 March 1990.

28. Most notably, THE HISTORICAL RESEARCH DEPARTMENT, *The Secret Relationship between Blacks and Jews* (Boston: Nation of Islam, 1991), vol. 1. The same HISTORICAL RESEARCH DEPARTMENT also publishes a newsletter, *Blacks and Jews News*.

29. There is another parallel, even stranger. New World Order also strikes fear among anti-American elements around the world, including communists in Russia and fundamentalist Muslims. Like the American Right, these see the New World Order as a terrifying conspiracy and locate its headquarters in the United Nations. They respond in precisely parallel ways—by attacking U.S. government buildings with truck bombs, the one destroying a Federal building in Oklahoma City, the other bringing down an embassy in Beirut. Despite these similarities, the two groups understand the term New World Order to have exactly opposite meanings: to Americans, it means a foreign takeover of the United States, to communists and fundamentalists, an American takeover of the rest of the world.

30. GARY H. KAH, *En Route to Global Occupation* (Lafayette, La.: Huntington House, 1991), p. 12.

31. *The New York Times*, 6 July 1995.

32. CALVIN GREENUP, a Montana Militiaman, quoted in Kenneth S. Stern, *A Force upon the Plain: The American Militia Movement and the Politics of Hate* (New York: Simon & Schuster, 1996), p. 87.

33. *The New York Times*, 6 July 1995.

34. ANDREW MACDONALD [pseud. of WILLIAM L. PIERCE], *The Turner Diaries* (Washington: National Alliance, 1978) and *Hunter* (Hillsborough, W.Va: National Vanguard, 1989).

35. *The Washington Post*, 24 April 1995.

36. *The New York Times*, 14 July 1992.

37. PATRICK J. BUCHANAN, "Will the American Nation Survive?" press release, n.d.

38. PATRICK J. BUCHANAN, "Investigate the NAFTA Bailout," press release, 1 February 1995.

39. Others (like LOUIS FARRAKHAN) note that two other institutions were established in that same fateful year: the Federal Bureau of Investigation and the Anti-Defamation League of B'nai B'rith. The Seventeenth Amendment, providing for the popular election of senators, was also ratified in 1913.

40. PAT ROBERTSON, *The New World Order* (Dallas: Word, 1991), p. 65. He deems the establishment of the Federal Reserve Board as the moment when "American finance was captured by European finance and their powerful American allies" (p. 127).

41. Ibid., pp. 65, 92, 37, 253, 216.

42. Ibid., p. 35. Other conspiracy theorists more boldly forward the idea of the U.S. government always being part of a plot: "Since Jefferson's time the citizens of the U.S.A. have gradually been conditioned for the day when the Illuminati decide to take over." WILLIAM GUY CARR, *The Conspiracy to Destroy All Existing Governments and Religions* (Metairie, La.: Sons of Liberty, [1960?]), p. 19.

43. ROBERTSON, *The New World Order*, p. 37. He recounts (on pp. 104–05) meeting President-elect Carter and giving him a list of evangelical Christian candidates for high office in his administration; Carter responded with tears, which Robertson understood as his response to the fact that "the appointment process is out of his hands" and the impossibility of his accepting the suggested individuals.
44. Ibid., p. 133.
45. Ibid., pp. 176–77.
46. Dennis King, *Lyndon LaRouche and the New American Fascism* (New York: Doubleday, 1989), p. 45.
47. JOSEPH BREWDA, "Saudi Bombing: It's the British Hitting the U.S.," *The New Federalist*, 8 July 1996.
48. *U.S. News & World Report*, 2 June 1992. In contrast, Gerald Posner sees conspiracism as "important but not the driving force" behind Perot's campaigns (telephone conversation, 5 December 1996).
49. *The New Yorker*, 15 June 1992.
50. *60 Minutes*, CBS-TV, 25 October 1992. Scott Barnes, one of Perot's campaign assistants, years later admitted to making up the wedding story (*The Dallas Morning News*, 28 March 1997).
51. *The New York Times*, 26 October 1992.
52. Letter dated 20 April 1988. Quoted in Paul Findley, "An Unresolved Question: Did AIPAC Unmask Agnew," *The Washington Report on Middle East Affairs*, November/December 1996, p. 21.
53. Jacob Cohen, "Conspiracy Fever," *Commentary*, October 1975, pp. 41, 33.
54. William Manchester, quoted in Gerald Posner, *Case Closed: Lee Harvey Oswald and the Assassination of JFK* (New York: Random House, 1993).
55. *The Washington Post*, 19 May 1991.
56. *Time*, 13 January 1992, reports 73 percent believing in a conspiracy and 72 percent suspecting an official cover-up; *The New York Times*, 4 February 1992, reports 77 percent and 75 percent, respectively.
57. Quoted in Tucker Carlson, "Trento's Last Case: From Boorda to Clinton," *The Weekly Standard*, 3 June 1996.
58. CHARLES BERLITZ and WILLIAM L. MOORE, *The Roswell Incident* (New York: Grosset & Dunlap, 1980).
59. HOWARD BLUM, *Out There: The Government's Secret Quest for Extraterrestrials* (New York: Simon & Schuster, 1990).
60. MILTON WILLIAM COOPER, *"Behold a Pale Horse"* (Sedona, Ariz.: Light Technology, 1991), p. 209.
61. *The New York Times Magazine*, 17 November 1996.
62. Posner, *Case Closed*, p. xi
63. JOHN A. STORMER, *None Dare Call It Treason . . . 25 Years Later* (Florissant, Mo.: Liberty Bell, 1990), p. vii. There is nothing new or characteristically American about conspiracism selling well. In the nineteenth century, AUGUSTIN DE BARRUEL, BENJAMIN DISRAELI, and LUCIEN DE LA HODDE, among other authors, enjoyed commercial success by satisfying this appetite; what differs are the order of magnitude of the numbers and the titillating nature of their arguments.
64. Umberto Eco, *Foucault's Pendulum* (London: Picador, 1990), p. 404.
65. ROBERT SHEA and ROBERT ANTON WILSON, *The Illuminatus! Trilogy*, 3 vols. (New York: Dell, 1975).
66. Michiko Kakutani, "Bound by Suspicion," *The New York Times Magazine*, 19 January 1997.

67. Charles Paul Freund, "If History Is a Lie," *The Washington Post*, 19 January 1992.
68. JONATHAN VANKIN, *Conspiracies, Cover-Ups, and Crimes: Political Manipulation and Mind Control in America* (New York: Paragon House, 1991), p. 259.
69. OLIVER STONE, "Splinters to the Brain," *New Perspectives Quarterly*, Spring 1992, p. 53.
70. Quoted in Freedom Review, May–June 1992, p. 40.

CHAPTER 2: A HOUSE OF MIRRORS

1. Henry Campbell Black, *Black's Law Dictionary*, 4th ed. (St. Paul, Minn.: West Publishing, 1951), p. 382.
2. NESTA H. WEBSTER, *Secret Societies and Subversive Movements* (New York: E. P. Dutton, 1924), p. xi.
3. The German term *Verschwörungsmythos* ("myth of conspiracy") serves better than the English *conspiracy theory*, for it more directly points to the imaginary content.
4. This point is often missed. Walter Laqueur writes in *Black Hundred: The Rise of the Extreme Right in Russia* (New York: HarperCollins, 1993), p. 34, that the conspiracy theory of history "is probably as old as historiography." Steven E. Ambrose is even more certain: "Conspiracy theories are as old as history." See "Writers on the Grassy Knoll: A Reader's Guide," *The New York Times Book Review*, 2 February 1992.
5. Richard S. Levy, *Antisemitism in the Modern World: An Anthology of Texts* (Lexington, Mass.: D. C. Heath, 1991), pp. 4, 122.
6. Spoken by John Coogan about his cousin Gertrude Coogan; quoted in Donald Warren, *Radio Priest: Charles Coughlin, the Father of Hate Radio* (New York: Free Press, 1996), p. 142.
7. MICHAEL HOWARD, *The Occult Conspiracy: Secret Societies—Their Influence and Power in World History* (Rochester, Vt.: Destiny Books, 1989), p. vii.
8. Dennis King, *Lyndon LaRouche and the New American Fascism* (New York: Doubleday, 1989), pp. 274–75.
9. Quoted in Heléne Lööw, "Racist Violence and Criminal Behavior in Sweden: Myths and Reality," in *Terror from the Extreme Right*, ed. Tore Bjørgo (London: Frank Cass, 1995), p. 127.
10. GARY H. KAH, *En Route to Global Occupation* (Lafayette, La.: Huntington House, 1991), p. 24.
11. Dan E. Moldea, *The Killing of Robert F. Kennedy: An Investigation of Motive, Means and Opportunity* (New York: W. W. Norton, 1995), p. 309. Moldea initially distrusted the official version that the convicted killer, Sirhan Bishara Sirhan, acted alone and instead accepted the conspiracist belief in a second gun and a wider conspiracy. But thorough research, including a revelatory interview with Sirhan himself, led him to conclude that Sirhan did act alone. "I now realize that even law-enforcement officials . . . *do* make mistakes." Moldea found he had previously expected too much of the authorities: "if one does not account for occasional official mistakes and incompetence, then nearly every . . . political murder could appear to be a conspiracy, particularly if a civilian investigator—with limited access and resources—is looking for one" (p. 307).
12. KAH, *En Route to Global Occupation*, p. 24.
13. Edward Crankshaw, *Khrushchev Remembers*, trans. and ed. Strobe Talbott (Boston: Little, Brown, 1970), pp. 596, 300.

14. Zhisui Li, *The Private Life of Chairman Mao: The Memoirs of Mao's Personal Physician*, trans. Hung-chao Tai (New York: Random House, 1994), p. 585. Li continues: "I saw myself as a doctor devoted to the Chairman's health. He saw me as an enemy."

15. *The Los Angeles Times*, 20 October 1996.

16. Years before, when on the staff of the *Cleveland Plain Dealer*, Webb wrote in that paper that promoters of the Cleveland Grand Prix had siphoned off nearly $1 million from the race revenues in breach of their agreement with the city. The race promoters brought a libel suit in 1990 against the *Plain Dealer* and won $13.6 million in damages, eventually settling out of court for an undisclosed amount.

17. LYNDON H. LAROUCHE, JR., *The Power of Reason: 1988, An Autobiography* (New York: Executive Intelligence Review, 1987), pp. 181–82.

18. Léon Poliakov, *Histoire de l'antisémitisme: de Voltaire à Wagner* (Paris: Calmann-Levy, 1968), trans. Miriam Kochan, *The History of Antisemitism*, vol. 3 (New York: Vanguard, 1975), p. 337.

19. Laqueur, *Black Hundred*, p. xv.

20. This explains why, not wanting to alienate Arabs, the Nazis from 1935 on did not use this term.

21. C. H. DOUGLAS in 1939, quoted in Michael B. Stein, *The Dynamics of Right-Wing Protest: A Political Analysis of Social Credit in Quebec* (Toronto: University of Toronto Press, 1973), p. 34, n. 50.

22. W. MARR, *Vom jüdischen Kriesschauplatz: Eine Streitschrift* (Bern: Rudolph Costenoble, 1879), p. 39.

23. V. SKURLATOV, *Sionism i Aparteid* (Kiev: Politizdat Ukrainy, 1975), p. 42. Quoted in Yaacov Tisgelman, "'The Universal Jewish Conspiracy' in Soviet Anti-Semitic Propaganda," in Theodore Freedman, ed., *Anti-Semitism in the Soviet Union: Its Roots and Consequences* (New York: Anti-Defamation League of B'nai B'rith, 1984), p. 416.

24. Johannes Rogalla von Bieberstein, *Die These von der Verschwörung, 1776–1945: Philosophen, Freimaurer, Juden, Liberale und Sozialisten als Verschwörer gegen die Sozialordnung* (Bern: Herbert Lang, 1976), p. 51.

25. CHARLES LOUIS CADET DE GASSICOURT, *Le Tombeau de Jacques Molay, ou, Le secret des conspirateurs, à ceux qui veulent tout savoir* (Paris: Chez les marchands de nouveautés, l'An 4 [1792]).

26. George Johnson, *Architects of Fear: Conspiracy Theories and Paranoia in American Politics* (Los Angeles: Jeremy P. Tarcher, 1983), p. 24.

27. McLaughlin Report, 26 August 1990.

28. *Komsomolskaya Pravda*, 4 October 1967.

29. *The Washington Post*, 3 February 1984.

30. Michael Billig, "Antisemitic Themes and the British Far Left," in Carl F. Graumann and Serge Moscovici, eds., *Changing Conceptions of Conspiracy* (New York: Springer, 1987), p. 132.

31. *Protocols of the Meetings of the Learned Elders of Zion*, trans. Victor E. Marsden (London: The Britons, 1923), p. 34. This fear reflects the 1890s origins of the *Protocols*, when subways were first constructed in major Western cities; and the alarm in antisemitic circles about the number of Jewish shareholders in the Paris Métro.

32. Charles Paul Freund, "If History Is a Lie," *The Washington Post*, 19 January 1992.

33. A long-time foreign resident in Haiti, quoted in Douglas Farah, "Letter from Haiti: Reality Check," *The Washington Post*, 7 December 1993.

34. Quoted in Gershom Scholem, "Toward an Understanding of the Messianic Idea in Judaism," in *The Messianic Idea in Judaism* (New York: Schocken Books, 1971), p. 29.

35. Quoted in ibid., pp. 342–43.

36. J. M. Roberts, *The Mythology of the Secret Societies* (New York: Charles Scribner's Sons, 1972), p. 101.

37. Paul Goodman, *Towards a Christian Republic: Antimasonry and the Great Transition in New England, 1826–1836* (New York: Oxford University Press, 1988), p. 21.

38. THE EARL OF BEACONSFIELD [BENJAMIN DISRAELI], *Coningsby: Or the New Generation*, new ed. (London: Longmans, Green, 1891), p. 250. In subsequent years, the "mighty revolution" was widely understood to have followed soon after, in 1848.

39. Ibid., p. 252. The most influential English edition of the *Protocols* quotes this passage in its introduction, then concludes that "those personages were all Jews." *Protocols*, p. 9.

40. Benjamin Disraeli, *Lord George Bentinck: A Political Biography* (London: Colburn, 1852), p. 498.

41. *Hansard's Parliamentary Debates* (House of Commons), 14 July 1856, col. 774.

42. *The Times* (London), 27 November 1875.

43. Quoted in HENRY WICKHAM STEED, *The Hapsburg Monarchy*, 2d ed. (London: Constable, 1914), p. 169.

44. CARROLL QUIGLEY, *Tragedy and Hope: A History of the World in Our Time* (New York: Macmillan, 1966), p. 950. See pp. 132–33, 582–83, 945–57, 991–92 for details on Toynbee Hall, "Milner's Kindergarten," the "Cliveden Set," the Rhodes Trust, and the Round Table Groups.

45. Richard Hofstadter, "The Paranoid Style in American Politics," in Richard Hofstadter, *The Paranoid Style in American Politics and Other Essays* (New York: Vintage, 1967), p. 36. Hofstadter appears to have coined the term *paranoid style*.

46. August Wolfsteig, *Bibliographie der freimaurerischen Literatur*, 3 vols. (Leipzig: Karl W. Hiersemann, 1923).

47. Bill Alexander, the ex-assistant district attorney of Dallas, discussing the Kennedy assassination. Quoted in Gerald Posner, *Case Closed: Lee Harvey Oswald and the Assassination of JFK* (New York: Random House, 1993), p. 467.

48. *The New York Times*, 4 March 1995. Those "original historical sources" are in fact secondary sources, and they indiscriminately mix legitimate studies with such staples of conspiracism as books cited here by ANATOLIY GOLITYSN, JOHN ROBISON, and NESTA WEBSTER.

49. ISAIAH BEN-DASAN [pseud. of SHICHIHEI YAMAMOTO], *The Japanese and the Jews*, trans. Richard L. Gage (Tokyo: Weatherhill, 1972).

50. MICHAEL BAIGENT, RICHARD LEIGH, AND HENRY LINCOLN, *Holy Blood, Holy Grail* (New York: Delacorte, 1982), pp. 79, 284–86.

51. MICHAEL BAIGENT, RICHARD LEIGH, AND HENRY LINCOLN, *The Messianic Legacy* (New York: Henry Holt, 1986), p. 324.

52. In JOSEPH DE HAMMER-PURGSTALL, *Mysterium Baphometis Revelatum* (Vienna: Heubner, 1818); JOSEPH VON HAMMER, *Die Geschichte der Assassinen aus morgenländischen Quellen* (Stuttgart: Cotta, 1818); JOSEPH VON HAMMER-PURGSTALL, *Die Schuld der Templer* in *Denkschriften der kaiserlichen Akademie der Wis-*

senschaften, Philosophisch-Historische Classe (Vienna: Kaiserlich-königlichen Hof- und Staatsdruckerei, 1855), 6: 175–210.

53. Gary Sick, *All Fall Down: America's Tragic Encounter with Iran* (New York: Random House, 1985), p. 33.

54. *New York Daily News,* 26 August 1988; *Rocky Mountain News,* 30 October 1988.

CHAPTER 3: UNMASKING THE CONSPIRACY THEORY

1. Quoted in Seymour Martin Lipset and Earl Raab, *The Politics of Unreason: Right-Wing Extremism in America, 1790–1970* (New York: Harper & Row, 1970), p. 255.

2. Christopher Andrew and Oleg Gordievsky, *KGB: The Inside Story of Its Foreign Operations from Lenin to Gorbachev* (New York: HarperCollins, 1990), p. 475.

3. David Brion Davis suggests that "the phenomenon of countersubversion might be studied as a special language or cultural form, apart from any preconceptions of its truth or falsity." See the introduction to his edited book, *The Fear of Conspiracy: Images of Un-American Subversion from the Revolution to the Present* (Ithaca, N.Y.: Cornell University Press, 1971), p. xv.

4. H. A. L. Fisher, *A History of Europe: Ancient and Mediaeval* (Boston: Houghton Mifflin, 1935), p. vii.

5. L. B. Namier, *Avenues of History* (London: Hamish Hamilton, 1952), p. 4.

6. David Kelley, *The Art of Reasoning,* exp. ed. (New York: W. W. Norton, 1990), p. 500.

7. Gerald Posner, *Case Closed: Lee Harvey Oswald and the Assassination of JFK* (New York: Random House, 1993), p. 202, note.

8. Kelley, *Art of Reasoning,* p. 502.

9. Niccolò Machiavelli, *The Prince,* chap. 19.

10. Karl R. Popper, *Conjectures and Refutations: The Growth of Scientific Knowledge* (London: Routledge and Kegan Paul, 1963), pp. 341–42.

11. Davis, Introduction to *The Fear of Conspiracy,* p. xv.

12. Tynetta Muhammad, "$4.4 Billion Dollars Is Not Enough!" *The Final Call,* 17 December 1996. Muhammad presumably means not "implemented" but "implicated."

13. Anon. [attributed to HIERONIM ZAHOROWSKI], *Monita Secreta Societatis Jesu* (Notobriage, 1612, meaning Cracow, 1614). For the text of Edwin Allen Sherman's 1883 translation into English, *The Engineer Corps of Hell: or, Rome's Sappers and Miners,* see <http://www.infidels.org/library/modern/>. For a listing of fabricated quotes often relied on by conspiracy theorists, see John George and Laird Wilcox, *American Extremists: Militias, Supremacists, Klansmen, Communists, and Others* (Amherst, N.Y.: Prometheus, 1996), pp. 383–419.

14. AGNES WATERS, quoted in John Roy Carlson [pseud. of Arthur Derounian], *Under Cover: My Four Years in the Nazi Underworld of America—The Amazing Revelation of How Axis Agents and Our Enemies Within Are Now Plotting to Destroy the United States* (New York: E. P. Dutton, 1943), p. 280.

15. *San Jose Mercury News,* 18–20 August 1996.

16. Charles Ward, *The Times-Picayune,* 1983, quoted in *Newsweek,* 23 December 1991.

17. Saviour's Day speech, Chicago, 26 February 1995.

18. Umberto Eco, *Foucault's Pendulum* (London: Picador, 1990), p. 200.

19. GARY SICK, *October Surprise: America's Hostages in Iran and the Election of Ronald Reagan* (New York: Times Books, 1991), p. 83.
20. Quoted in Paul Goodman, *Towards a Christian Republic: Antimasonry and the Great Transition in New England, 1826–1836* (New York: Oxford University Press, 1988), p. 58.
21. *Protocols of the Meetings of the Learned Elders of Zion*, trans. Victor E. Marsden (London: The Britons, 1923), p. 11.
22. WILLIAM GUY CARR, *The Red Fog over America* (Willowdale, Ont.: National Federation of Christian Laymen, 1955), p. 6.
23. PAT ROBERTSON, *The New World Order* (Dallas: Word, 1991), p. 31.
24. NESTA H. WEBSTER, *Secret Societies and Subversive Movements* (New York: E. P. Dutton, 1924), p. 403.
25. LÉON MEURIN, *La Franc-Maçonnerie, synagogue de satan* (Paris: Victor Retaux, 1893), p. 210.
26. WILLIAM GUY CARR, *The Conspiracy to Destroy All Existing Governments and Religions* (Metairie, La.: Sons of Liberty, [1960?]), p. 14.
27. JONATHAN VANKIN, *Conspiracies, Cover-Ups and Crimes: Political Manipulation and Mind Control in America* (New York: Paragon House, 1991), p. 221.
28. ROBERTSON, *The New World Order*, p. 95.
29. Quoted in Carlston, *Under Cover*, p. 458.
30. Lipset and Raab, *Politics of Unreason*, p. 62.
31. Richard Hofstadter, "The Paranoid Style in American Politics," in Richard Hofstadter, *The Paranoid Style in American Politics and Other Essays* (New York: Vintage, 1967), p. 29.
32. Karl R. Popper, *The Open Society and Its Enemies*, 5th rev. ed. (Princeton, N.J.: Princeton University Press, 1966), vol. 2, p. 95.
33. ROBERTSON, *The New World Order*, p. 9.
34. WILLIAM GUY CARR, *Pawns in the Game*, 2d. ed. (Toronto: National Federation of Christian Laymen, 1956), p. 86.
35. Quoted in Michael Billig, *Fascists: A Social Psychological View of the National Front* (London: Academic Press, 1978), pp. 315–16.
36. *The New York Times*, 31 May 1995.
37. Quoted in Andrew and Gordievsky, *KGB*, p. 118.
38. *The Thunderbolt*, quoted in Lipset and Raab, *Politics of Unreason*, p. 282.
39. Bernard Bailyn, *The Ideological Origins of the American Revolution* (Cambridge, Mass.: Harvard University Press, 1967), p. 95.
40. Steven Emerson, "Ross Perot's Conspiracy Fever—and Ours," *The Wall Street Journal*, 28 October 1992.
41. Richard Pipes, Introduction to Richard Pipes, ed., *The Unknown Lenin: From the Secret Archive* (New Haven: Yale University Press, 1996), p. 13.
42. Quoted in Andrew and Gordievsky, *KGB*, pp. 127–28.
43. *Protocols*, p. 32.
44. NESTA H. WEBSTER, *World Revolution: The Plot against Civilization* (London: Constable, 1921), p. 95. For more along these lines, see JUNE GREM, *Karl Marx, Capitalist* (Oak Park, Ill.: Enterprise Publications [1972]).
45. OSWALD SPENGLER, *Der Untergang des Abendlandes: Unrisse einer Morphologie der Weltgeschichte* (Munich: C. H. Beck, 1922), vol. 2, p. 502.
46. ROBERT WELCH, writing in *American Opinion*, November 1966. Quoted in George Johnson, *Architects of Fear: Conspiracy Theories and Paranoia in American Politics* (Los Angeles: Jeremy P. Tarcher, 1983), p. 134.

47. ROBERTSON, *The New World Order*, p. 31. At other times, Robertson explains this collusion on the grounds that the bankers and communists share "larger goals" (ibid., p. 71). See also pp. 177–78.

48. JOHN LOFTUS and MARK AARONS, *The Secret War against the Jews: How Western Espionage Betrayed the Jewish People* (New York: St. Martin's Press, 1994), p. 4.

49. Quoted in James V. Compton, *The Swastika and the Eagle: Hitler, the United States, and the Origins of World War II* (Boston: Houghton Mifflin, 1967), p. 32.

50. Quoted in ibid., p. 34.

51. DAN SMOOT, *The Invisible Government*, 2d ed. (Boston: Western Islands 1977), p. 131. On p. 130, Smoot acknowledges that "The Council does not *own* its members."

52. SIDNEY AND BEATRICE WEBB, *Soviet Communism: A New Civilisation?* (New York: Charles Scribner's Sons, 1936), vol. 1, p. 282, n. 2.

53. For their statements, as well as those of many other foreign observers, see Robert Conquest, *The Great Terror: A Reassessment* (New York: Oxford University Press, 1990), pp. 499–513.

54. WILLIAM GUY CARR, *Pawns in the Game*, 2d ed. (Toronto: National Federation of Christian Laymen, 1956), pp. 151, 147.

55. LOUIS J. HALLE, *The Cold War as History* (New York: Harper & Row, 1967), p. 414.

56. ROBERT JEWETT, *The Captain America Complex: The Dilemma of Zealous Nationalism* (Philadelphia: Westminster, 1973), p. 132.

57. JOEL KOVEL, *Red Hunting in the Promised Land: Anticommunism and the Making of America* (New York: Basic Books, 1994), p. xi.

58. Quoted in JONATHAN VANKIN, *Conspiracies, Cover-Ups, and Crimes: Political Manipulation and Mind Control in America* (New York: Paragon House, 1991), pp. 100–01. Vankin himself "looks on conspiracy theories as the stuff that conventional political science refuses to deal with" (p. 251).

59. The classic volume in English was John Cleland's story of Fanny Hill in *Memoirs of a Woman of Pleasure* (London: R. Griffiths, 1749). On this and other writings, see Lynn Hunt, ed., *The Invention of Pornography: Obscenity and the Origins of Modernity, 1500–1800* (New York: Zone, 1993), pp. 31–32.

60. Richard S. Levy feels compelled to assure the reader that his selections from the *Protocols of the Elders of Zion* will do no mischief: "A brief excerpt from the *Protocols* text itself is reproduced here to contribute to readers' understanding, but it will be of little use to those who would circulate the *Protocols* for the usual destructive purposes." Preface to Benjamin W. Segel, *Welt-Krieg, Welt-Revolution, Welt-Verschwörung, Welt-Oberregierung* (Berlin: Philo, 1926), trans. and ed. Richard S. Levy, *A Lie and a Libel: The History of the Protocols of the Elders of Zion* (Lincoln: University of Nebraska Press, 1966), p. ix.

61. Billig, *Fascists*, p. 300.

62. Quoted in Armin Pfahl-Traughber, *Der antisemitisch-antifreimaurerische Verschwörungsmythos in der weimarer Republik und im NS-Staat* (Vienna: Braumüller, 1993), p. 39. Schirach was sentenced to twenty years in prison.

63. Richard S. Levy, *Antisemitism in the Modern World: An Anthology of Texts* (Lexington, Mass.: D. C. Heath, 1991), p. 2.

CHAPTER 4: THE ORIGINS, TO 1815

1. Quoted in James Parkes, *The Jew in the Medieval Community*, 2d ed. (New York: Hermon Press, 1976), p. 334.

2. Quoted in Malcolm Barber, *The Trial of the Templars* (Cambridge, Eng.: Cambridge University Press, 1978), p. 45.

3. Salo Wittmayer Baron, *A Social and Religious History of the Jews*, vol. 4, *Meeting of East and West*, 2d ed. (New York: Columbia University Press and Philadelphia: Jewish Publication Society, 1957), pp. 94–95.

4. Some trace it back right to the very beginning: "If the chronology of the third chapter of Genesis is correct, conspiracy was the first spontaneous activity in which any creatures participated after the Creation, antedating even sex, which does not make an appearance till Chapter IV." Robert Wernick, "Don't Look Now—But All Those Plotters Might Be Hiding under Your Bed," *Smithsonian*, March 1994, p. 109.

5. Origen, *Contra Celsum*, 4, 23, quoted in Léon Poliakov, *Histoire de l'antisémitisme: du temps de Christ aux Juifs de cour* (Paris: Calmann-Levy, 1965), trans. Richard Howard, *The History of Antisemitism*, vol. 1 (New York: Vanguard, 1965), p. 23.

6. Robert Chazan, *European Jewry and the First Crusade* (Berkeley: University of California Press, 1987), p. 64.

7. Quoted in ibid., pp. 78–79.

8. Ibid., p. 132.

9. Poliakov, *History of Antisemitism*, vol. 1, p. 62.

10. Norman Cohn, *Warrant for Genocide: The Myth of the Jewish World Conspiracy and the Protocols of the Elders of Zion* (New York: Harper & Row, 1969), p. 254.

11. Martin Luther, "On the Jews and Their Lies," *Luther's Works*, ed. Franklin Sherman, vol. 47, *The Christian in Society*, IV (Philadelphia: Fortress Press, 1971), pp. 262, 293.

12. Ibid., pp. 267, 288.

13. Mark R. Cohen, *Under Crescent and Cross: The Jews in the Middle Ages* (Princeton, N.J.: Princeton University Press, 1994), p. xix.

14. 'Abd al-Masih al-Kindi, *Ar-Risala*, trans. into Latin, quoted in Salo Wittmayer Baron, *A Social and Religious History of the Jews*, vol. 5, *High Middle Ages, 500–1200*, 2d ed. rev. (New York: Columbia University Press, 1957), p. 124.

15. Luther, "On the Jews and Their Lies," p. 293.

16. Allan Harris Cutler and Helen Elmquist Cutler, *The Jew as Ally of the Muslim: Medieval Roots of Anti-Semitism* (Notre Dame, Ind.: University of Notre Dame Press, 1986), p. 82.

17. Ibid., pp. 96, 6.

18. Marion Melville, "Les Débuts de l'Ordre du Temple," in Josef Fleckenstein and Manfred Hellman, eds., *Die geistlichen Ritterorden Europas* (Sigmaringen, Germany: Jan Thorbecke, 1980), p. 23.

19. Quoted in Barber, *Trial of the Templars*, p. 11.

20. Ibid., p. 246. Others find the Templars not guilty: "the stories they told do not add up to a consistent description of heresy." Joseph R. Strayer, *The Reign of Philip the Fair* (Princeton, N.J.: University Press, 1980), p. 291.

21. DENIS LEBEY DE BATILLY (1551–1607), *Traicte de l'origine des anciens Assassins porte-couteaux* (Lyon: V. Vaspase, 1603), appears to be the first to trace the Templars' origins back to Alexander the Great's time.

22. Umberto Eco, *Foucault's Pendulum* (London: Picador, 1990), p. 375.

23. Peter Partner, *The Murdered Magicians: The Templars and Their Myth* (Oxford: Oxford University Press, 1982), p. 101.

24. In a similar spirit, the Russian Right focuses on Jews rather than Chinese, Arabs and Iranians dwell on Israel rather than India, and American militiamen get worked up over the United Nations rather than drug traffickers.

25. NESTA H. WEBSTER, *World Revolution: The Plot against Civilization* (London: Constable, 1921), p. 4.

26. JOHN J. ROBINSON, *Born in Blood: The Lost Secrets of Freemasonry* (New York: M. Evans, 1989), p. xix.

27. Mervyn Jones, "Freemasonry," in Norman MacKenzie, ed., *Secret Societies* (New York: Holt, Rinehart and Winston, 1967), p. 167.

28. Quoted in J. M. Roberts, *The Mythology of the Secret Societies* (New York: Charles Scribner's Sons, 1972), p. 54.

29. In 1958, Pope Pius XII blamed Freemasonry for the "modern decline of religious faith." In 1983, on orders of Pope John Paul II, Cardinal Joseph Ratzinger reaffirmed this condemnation in a document from the Sacred Congregation for the Doctrine of the Faith: "the Church's negative judgment in regard to Masonic associations remains unchanged. . . . The [Catholic] faithful who enroll in Masonic associations are in a state of grave sin and may not receive Holy Communion."

30. NICHOLAS DE BONNEVILLE (1760–1828) made this a major theme of his study, *Les Jésuites chassés de la Maçonneries, et leur poignard brisé par les Maçons,* 2 vols. (Paris: C. Volland, 1788).

31. ABBÉ LARUDAN, *Les Francs-Maçons Ecrasés* (Amsterdam, 1747).

32. Quoted in Paul Goodman, *Towards a Christian Republic: Antimasonry and the Great Transition in New England, 1826–1836* (New York: Oxford University Press, 1988), p. 237.

33. For details, see Richard von Dülmen, *Der Geheimbund der Illuminaten* (Stuttgart: Frommann-Holzboog, 1977). For a less dismissive view, see James H. Billington, *Fire in the Minds of Men: Origins of the Revolutionary Faith* (New York: Basic Books, 1980), pp. 94–99.

34. Klaus Epstein, *The Genesis of German Conservatism* (Princeton, N.J.: Princeton University Press, 1966), p. 517.

35. Partner, *Murdered Magicians,* p. 126.

36. Anon. [MARQUIS DE LUCHET], *Essai sur la secte des Illuminés* (Paris: n.p., 1788), p. 46. Confusion about the term *illuminist* has done much to enhance the Illuminati mystique, making this small organization appear active even where it has no presence at all.

37. Roberts, *Mythology of the Secret Societies,* pp. 134, 144.

38. René le Forestier, *Les Illuminés de Bavière et la Franc-maçonnerie allemande* (Paris: Hachette, 1914), pp. 613, 622.

39. Vernon Stauffer, *New England and the Bavarian Illuminati* (New York: Columbia University Press, 1918), p. 113.

40. WEBSTER, *World Revolution,* p. 289.

41. Quoted in Donald Warren, *Radio Priest: Charles Coughlin, the Father of Hate Radio* (New York: Free Press, 1996), pp. 32. 132–33.

42. WILLIAM GUY CARR, *Pawns in the Game,* 2d ed. (Toronto: National Federation of Christian Laymen, 1956), p. 13.

43. ROBERT WELCH in *Birch Society Bulletin*, August 1968. Quoted in Seymour Martin Lipset and Earl Raab, *The Politics of Unreason: Right-Wing Extremism in America, 1790–1970* (New York: Harper & Row, 1970), p. 253.

44. PAT ROBERTSON, *The New World Order* (Dallas: Word, 1991), p. 180.

45. ANON., *Théorie des Conspirations* (Paris, 1797?), p. 6. Quoted in Johannes Rogalla von Bieberstein, *Die These von der Verschwörung, 1776–1945: Philosophen, Freimaurer, Juden, Liberale und Sozialisten als Verschwörer gegen die Sozialordnung* (Bern: Herbert Lang, 1976), p. 56.

46. WEBSTER, *World Revolution*, p. 72.

47. Roberts, *Mythology of the Secret Societies*, p. 145.

48. Steven L. Kaplan, *The Famine Plot Persuasion in Eighteenth-Century France* (Philadelphia: The American Philosophical Society, 1982).

49. Roberts, *Mythology of the Secret Societies*, pp. 148–49.

50. Quoted in Epstein, *The Genesis of German Conservatism*, p. 537.

51. JACQUES FRANÇOIS LEFRANC, *Le Voile levé pour les curiex, ou Les secrets de la Révolution de France révélés à l'aide de la Franc-Maçonnerie* ([Paris: Valade], 1791). On this being the earliest account, see Marcelin Défourneaux, "Complot maçonnique et complot jésuitique," *Annales historiques de la Révolution française* (1965): 175.

52. CHARLES LOUIS CADET DE GASSCOURT, *Le Tombeau de Jacques Molay, ou, Le secret des conspirateurs, à ceux qui veulent tout savoir* (Paris: Chez les merchands de nouveautés, l'An 4 [1792]). CADET DE GASSICOURT published variant versions of this book, with slightly different titles, a year later; in 1799, he wrote a pamphlet against the Freemasons, *Les Franc-Maçons, ou, Les Jacobins demasqués: fragmens pour l'histoire*.

53. N. DESCHAMPS, *Les Sociétés secrètes et la société, ou philosophie de l'histoire contemporaine*, 3d ed. (Avignon: Seguin Frères, 1880); vol. 1, pp. 313–32, provides copious details. See ROBINSON, *Born in Blood*, for a recent example of this approach. In addition, the notion that "every true Mason is a Knight Templar" goes back to the Baron Hunde in the 1740s.

54. JOHN ROBISON, *Proofs of a Conspiracy against All the Religions and Governments of Europe, Carried on in the Secret Meetings of the Free Masons, Illuminati, and Reading Societies, Collected from Good Authorities* (Edinburgh: William Creech, 1797). The John Birch Society reprinted the book in 1967, and it remains in print thirty years later.

55. *Porcupine's Gazette*, 14 July 1798. Quoted in Vernon Stauffer, *New England and the Bavarian Illuminati* (New York: Columbia University Press, 1918), p. 285.

56. David Brion Davis, "Some Ideological Functions of Prejudice in Ante-Bellum America," *American Quarterly* 15 (1963): 119.

57. Abbé Barruel, *Mémoires pour servir à l'histoire du Jacobinisme*, 4 vols. (London: De l'imprimerie françoise, chez P. le Boussonnier, 1797–98). The book has been reprinted more than once in recent years, including Chiré-en-Montreuil: Diffusion de la Pensée Française, 1973. On de Barruel, see Sylva Schaeper-Wimmer, *Augustin Barruel, S. J. (1741–1820): Studien zu Biographie und Werk* (Frankfurt: Peter Lang, 1985); Michel Riquet, *Augustin de Barruel: Un jésuite face aux Jacobins francs-maçons, 1741–1820* (Paris: Beauchesne, 1989).

58. Le Forestier, *Les Illuminés de Bavière*, p. 688.

59. Letter of 1 May 1797, in R. B. McDowell, ed., *The Correspondence of Edmund Burke* (Cambridge, Eng.: At the University Press, 1970), vol. 9, pt. 1, p. 319.

60. Walter Edwin Peck, "Shelley and the Abbe Barruel," *Modern Language Association of America, Publications* 36 (1921): 348.

61. Thomas De Quincey, "Secret Societies," in David Masson, ed., *The Collected Writings of Thomas de Quincey* (London: A. and C. Black, 1897), vol. 7, pp. 173–85. This article first appeared in *Taft's Magazine* in 1847.

62. "[C]elle pourriture de l'illuminisme est un effect et non un cause," quoted in Roberts, *Mythology of the Secret Societies*, p. 296.

63. Jean-Joseph Mounier, *De l'influence attribuée aux Philosophes, aux Francs-Maçons et aux Illuminés sur la Révolution Française* (Tübingen: Cotta, 1801), trans. J. Walker, *The Influence Attributed to Philosophers, Free-Masons, and to the Illuminati on the Revolution of France* (London: W. and C. Spilsbury, 1801), p.v.

64. George Farquhar, *The Beaux' Stratagem*, act 4, scene 1.

65. Jacques Droz, "La Légende due complot illuministe et les origines du romantisme politique en Allemagne," *Revue historique* 226 (1961): 313–38.

66. Partner, *Murdered Magicians*, p. 131.

67. Roberts, *Mythology of the Secret Societies*, p. 193.

68. JOHANN AUGUST STARCK, *Der Triumph der Philosophie im achtzenten Jahrhundert*, 2 vols. (Augsburg: Bolling, 1803). He had previously published *Über die alten und neuen Mysterien* (Berlin: Friedrich Maurer, 1782).

69. Léon Poliakov, *Histoire de l'antisémitisme: de Voltaire à Wagner* (Paris: Calmann-Levy, 1968), trans. Miriam Kochan, *The History of Antisemitism*, vol. 3 (New York: Vanguard, 1975), p. 221.

70. For Simonini's letter, see "Les Souvenirs du P. Grivel sur les PP. Barruel et Feller," *Le Contemporain*, July 1878, pp. 58–61. De Barruel was already thinking along these lines; a footnote to the German translation of the *Memoirs*, published in 1800, refers to the "Jewishness of the Freemasons." Augustin Barruel, *Denkwürdigkeiten zur Geschichte des Jakobinisumus*, 4 vols. (Münster, 1800–03), vol. 1, p. 349.

71. Poliakov, *History of Antisemitism*, vol. 3, p. 283.

72. Cohn, *Warrant for Genocide* (London: Eyre & Spottiswoode, 1967), p. 30.

CHAPTER 5: FLORESCENCE, 1815–1945

1. Quoted in WERNER SOMBART, *The Jews and Modern Capitalism*, trans. M. Epstein (Glencoe, Ill.: Free Press, 1951), p. 99.

2. Report of a conversation, 14 December 1940, quoted in Donald Warren, *Radio Priest: Charles Coughlin, the Father of Hate Radio* (New York: Free Press, 1996), p. 113.

3. Although this famous statement captures a nineteenth-century sentiment, it was made in 1929 by Secretary of State Henry L. Stimson as he shut the "Black Chamber," the State Department's code-breaking office.

4. J. M. Roberts, *The Mythology of the Secret Societies* (New York: Charles Scribner's Sons, 1972), p. 347.

5. Richard Pipes, *The Russian Revolution* (New York: Alfred A. Knopf, 1990), p. 142. Others consider the Assassins, a medieval Muslim group, to have been history's first political terrorist organization.

6. Vladimir Dedijer, *The Road to Sarajevo* (New York: Simon & Schuster, 1966), p. 178.

7. Roberts, *Mythology of the Secret Societies*, p. 222.

8. Ibid., pp. 300, 14.
9. Peter Partner, *The Murdered Magicians: The Templars and Their Myth* (Oxford: Oxford University Press, 1982), p. 168.
10. Dedijer, *The Road to Sarajevo*, pp. 449–51.
11. FRIEDRICH WICHTL, *Weltfreimaurerei—Weltrevolution—Weltrepublik: Eine Untersuchung über Ursprung und Endziele des Weltkrieges* (Munich: J. F. Lehmann, 1919), p. 183.
12. "Die Freimaurerei als Generalstab des Marxismus," *Völkischer Beobachter*, 15 March 1927.
13. Nirad C. Chaudhuri, *Autobiography of an Unknown Indian* (Berkeley: University of California Press, 1968), p. 104. Similarly, "We heard that the English had won the battle of Waterloo by bribing Grouchy" (ibid.).
14. *Al-Ahram* (Cairo), 21 May 1993.
15. This paragraph relies on Dan Diner, *America in the Eyes of the Germans: An Essay on Anti-Americanism*, trans. Allison Brown (Princeton, N.J.: Markus Weiner, 1997), esp. pp. 55–77.
16. J. A. HOBSON, *Imperialism: A Study*, 3d ed. (London: George Allen & Unwin, 1968), pp. 46, 48, 53, 57.
17. V. I. LENIN, "Preface" dated 1920, in *Imperialism, the Highest Stage of Capitalism: A Popular Outline* (New York: International Publishers, 1933), pp. 13, 109.
18. Diner, *America in the Eyes of the Germans*, p. 64.
19. ANDRÉ GUNDER FRANK, *Capitalism and Underdevelopment in Latin America* (New York: Monthly Review Press, 1967); IMMANUEL WALLERSTEIN, *The Modern World System*, 3 vols. (San Diego: Academic Press, 1974–89).
20. HEINRICH AUGUST WINKLER, ed., *Organisierte Kapitalismus: Voraussetzungen und Anfänge* (Göttingen: Vandenhoeck & Ruprecht, 1974), p. 7.
21. SIR JOHN RETCLIFFE [pseud. of HERMANN GOEDSCHE], *Biarritz, historisch-politischer Roman* (Berlin: Kogge & Fritze, 1868).
22. Binjamin W. Segel, *Welt-Krieg, Welt-Revolution, Welt-Verschwörung, Welt-Oberregierung* (Berlin: Philo, 1926); trans. and ed. Richard S. Levy, *A Lie and a Libel: The History of the* Protocols of the Elders of Zion (Lincoln: University of Nebraska Press, 1996), p. 75.
23. For these and other key texts in English translation, see Herman Bernstein, *The Truth about "The Protocols of Zion": A Complete Exposure* (New York: Covici, Friede, 1935).
24. For an informed dissenting view, seeing Rachkovsky as "a gigantic red herring" and placing the responsibility on Yuliana Glinka, see James Webb, *The Occult Establishment*, vol. 2 of *The Age of the Irrational* (La Salle, Ill.: Open Court, 1976), chap. 4.
25. *Protocols of the Meetings of the Learned Elders of Zion*, trans. Victor E. Marsden (London: The Britons, 1923), pp. 22, 27, 41.
26. SERGEI ALEKSANDROVICH NILUS, *Velikoe v Malom i Antikrist, kak Blizkaia Politicheskaia Vozmozhnost'*, 3d ed. (Tsarskoe Selo: Tipografiia Tsarskosel'skago Komiteta Krasnago Kresta, 1905). "Antichrist" here means "global Jewish hegemony."
27. According to one count, the *Protocols* has been published afresh 8 times in the 1950s, 16 times in the 1960s, 23 times in the 1970s, 20 in the 1980s, and 4 times in the early 1990s—or once every eight months since Hitler committed suicide.
28. Umberto Eco, *Foucault's Pendulum* (London: Picador, 1990), p. 490.

29. DIETRICH ECKART, *Der Bolschewismus von Moses bis Lenin: Zwiegesprach zwischen Adolf Hitler und mir* (Munich: Hoheneichen, 1924).

30. JENS JÜRGENSEN, *Die entdeckten "Henker und Brandstifter der Welt" und ihr 2000jähriges Verschwörungssystem: der Schlüssel zur Weltgeschichte und Weltpolitik, aus Geheimarchiven und Bekenntnissen von einem Eingeweihten* (Munich, 1928).

31. WILLIAM GUY CARR, *Pawns in the Game*, 2d ed. (Toronto: National Federation of Christian Laymen, 1956), p. 114.

32. GRIGORY KLIMOFF, interviewed in *Moladaya Guardia*, reported in *The Forward*, 19 July 1991. In contrast, the Nazis called Roosevelt "the Freemason president." Quoted in Armin Pfahl-Traughber, *Der antisemitisch-antifreimaurerische Verschwörungsmythos in der weimarer Republik und im NS-Staat* (Vienna: Braumüller, 1993), p. 111.

33. *Komsomolskaya Pravda*, 4 October 1967.

34. Marx tormented Jews in several ways: atheism denied them their own heritage within the Soviet bloc; the Left adopted his anti-Jewish attitudes; the Right saw him as a Jew and blamed socialism on Jewish scheming. (He was born Jewish but his father had him baptized at age six as a Protestant.)

35. Book title quoted in David G. Goodman and Masanori Miyazawa, *Jews in the Japanese Mind: The History and Uses of a Cultural Stereotype* (New York: Free Press, 1995), p. 245.

36. HOBSON, *Imperialism*, p. 57.

37. *The Pakistan Times*, 4 February 1991.

38. THE HISTORICAL RESEARCH DEPARTMENT, *The Secret Relationship between Blacks and Jews* (Boston: Nation of Islam, 1991), vol. 1, p. 111.

39. David Brion Davis, Introduction to David Brion Davis, ed., *The Fear of Conspiracy: Images of Un-American Subversion from the Revolution to the Present* (Ithaca, N.Y.: Cornell University Press, 1971), p. xiii.

40. David Brion Davis, *The Slave Power Conspiracy and the Paranoid Style* (Baton Rouge: Louisiana State University Press, 1969), pp. 3–4.

41. Bernard Bailyn, *The Ideological Origins of the American Revolution* (Cambridge, Mass.: Harvard University Press, 1967), p. ix.

42. Ibid., p. 95.

43. Ibid., p. 121.

44. Quoted in ibid., p. 119.

45. Ira D. Gruber, "The American Revolution as a Conspiracy: The British View," *William and Mary Quarterly*, ser. 3, 26 (1969): 369.

46. Robert S. Levine, *Conspiracy and Romance: Studies in Brockden Brown, Cooper, Hawthorne, and Melville* (Cambridge, Eng.: Cambridge University Press, 1989), p. 5.

47. Text in Felix Gilbert, *To the Farewell Address: Ideas of Early American Foreign Policy* (Princeton, N.J.: Princeton University Press, 1961), p. 147.

48. Proclamation dated 6 March 1799, in Charles Francis Adams, ed., *The Works of John Adams, Second President of the United States: With a Life of the Author, Notes and Illustrations* (Boston: Little, Brown, 1854), vol. 9, p. 172.

49. Alexander Hamilton, "The Public Conduct and Character of John Adams, Esq., President of the United States," in Henry Cabot Lodge, ed., *The Works of Alexander Hamilton* (New York: G. P. Putnam's Sons, 1904), vol. 7, p. 324.

50. Quoted in William Preston Vaughn, *The Antimasonic Party in the United States, 1826–1843* (Lexington: University Press of Kentucky, 1983), p. 15.

51. Quoted in Paul Goodman, *Towards a Christian Republic: Antimasonry and the Great Transition in New England, 1826–1836* (New York: Oxford University Press, 1988), p. 57.
52. David Brion Davis, "Some Ideological Functions of Prejudice in Ante-Bellum America," *American Quarterly* 15 (1963): 124.
53. Serge Moscovici, "The Conspiracy Mentality," in Carl F. Graumann and Serge Moscovici, eds., *Changing Conceptions of Conspiracy* (New York: Springer, 1987), p. 153.
54. Quoted in Pfahl-Traughber, *Der antisemitisch-antifreimaurerische Verschwörungs-mythos*, p. 55.
55. Webb, *Occult Establishment*, p. 295.
56. WILLIAM DUDLEY PELLEY, "This Book," in ERNEST F. ELMHURST [pseud. of HERMANN FLEISCHKOPF], *The World Hoax* (n.p., 1938), pp. 2, 3.
57. Quoted in Webb, *Occult Establishment*, p. 130.
58. Quoted in Robert Lacey, *The Kingdom* (London: Hutchinson, 1981), p. 386.
59. Richard Pipes, *Russia under Bolshevik Regime* (New York: Alfred A. Knopf, 1993), p. 258.
60. Alldeutscher Verband, Deutschvölkische Schutz- und Trutzbund, Nationalsocialistische Deutsche Arbeitspartei, Reichshammerbund, Verband gegen Überhebung des Judentums.
61. GOTTFRIED ZUR BECK [pseud. of LUDWIG MÜLLER VON HAUSEN], *Gehiemnisse der Weisen von Zion* (Charlottenburg: Auf Vorposten, 1919). Though dated 1919, the book appeared in 1920.
62. HENRY WICKHAM STEED, "A Disturbing Pamphlet: A Call for Enquiry," *The Times*, 8 May 1920. Those "uncanny" prophecies were written not in 1897 but in 1919, then added to the text.
63. For details of this article's remarkable impact, see Pierre-André Taguieff, *Les Protocols des Sages de Sion* (Paris: Berg International, 1992), vol. 1, pp. 39–98.
64. ALFRED ROSENBERG, *Die Protokolle der Weisen von Zion und die jüdische Weltpolitik* (Munich: Deutsche Volksverlag, 1923).
65. Segel, *Welt-Krieg*, p. 62.
66. Quoted in Pfahl-Traughber, *Der antisemitisch-antifreimaurerische Verschwörungs-mythos*, p. 109.
67. Quoted in Christopher Andrew and Oleg Gordievsky, *KGB: The Inside Story of Its Foreign Operations from Lenin to Gorbachev* (New York: HarperCollins, 1990), p. 46.
68. Edward Crankshaw, *Khrushchev Remembers*, trans. and ed. Strobe Talbott (Boston: Little, Brown, 1970), p. 309.
69. Quoted in Edvard Radzinsky, *Stalin*, trans. H. T. Willetts (New York: Doubleday, 1996), p. 448.
70. Léopold Trepper, in collaboration with Patrick Rotman, *Le Grand jeu* (Paris: Albin Michel, 1975), trans. as *The Great Game: Memoirs of the Spy Hitler Couldn't Silence* (New York: McGraw-Hill, 1977), p. 39.
71. *Pravda*, 29 May 1948. Quoted in Amitzur Ilan, *The Origins of the Arab-Israeli Arms Race: Arms, Embargo, Military Power and Decision in the 1948 Palestine War* (New York: New York University Press, 1996), p. 246.
72. Louis Rapoport, *Stalin's War against the Jews: The Doctors' Plot and the Soviet Solution* (New York: Free Press, 1990), p. xiii.
73. Ibid., p. 158.

74. Radzinsky, *Stalin*, p. 551.
75. ERICH LUDENDORFF, *Kriegshetze und Völkermorden in den letzen 150 Jahren im Dienste des "allmächtigen Baumeisters aller Welten"* (Munich: Selbstverlag des Verfassers, 1928), p. 29.
76. MATHILDE LUDENDORFF, *Erlösung von Jesu Christu* (Munich: Ludendorff, 1935), p. 245; a summary appeared in English under the title *Getting Rid of Jesus Christ* (London: Friends of Europe, [1937]).
77. Quoted in Carlson, *Under Cover*, p. 37.
78. Pfahl-Traughber, *Der antisemitisch-antifreimaurerische Verschwörungsmythos*, p. 92.
79. RICHARD HEYDRICH, quoted in Pfahl-Traughber, *Der antisemitisch-antifreimaurerische Verschwörungsmythos*, p. 99.
80. Congressman JOHN E. RANKIN quoted in Carlson, *Under Cover*, pp. 233–34.
81. Quoted in ibid., p. 431.
82. Cited above, note 11.
83. Pfahl-Traughber, *Der antisemitisch-antifreimaurerische Verschwörungsmythos*, pp. 33–34. This section relies heavily on Pfahl-Traughber's well-documented study.
84. KARL HEISE, *Die Entente-Freimaurerei und Weltkrieg: ein Beitrag zur Geschichte des Weltkrieges und zum Verständnis der wahren Freimaurerei* (Basel: E. Finckh, 1919).
85. ERICH LUDENDORFF, *Vernichtung der Freimaurerei durch Enthüllung ihrer Geheimnisse* (Munich: Im Selbstverlage des Verfassers, 1927).
86. See Helmut Neuberger, *Freimaurerei und Nationalsozialismus: die Verfolgung der deutschen Freimaurerei durch völkische Bewegung und Nationalsozialismus, 1918–1945*, 2 vols. (Hamburg: Bauhutten, 1980). All others—the Left, intellectuals, moderates, financiers—were seen as offshoots of Jews or Freemasons.
87. Quoted in Pfahl-Traughber, *Der antisemitisch-antifreimaurerische Verschwörungsmythos*, p. 56.
88. "Das Ende der Freimaurerei in Deutschland," *Völkischer Beobachter*, 9 August 1935.
89. Quoted in William L. Shirer, *The Rise and Fall of the Third Reich: A History of Nazi Germany* (New York: Simon & Schuster, 1960), p. 784.
90. GISELHER WIRSING, *Der masslose Kontinent: Roosevelts Kampf um die Weltherrschaft* (Jena: Eugen Diederich, 1942), p. 188. Quoted in Diner, *America in the Eyes of the Germans*, p. 95.
91. Otto SCHÄFER, *Imperium Americanum: Die Ausbreitung des Machtbereichs der Vereinigten Staaten* (Essen: Essener Verlagsanstalt, 1943), p. 191. Quoted in ibid., p. 81. For other examples, see ibid., pp. 82, 84, 95–98, 116.
92. Quoted in Robert C. Tucker, *Stalin in Power: The Revolution from Above, 1928–1941* (New York: W. W. Norton, 1990), p. 415.
93. Hitler compounded this mistake a half-year later when he gratuitously declared war on the United States, in effect opening up a third front.
94. Dmitri Volkogonov, *Triyumf i Tragediya: politicheskii portret I. V. Stalina* (Moscow: Novosti, 1989), ed. and trans. as *Stalin: Triumph and Tragedy*, by Harold Shukman (London: Weidenfeld and Nicolson, 1991), p. 524.
95. R. J. Rummel, *Lethal Politics: Soviet Genocide and Mass Murder since 1917* (New Brunswick, N.J.: Transaction, 1990). This count ends in 1987.
96. Andrew and Gordievsky, *KGB*, p. 114.
97. Tucker, *Stalin in Power*, p. 591.
98. Quoted in Volkogonov, *Stalin: Triumph and Tragedy*, p. xxi.
99. Andrew and Gordievsky, *KGB*, p. 114; also pp. 128, 144, 146.

100. Nora Levin, *The Jews of the Soviet Union since 1917: Paradox of Survival* (New York: New York University Press, 1988), p. 483.

101. Walter Laqueur, *Black Hundred: The Rise of the Extreme Right in Russia* (New York: HarperCollins, 1993), p. 103.

102. Ron Rosenbaum, "Explaining Hitler," *The New Yorker,* 1 May 1995, p. 67.

103. Norman Cohn, *Warrant for Genocide: The Myth of the Jewish World Conspiracy and the* Protocols of the Elders of Zion (London: Eyre & Spottiswoode, 1967), p. 192.

CHAPTER 6: MIGRATION TO THE PERIPHERY, SINCE 1945

1. Pavel Sudoplatov and Anatoli Sudoplatov with Jerrold L. and Leona P. Schecter, *Special Tasks: The Memoirs of an Unwanted Witness—A Soviet Spymaster* (Boston: Little, Brown, 1994), p. 4.

2. Quoted in William Korey, "The Soviet *Protocols of the Elders of Zion*," in Theodore Freedman, ed., *Anti-Semitism in the Soviet Union: Its Roots and Consequences* (New York: Anti-Defamation League of B'nai B'rith, 1984), p. 152.

3. For a point-by-point comparison showing the near-identity of tsarist-period, Nazi, and Soviet antisemitism, see the impressive work by Ruth Okuneva, "Anti-Semitic Notions: Strange Analogies," in Freedman, ed., *Anti-Semitism in the Soviet Union*, pp. 266–381.

4. Quoted in Abdel Magid Farid, *Nasser: The Final Years* (Reading, Eng.: Ithaca Press, 1994), p. 22.

5. Quoted in Korey, "Soviet *Protocols*," in Freedman, ed., *Anti-Semitism in the Soviet Union*, p. 154.

6. TROKHYM KORNIIOVYCH KICHKO, *Iudaizm bez Prykras* (Kiev: Vyd-vo Akademii nauk URSR, 1963).

7. Josef Frolik, *The Frolik Defection* (London: Lee Cooper, 1975), p. 9.

8. Quoted in Tore Bjørgo, "Extreme Nationalism and Violent Discourses in Scandinavia: 'The Resistance,' 'Traitors,' and 'Foreign Invaders,'" in *Terror from the Extreme Right*, ed. Tore Bjørgo (London: Frank Cass, 1995), p. 197.

9. James H. Hutson, "The Origins of 'The Paranoid Style in American Politics': Public Jealousy from the Age of Walpole to the Age of Jackson," in David D. Hall et al., eds., *Saints and Revolutionaries: Essays on Early American History* (New York: W. W. Norton, 1984), p. 369. Hutson uses *jealousy* in its archaic sense of suspicion or anxiety.

10. Léon Poliakov, *Histoire de l'antisémitisme: de Voltaire à Wagner* (Paris: Calmann-Levy, 1968), trans. Miriam Kochan, *The History of Antisemitism*, vol. 3 (New York: Vanguard, 1975), p. 469.

11. Julius Gould, "Impugning Israel's Legitimacy: Anti-Zionism and Antisemitism," in Robert S. Wistrich, ed., *Anti-Zionism and Antisemitism in the Contemporary World* (New York: New York University Press, 1990), p. 181.

12. Richard S. Levy, *Antisemitism in the Modern World: An Anthology of Texts* (Lexington, Mass.: D. C. Heath, 1991), p. 261.

13. Michel Gurfinkiel, "Islam in France: The French Way of Life Is in Danger," *Middle East Quarterly,* March 1997, pp. 19–30.

14. Michael Billig, "The Extreme Right: Continuities in Anti-Semitic Conspiracy Theory in Post-War Europe," in Roger Eatwell and Noël O'Sullivan, eds., *The Nature of the Right: American and European Policies and Political Thought since 1789* (Boston: Twayne, 1989), p. 162.

15. *The New York Times*, 13 August 1993.
16. Ibid., 23 September 1993.
17. Ibid., 11 January 1997.
18. For examples, see Armin Pfahl-Traughber, "Die neue/alte Legende vom Komplott der Juden und Freimaurer," *Osteuropa* 41 (1991): 122–33.
19. John F. Dunn, "Hard Times in Russia Give Rise to Conspiracy Theories," *Post-Soviet/East European Report*, 17 November 1992.
20. Quoted in David Aikman, "Zyuganov the Terrible," *The American Spectator*, May 1996, p. 49.
21. Ibid. See also Adrian Karatnycky, "Gennady Zyuganov: Russia's Pragmatic Extremist," *Freedom Review*, May-June 1996, pp. 27–40.
22. *The Washington Post*, 8 December 1991.
23. ANATOLIY GOLITSYN, *New Lies for Old: The Communist Strategy of Deception and Disinformation* (New York: Dodd, Mead, 1984), p. 231.
24. In *The Perestroika Deception* (London: Edward Harle, 1995), GOLITSYN argues that the Leninists are still in control of Russia and have monumentally duped the West into letting down its guard.
25. Quoted in David Brion Davis, ed., *The Fear of Conspiracy: Images of Un-American Subversion from the Revolution to the Present* (Ithaca, N.Y.: Cornell University Press, 1971), p. 279.
26. 14 June 1951, *Congressional Record*, 82d Cong. 1st sess. vol. 97, pt. 5, p. 6602.
27. DAN SMOOT, *The Invisible Government*, 2d ed. (Boston: Western Islands, 1977), p. 115. PTA stands for Parent-Teachers Association, a group that organizes parents' involvement in the schools their children attend.
28. GARY H. KAH, *En Route to Global Occupation* (Lafayette, La.: Huntington House, 1991), p. 36.
29. SMOOT, *Invisible Government*, pp. 3, xvi.
30. Ibid., p. 141.
31. This presumably explains why my name is listed in JAMES PERLOFF, *The Shadows of Power: The Council on Foreign Relations and the American Decline* (Appleton, Wisc.: Western Islands, 1988), p. 261.
32. PAT ROBERTSON, *The New World Order* (Dallas: Word, 1991), pp. 135–36.
33. KAH, *En Route to Global Occupation*, p. 55.
34. ROBERT WELCH, *The Politician* (Belmont, Mass.: Privately printed, 1963), pp. 83, 17, 6.
35. Father Louis Rohr, quoted in Donald Warren, *Radio Priest: Charles Coughlin, the Father of Hate Radio* (New York: Free Press, 1996), p. 296.
36. ROBERT K. SPEAR, *Surviving Global Slavery: Living under the New World Order* (Leavenworth, Kan.: Universal Force Dynamics, 1992), p. 5.
37. MURRAY ROTHBARD, quoted in Peter Schwartz, "Libertarianism: The Perversion of Liberty," in Leonard Peikoff, ed., *The Voice of Reason: Essays in Objectivist Thought* (New York: New American Library, 1988), p. 321.
38. BARBARA CONRY, "U.S. 'Global Leadership': A Euphemism for World Policeman," CATO Institute Policy Analysis, 5 February 1997.
39. *The Washington Post*, 10 April 1984.
40. *Christian Posse Comitatus Newsletter*, n.d., quoted in Kenneth S. Stern, *A Force upon the Plain: The American Militia Movement and the Politics of Hate* (New York: Simon & Schuster, 1996), p. 50.

41. Ilan Peleg, "Censorship in Global and Comparative Perspective: An Analytical Framework," in Ilan Peleg, *Patterns of Censorship around the World* (Boulder, Colo.: Westview, 1993), p. 7.

42. The English version can be found at <http://www.webcom.com/~ezundel/english/a.acht.html>.

43. At times, influence spreads in the other direction too; the skinheads, for example, are a British import.

44. MARVIN S. ANTELMAN, *To Eliminate the Opiate* (New York: Zahavia, 1974), pp. 155, title page, 157.

45. *The New York Times*, 16 September 1990.

46. FOUAD AYOUB, letter to the *Washington Post*, 18 December 1990, responding to an alleged Iraqi-Jordanian-Yemeni plan to seize Saudi Arabia.

47. *Cumhuriyet*, 13 February 1993.

48. Daniel Pipes, *The Hidden Hand: Middle East Fears of Conspiracy* (New York: St. Martin's, 1996). Only after publication of this work did another study on this general topic come to my attention: Tore Bjørgo, *Conspiracy Rhetoric in Arab Politics: The Palestinian Case* (Oslo: Norsk utenrikspolitsk institutt, 1987). The vital case of conspiracy theories in the June 1967 Arab-Israeli war is discussed at length in Richard B. Parker, ed., *The Six-Day War: A Retrospective* (Gainesville: University of Florida Press, 1996), pp. 237–88.

49. "Les Souvenirs du P. Grivel sur les PP. Barruel et Feller," *Le Contemporain*, July 1878, pp. 58–61.

50. Walther Rathenau, *Zur Kritik der Zeit* (Berlin: S. Fischer, 1919).

51. According to a 1956 book, "less than THREE HUNDRED MEN have controlled" politics for "several hundred years." See the foreword to WILLIAM GUY CARR, *Pawns in the Game*, 2d ed. (Toronto: National Federation of Christian Laymen, 1956). American militias sell videotapes of *The Committee of 300*. A participant at Ross Perot's Reform party convention selecting a 1996 presidential candidate told a journalist that $1.4 trillion disappears each year from the United States. "Where do you think it goes?" asked the journalist. "Probably to some kind of committee of 300 in Europe—the powers that be or something like that. They use it for their own agenda." *The Wall Street Journal*, 13 August 1996.

52. 28 September 1958 interview. Text in *President Gamal Abdel Nasser's Speeches and Press Interviews during the Year 1958* (Cairo: U.A.R. Information Department, 1959), p. 402.

53. NESTA H. WEBSTER, *Secret Societies and Subversive Movements* (New York: E. P. Dutton, 1924), p. xii, note. The neologism *antisemitism* was actually coined by the antisemite WILHELM MARR or his rivals; see Moshe Zimmerman, *Wilhelm Marr: The Patriarch of Anti-Semitism* (New York: Oxford University Press, 1986), pp. 88–95, 112.

54. IBRAHIM AL-HARDALLO, *Antisemitism: A Changing Concept* (Khartoum: Khartoum University Press, 1970), p. 9.

55. Quoted in Richard S. Levy, *Antisemitism in the Modern World: An Anthology of Texts* (Lexington, Mass.: D. C. Heath, 1991), p. 218.

56. Voice of the Islamic Republic, 14 February 1993, 3 September 1993.

57. *The Jerusalem Report*, 6 June 1991.

58. Frank Dikötter, *The Discourse of Race in Modern China* (London: Hurst, 1992), p. 114.

59. This definition of Japanese antisemitism is in David G. Goodman and Masanori Miyazawa, *Jews in the Japanese Mind: The History and Uses of a Cultural Stereotype* (New York: Free Press, 1995), p. 11.

60. Quoted in ibid., p. 106.

61. HOKUZAN ATAGO quoted in ibid., pp. 107, 226, 245.

62. *Mainichi shimbun*, 12 September 1944 and *Yomiuri shimbun*, 22 January 1944. Quoted in ibid., pp. 108–09.

63. MASAO MASUDA, writing in November 1942. Quoted in ibid., pp. 120–21.

64. UNO MASAMI, *Yudaya ga wakaru to Nihon ga miete kuru* (Tokyo: Tokuma shoten, 1986) idem, and *Yudaya ga wakaru to sekai ga miete kuru* (Tokyo: Tokuma shoten, 1986). Translated, the titles are "If You Understand the Jews, You Will Understand Japan" and "If You Understand the Jews, You Will Understand the World."

65. Carlos Rangel, *Del buen salvaje al buen revolucionario: mitos y realidades de America Latina* (Caracas: Monte Avila, 1976), p. 42.

66. ANDREO MATIAS, *CIA, Sendero Luminoso: Guerra politica* (Lima: Universo Grafico, 1988).

67. *The New York Times*, 28 November 1988.

68. Douglas Farah, "Letter from Haiti: Reality Check," *The Washington Post*, 7 December 1993.

69. Alan Berlow, "Way Off Base," *The New Republic*, 31 December 1990.

70. *The Times of India*, 2 April 1993.

71. Mary Clabaugh Wright, *The Last Stand of Chinese Conservatism: The Tung-Chih Restoration, 1862–1874* (Stanford: Stanford University Press, 1957), p. 44, n. b.

CHAPTER 7: TWO CONSPIRACIST TRADITIONS

1. Armin Pfahl-Traughber, *Der antisemitisch-antifreimaurerische Verschwörungsmythos in der weimarer Republik und im NS-Staat* (Vienna: Braumüller, 1993), p. 21.

2. Robert Welch, writing in *American Opinion*, November 1966. Quoted in George Johnson, *Architects of Fear: Conspiracy Theories and Paranoia in American Politics* (Los Angeles: Jeremy P. Tarcher, 1983), p. 136.

3. GARY ALLEN, *None Dare Call It Conspiracy* (Rossmoor, Calif.: Concord Press, [1972]), p. 39.

4. WILLIAM GUY CARR, *The Red Fog over America* (Willowdale, Ont.: National Federation of Christian Laymen, 1955), p. 186.

5. NESTA H. WEBSTER, *World Revolution: The Plot against Civilization* (London: Constable, 1921), pp. 296, 297–304, 305.

6. CARR, *Red Fog over America*, pp. 4, 7. CARR also explains that *goy* does not mean "non-Jews" but "*all* people of *all* races and *all* creeds" who are not members of the Illuminati. Elsewhere, WILLIAM GUY CARR, *Pawns in the Game*, 2d ed. (Toronto: National Federation of Christian Laymen, 1956), pp. 27–31, 157, presents the *Protocols* as an "enlargement" of a plot originally forwarded by Mayer Rothschild in 1773 to a group of non-Jewish bankers and industrialists.

7. MILTON WILLIAM COOPER, *"Behold a Pale Horse"* (Sedona, Ariz.: Light Technology, 1991), p. 267. Cooper includes the entire text of the *Protocols* (in the Marsden translation) in his book.

8. Steven L. Kaplan, *The Famine Plot Persuasion in Eighteenth-Century France* (Philadelphia: American Philosophical Society, 1982), p. 2.

9. David Brion Davis, Introduction to David Brion Davis, ed., *The Fear of Conspiracy: Images of Un-American Subversion from the Revolution to the Present* (Ithaca, N.Y.: Cornell University Press, 1971), pp. xv, 37.

10. Robert S. Wistrich, *Antisemitism: The Longest Hatred* (New York: Pantheon, 1991), p. xxiv.

11. Norman Cohn, *Warrant for Genocide: The Myth of the Jewish World Conspiracy and the Protocols of the Elders of Zion* (London: Eyre & Spottiswoode, 1967), p. 277.

12. Serge Moscovici, "The Conspiracy Mentality," in Carl F. Graumann and Serge Moscovici, eds., *Changing Conceptions of Conspiracy* (New York: Springer, 1987), pp. 157, 168.

13. GARY H. KAH, *En Route to Global Occupation* (Lafayette, La.: Huntington House, 1991), p. 120; CARR, *Red Fog over America*, p. 5.

14. Would it not make more sense to see Freemasonry as a British stalking horse? It did originate in London, after all. But other than some Nazis, conspiracy theorists seem oblivious to this connection.

15. Quoted in ARTHUR SINGER, *Der Kampf Roms gegen die Freimaurerei: Geschichtliche Studie* (Leipzig: Ernst Oldenburg, 1925), p. 37. The title of this book, it bears noting is, "Rome's Battle against the Freemasons." This idea remains alive in some circles: CARR writes in *Pawns in the Game*, pp. 12–13 that "It was the Illuminati, and the false priests and elders in their pay, who hatched the plot by which Christ would be executed by the Roman soldiers." Then, "after the foul deed had been done," the Illuminati shifted the blame they bore to the Jews.

16. Quoted in Paul Goodman, *Towards a Christian Republic: Antimasonry and the Great Transition in New England, 1826–1836* (New York: Oxford University Press, 1988), p. 59. This opinion was not universal in the Antimasonic party, where others deemed Freemasonry an anti-Christian effort shaped by Jews in combination with "Jesuits and French atheists." Quoted in William Preston Vaughn, *The Antimasonic Party in the United States, 1826–1843* (Lexington: University Press of Kentucky, 1983), p. 15.

17. In particular, EDUARD EMIL ECKERT, *Die Freimaurer-Orden in seiner wahren Bedeutung* (Magdeburg: Fabricius & Schaefer, 1848), translated (and increased in size from 30 pages to over 800) as *La Franc-Maçonnerie dans sa véritable signification, ou son organisation, son but et son histoire* (Liege: J.-G. Lardinois, 1854).

18. BENJAMIN DISRAELI, *Lord George Bentinck: A Political Biography* (London: Colburn, 1852), p. 497.

19. GOUGENOT DE MOUSSEAUX, *Le Juif, le Judaïsme et la judaisation des peuples chrétiens* (Paris: Henri Plon, 1869), pp. 340, n. 1, 342, 347, 515–16.

20. C. C. DE SAINT-ANDRE [pseud. of E. H. CHABAUTY], *Franc-Maçons et Juifs, sixième age de l'église d'après l'Apocalypse* (Paris: Societé générale de librarie catholique, 1880), p. 652.

21. LÉON MEURIN, *La Franc-Maçonnerie, synagogue de satan* (Paris: Victor Retaux, 1893), p. 260.

22. Jacob Katz, *Jews and Freemasons in Europe, 1723–1939*, trans. Leonard Oschry (Cambridge, Mass.: Harvard University Press, 1970), p. 162.

23. Quoted in Richard Pipes, *Russia under Bolshevik Regime* (New York: Alfred A. Knopf, 1993), p. 257.

24. WEBSTER, *World Revolution*, p. 307.

25. *Münchener Beobachter*, 9 November 1918.

26. FRIEDRICH WICHTL, *Freimaurerei—Zionismus—Kommunismus—Spartakismus—Bolschewismus* (Hamburg: Deutschvolkische Verlagsanstalt, [1920]).

27. Quoted in Pfahl-Traughber, *Der antisemitisch-antifreimaurerische Verschwörungsmythos*, p. 66.

28. Katz, *Jews and Freemasons*, p. 221. In some conspiracist circles, such as the Nation of Islam, that identification remains.

29. Examples in this and the next paragraph derive, except where noted, from H. D. Schmidt, "Anti-Western and Anti-Jewish Tradition in German Historical Thought," *Leo Baeck Institute Year Book* 4 (1959): 37–60.

30. A passage tactfully dropped from the English-language edition; quoted in Herman Bernstein, *The Truth about "The Protocols of Zion": A Complete Exposure* (New York: Covici, Friede, 1935), p. 65.

31. ÉMILE FLOURENS, *La France conquise: Édouard VII et Clemenceau* (Paris: Garnier Frères, [1907]), pp. 17, 28.

32. V. I. LENIN, *Imperialism, the Highest Stage of Capitalism: A Popular Outline* (New York: International Publishers, 1933), p. 73.

33. MARY E. LEASE, *The Problem of Civilization Solved* (Chicago: Laird and Lee, 1895), pp. 319–20. Quoted in Richard Hofstadter, *The Age of Reform: From Bryan to F.D.R.* (New York: Alfred A. Knopf, 1955), p. 79.

34. G. BUTMI, *Vragi Roda Cheloviecheskago Posviashchaetsia Soiuzu Russkago Naroda*, 3d ed. (St. Petersburg: Tipografiia Uchilishcha Glukhoniemykh, 1906), p. 109. Quoted in John S. Curtiss, *An Appraisal of the Protocols of Zion* (New York: Columbia University Press, 1942), p. 24.

35. 29 May 1920. Reprinted in *The International Jew: The World's Foremost Problem* (Dearborn, Mich.: Dearborn Independent, 1920), p. 30.

36. Quoted in Dan Diner, *America in the Eyes of the Germans: An Essay on Anti-Americanism*, trans. Allison Brown (Princeton, N.J.: Markus Weiner, 1997), pp. 20, 62.

37. *The New York Times Magazine*, 29 April 1984.

38. Paul Hollander, *Anti-Americanism: Critiques at Home and Abroad, 1965–1990* (New York: Oxford University Press, 1992), p. 364.

39. *The Washington Times*, 30 January 1992.

40. Diner, *Americans in the Eyes of the Germans*. For more early examples, see pp. 66–67, 70–73.

41. WILLIAM HOPE HARVEY, *Coin's Financial School* (Chicago: Coin Publishing, 1894), p. 124.

42. "It does happen that 90 percent of the Soviet government is Jewish," Father Charles Coughlin told the House of Representatives in 1930. Quoted in Donald Warren, *Radio Priest: Charles Coughlin, the Father of Hate Radio* (New York: Free Press, 1996), p. 33.

43. Jewish background but not Jewish identification; they saw themselves as international socialists and retained no ties, emotional or other, to the Jewish community.

44. And Vladimir Lenin. Many antisemites falsely turned Lenin into a Jew named Chaim Goldman. But until the Soviet Union was in an advanced state of collapse, Lenin and the Communist party successfully hid the fact that his maternal grandfather, Israel Dymitrovich Blank, was a Jew who converted to the Russian Orthodox faith in 1820, taking the name Alexander. This was revealed in M. Stein, "Genealogiya rod Ulyanovikh," *Literator*, 12 September 1990.

45. W. S. CHURCHILL, "Zionism versus Bolshevism," *Sunday Illustrated Herald*, 8 February 1920. Weishaupt used the pseudonym Spartacus.

46. In *Zionism in the Age of the Dictators* (London: Croom Helm, 1983).

47. Zionists leaders were prepared "to sacrifice the Jews of the Diaspora" and so pursued a "policy of making deals with the Nazis." *Perdition: A Play in Two Acts* (London: Ithaca Press, 1987), p. 35.

48. C.C. DE SAINT-ANDRE [pseud. of E.H. CHABAUTY], *Franc-Maçons et Juifs, sixième age de l'église d'après l'Apocalypse* (Paris: Societé générale de librarie catholique, 1880), p. 539.

49. For example, MICHAEL SABA, *The Armageddon Network* (Brattleboro, Vt.: Amana Books, 1984) and PAUL FINDLEY, *They Dare to Speak Out: People and Institutions Confront Israel's Lobby*, rev. ed. (Chicago: Lawrence Hill, 1989).

50. For example, Iliya Abu Ruways, *Al-Yuhudiya al-'Alamiya wa-Harbiha al-Mustamirra 'ala al-Masihiya* (Beirut: Dar at-Tali'a, 1993) and *Ihdharu al-Khadi'a al-Yuhudiya* (Beirut: n.p., 1988). These titles translate, respectively, as "World Jewry and the Ongoing War against Christianity" and "Beware the New Jewish Deception."

51. YASUMASA KURODA, "Bush's New World Order: A Structural Analysis of Instability and Conflict in the Gulf," in Tareq Y. Ismael and Jacqueline S. Ismael, eds., *The Gulf War and the New World Order* (Gainesville: University of Florida Press, 1994), p. 69.

52. Dean Rusk, as told to Richard Rusk, *As I Saw It* (New York: W. W. Norton, 1990), pp. 380–81. For a detailed look at Arab and Iranian puzzlement about U.S.-Israel relations, see Daniel Pipes, *The Hidden Hand: Middle East Fears of Conspiracy* (New York: St. Martin's, 1996), chap. 8.

53. JOSEPH BREWDA, "Rabin Assassination Part of London's Terror Wave," *The New Federalist*, 13 November 1995.

54. Mattias Gardell, *In the Name of Elijah Muhammad: Louis Farrakhan and the Nation of Islam* (Durham, N.C.: Duke University Press, 1996), p. 411.

55. Dennis King, *Lyndon LaRouche and the New American Fascism* (New York: Doubleday, 1989), p. 273.

56. Kenneth S. Stern, *A Force upon the Plain: The American Militia Movement and the Politics of Hate* (New York: Simon & Schuster, 1996), p. 247; more specifically, Stern writes (p. 69) of the man who founded the Militia of Montana: "When he said 'shadow government' or 'banking elite,' people knew he meant 'Jews.'"

57. MICHAEL LIND, *Up from Conservatism: Why the Right Is Wrong for America* (New York: Free Press, 1996), p. 8. "ZOG" stands for Zionist Occupied Government.

58. For example, PAT ROBERTSON, *The New World Order* (Dallas: Word, 1991), pp. 74, 208, 243, 256–57.

59. Michael Lind, "Rev. Robertson's Grand International Conspiracy Theory," *The New York Review of Books*, 2 February 1995, esp. p. 22, col. 3; and LIND, *Conservatism*, p. 101.

60. *The New York Times*, 4 March 1995.

61. JAMES PERLOFF, *The Shadows of Power: The Council on Foreign Relations and the American Decline* (Appleton, Wisc.: Western Islands, 1988), pp. 19, 217.

62. Robert S. Wistrich, *Antisemitism: The Longest Hatred* (New York: Pantheon, 1991), p. 181.

63. *Protocols of the Meetings of the Learned Elders of Zion*, trans. Victor E. Marsden (London: The Britons, 1923), p. 33.

64. WEBSTER, *World Revolution*, p. 280.

65. ROBERTSON, *New World Order*, p. 68.

66. Ishmael Reed, *Mumbo-Jumbo* (Garden City, N.Y.: Doubleday, 1972), pp. 19–20.

67. John Daniel, *Scarlet and the Beast: A History of the War between English and French Freemasonry*, 3 vols. (Tyler, Texas: Jon Kregel, 1995).

68. Unless written by Jews. For examples, see Jeffrey Goldberg, "The Protocols of the Teenagers of Zion," *Jerusalem Post International Edition*, 7 December 1991; and Ze'ev Chafets, "Say It Ain't So, Lefty," *The Jerusalem Report*, 19 May 1994.

69. "The Great Conspiracy," *The New York Times*, 2 July 1894.

70. Fred E. Foldvary, "Blaming It All on Stamp Collectors," *The American Philatelist*, December 1991, pp. 1116–17.

71. Vladimir Nabokov, *Pale Fire* (New York: G. P. Putnam's Sons, 1962).

72. Text by Michael Litchfield (Berkeley, Cal.: EarthWorks Press, 1992). Other recent examples of cheerful conspiracism include Michael Howard, *The Occult Conspiracy: Secret Societies—Their Influence and Power in World History* (Rochester, Vt.: Destiny Books, 1989); Robert Eringer, *The Conspiracy Peddlers: A Review of the Conspiracy Media in the United States* (Mason, Mich.: Loompanics, 1981); and Jonathan Vankin and John Whalen, *50 Greatest Conspiracies of All Time: History's Biggest Mysteries, Coverups, and Cabals* (Secaucus, N.J.: Carol, 1995), with an associated World Wide Web site (see appendix C).

73. Calvin Trillin, "Tracing a Conspiracy of Cuckoos," *The Philadelphia Inquirer*, 29 July 1995.

74. David Cogswell and Paul Gordon, *Chomsky for Beginners* (New York: Writers and Readers, 1996).

75. Peter Partner, *The Murdered Magicians: The Templars and Their Myth* (Oxford: Oxford University Press, 1982), pp. 175–76, 179.

76. Webster, *World Revolution*, pp. 314, 203, 309.

77. Address of 8 April 1917, quoted in Richard Pipes, *The Russian Revolution* (New York: Alfred A. Knopf, 1990), p. 397.

78. Ibid., pp. 396, 352.

79. Quoted in James V. Compton, *The Swastika and the Eagle: Hitler, the United States, and the Origins of World War II* (Boston: Houghton Mifflin, 1967), p. 259.

80. *Dearborn Independent*, 29 May 1920. Reprinted in *The International Jew: The World's Foremost Problem* (Dearborn, Mich.: Dearborn Independent, 1920), p. 29.

81. Gary Allen, *None Dare Call It Conspiracy* (Rossmoor, Calif.: Concord Press, [1972]), pp. 18, 131. Allen reiterates the same theme on pp. 59, 62, 98, 102–03, 106–07.

82. Quoted in Robert S. Wistrich, ed., *The Left Against Zion: Communism, Israel and the Middle East* (London: Valentine, Mitchell, 1979), p. 225.

83. Alberto Rivera and Jack T. Chick, *My Name? . . . In the Vatican?* Cited in Johnson, *Architects of Fear*, p. 88.

84. This statement can be heard on <http://www.conspire.com/conspire/chick.au>.

85. Quoted in Warren, *Radio Priest*, p. 189.

86. Carr, *Pawns in the Game*, p. 20.

87. Quoted in Carlson, *Under Cover*, p. 44.

88. Quoted in Warren, *Radio Priest*, p. 135.

89. James Dale Davidson and William Rees-Mogg, *The Great Reckoning: How the World Will Change in the Depression of the 1990s* (New York: Summit, 1991), p. 213.

90. *The Washington Times*, 27 December 1995.

91. For a French example, see Jean-Claude Barreau, *La France va-t-elle disparaître?* (Paris: Bernard Grasset, 1997).

92. Quoted in Michael Billig, "Rhetoric of the Conspiracy Theory: Arguments in National Front Propaganda," *Patterns of Prejudice*, Summer 1988, p. 28.

93. Tore Bjørgo, "Extreme Nationalism and Violent Discourses in Scandinavia: 'The Resistance,' 'Traitors,' and 'Foreign Invaders,'" in *Terror from the Extreme Right*, ed. Tore Bjørgo (London: Frank Cass, 1995), p. 209.

94. VLADIMIR ZHIRINOVSKY, *Posledniy Brosok na Yug* (Moscow: LDP, 1993), p. 129. Quoted in Paul Quinn-Judge, "Zhirinovsky vs. the Turks," *Middle East Quarterly*, June 1994, p. 88.

95. "Playboy Interview: Vladimir Zhirinovsky," *Playboy*, March 1995, p. 59.

96. Alan J. Koman, "The Last Surge to the South: The New Enemies of Russia in the Rhetoric of Zhirinovsky," *Studies in Conflict & Terrorism* 19 (1996): 310. Others speculate that Zhirinovsky received right-wing German money in return for the anti-Turkish rhetoric.

97. Field Marshall AUGUST NEITHARDT GNEISENAU (1760–1831), text in Franz Kobler, *Juden und Judentum in deutschen Briefen aus drei Jahrhunderten* (Vienna: Saturn, 1935), p. 209.

98. ADOLF STOECKER, "Unsere Forderungen an das moderne Judentum," *Christlich-Sozial: Reden und Aufsätze* (Bielefeld: Velhagen & Klasing, 1885), p. 144.

99. WILHELM MARR, *Der Sieg des Judenthums über das Germanenthum: Vom nicht confessionellen Standpunkt aus betrachtet* (Bern: Rudolph Costenoble, 1879), p. 22.

100. Quoted in Warren, *Radio Priest*, p. 106.

101. Quoted in John Roy Carlson [pseud. of Arthur Derounian], *Under Cover: My Four Years in the Nazi Underworld of America—The Amazing Revelation of How Axis Agents and Our Enemies Within Are Now Plotting to Destroy the United States* (New York: E. P. Dutton, 1943), p. 350.

102. Goodman, *Towards a Christian Republic*, pp. 36, 23.

CHAPTER 8: RIGHT-WING NUTS, LEFTIST SOPHISTICATES

1. The facts of the case were not clear until established by Fritz Tobias in his monumental study, *Der Reichstagsbrand; Legende und Wirklichkeit* (Rastatt: Grote 1962).

2. In WORLD COMMITTEE FOR VICTIMS OF GERMAN FASCISM, *Braunbuch uber Reichstagsbrand und Hitler-Terror* (Basel: Universumbucherei, 1933); *The Brown Book of the Hitler Terror and the Burning of the Reichstag* (London: Victor Gollancz, 1933; New York: A. A. Knopf, 1933) and *The Reichstag Fire Trail: The Second Brown Book of the Hitler Terror* (London: Bodley Head, 1934). The WORLD COMMITTEE was actually a communist front run by the ace Soviet propagandist, Willi Münzenberg.

3. The Hollywood movie *Foreign Affair* (1948) retells this interpretation.

4. For example, Robert Leckie, *Delivered from Evil: The Saga of World War II* (New York: Harper & Row, 1987), p. 60.

5. Michael Kelly, "The Road to Paranoia," *The New Yorker*, 19 June 1995.

6. Robert S. Wistrich, Introduction to Robert S. Wistrich, ed., *The Left against Zion: Communism, Israel and the Middle East* (London: Valentine, Mitchell, 1979), p. viii.

7. GENNADY ZYUGANOV, *Za Gorizontom* (Moscow: Informpechat', 1995).

8. PETER LANGAN of the Aryan Republican Army, Associated Press, 10 February 1997.

9. THE HISTORICAL RESEARCH DEPARTMENT, *The Secret Relationship between Blacks and Jews* (Boston: Nation of Islam, 1991), vol. 1, p. vii.

10. *The Final Call,* 22 April 1991. Quoted in Mattias Gardell, *In the Name of Elijah Muhammad: Louis Farrakhan and the Nation of Islam* (Durham, N.C.: Duke University Press, 1996), p. 278.

11. Quoted in Kenneth S. Stern, *A Force upon the Plain: The American Militia Movement and the Politics of Hate* (New York: Simon & Schuster, 1996), p. 97.

12. Quoted in Arthur J. Magida, *Prophet of Rage: A Life of Louis Farrakhan and His Nation* (New York: Basic Books, 1996), p. 155.

13. *The New York Times,* 12 October 1985.

14. ADOLF HITLER, *Mein Kampf* (Munich: Zentralverlag der NSDAP, 1935), p. 356. This book was first published in 1925–27.

15. Quoted in Ran Marom, "The Bolsheviks and the Balfour Declaration 1917–1920," *The Wiener Library Bulletin,* vol. 29, nos. 37/38 (1976): 22.

16. TODD GITLIN, "The Stoning of Oliver and the Fascination of JFK," *Tikkun,* March-April 1992, p. 54.

17. Richard S. Levy, *Antisemitism in the Modern World: An Anthology of Texts* (Lexington, Mass.: D. C. Heath, 1991), p. 7.

18. Walter Laqueur, *Black Hundred: The Rise of the Extreme Right in Russia* (New York: HarperCollins, 1993), p. xv.

19. Michael Lerner, *The Socialism of Fools: Anti-Semitism on the Left* (Oakland, Calif.: Tikkun Books, 1992), pp. v, 39.

20. Michael Billig, "The Extreme Right: Continuities in Anti-Semitic Conspiracy Theory in Post-War Europe," in Roger Eatwell and Noël O'Sullivan, eds., *The Nature of the Right: American and European Policies and Political Thought since 1789* (Boston: Twayne, 1989), p. 149.

21. Richard Hofstadter, "The Paranoid Style in American Politics," in Richard Hofstadter, *The Paranoid Style in American Politics and Other Essays* (New York: Vintage, 1967), pp. 1, 3. This chapter, it bears noting, is in a section titled "Studies in the American Right."

22. Seymour Martin Lipset and Earl Raab, *The Politics of Unreason: Right-Wing Extremism in America, 1790–1970* (New York: Harper & Row, 1970).

23. George Johnson, *Architects of Fear: Conspiracy Theories and Paranoia in American Politics* (Los Angeles: Jeremy P. Tarcher, 1983), p. 199, also pp. 13–14, 69, 166.

24. Dennis King, *Lyndon LaRouche and the New American Fascism* (New York: Doubleday, 1989).

25. The intrawar period witnessed quite a few exceptions, and not just in Germany; the English-speaking world, for example, had such distinguished literary figures as HILAIRE BELLOC, G. K. CHESTERTON, EZRA POUND, and HUGH WALPOLE espousing rightist conspiracism.

26. MARY STEWART RELFE, *When Your Money Fails . . . the "666 System" Is Here* (Montgomery, Ala.: Ministries, Inc., 1981), pp. 127–28.

27. "The following document [in which the Illuminati declare war on the United States] dated May 1979 was found on July 7, 1986, in an IBM copier that had been purchased at a surplus sale." MILTON WILLIAM COOPER, *"Behold a Pale Horse"* (Sedona, Ariz: Light Technology, 1991), p. 36.

28. After their invasion of Kuwait, the Iraqis turned up a self-evidently bogus memorandum from the Kuwaiti archives that established joint Kuwaiti-CIA efforts

to undermine the Iraqi economy that SALINGER and ERIC LAURENT reprinted in its entirety and relied on heavily in their book, *Guerre du Golfe: Le dossier secret* (Paris: Olivier Orban, 1991); trans. Howard Curtis, *Secret Dossier: The Hidden Agenda behind the Gulf War* (Harmondsworth, Eng.: Penguin, 1991).

29. Robert F. Barsky, *Noam Chomsky: A Life of Dissent* (Cambridge, Mass.: MIT Press, 1997), p. 3.

30. WILLIAM GUY CARR, *The Red Fog over America* (Willowdale, Ont.: National Federation of Christian Laymen, 1955), pp. 170, 172. See also WILLIAM GUY CARR, *The Devil's Poison: Or "The Truth about Fluorine"* (Willowdale, Ont.: National Federation of Christian Laymen, [1956]). The same organization interpreted the "publication of Crime and Sex comics" as "part of the Communist psychological warfare." See WILLIAM GUY CARR, *Pawns in the Game*, 2d ed. (Toronto: National Federation of Christian Laymen, 1956), p. 127.

31. RELFE, *When Your Money Fails*. Some Christians consider the number 666 to be the "mark of the beast" of Revelations 13:16–17 (because that is the numerical value in Hebrew of the name Nero Caesar). In a curious parallel, SERGEI NILUS, the first person to publish the *Protocols* in a book, had a system by which he detected signs of the Antichrist in commercial trademarks.

32. *The Washington Times*, 28 April 1996. (Mason jars? It already sounds suspicious.)

33. *The New York Times*, 18 September 1996. A few months later, in a more sober mood, Boutros-Ghali ascribed the American veto of his second term in part to the black helicopters.

34. TONY MARTIN at Wellesley College in Massachusetts holds Jews responsible for the slave trade. LEONARD JEFFRIES, Jr., at City University of New York sees Jews engaged in a "conspiracy, planned and plotted in Hollywood" for "the destruction of black people" (ibid., 11 August 1991).

35. Especially influential is MARTIN BERNAL, *Black Athena: The Afroasiatic Roots of Classical Civilization*, 2 vols. (New Brunswick, N.J.: Rutgers University Press, 1987–91). It even sparked a serious, full-length refutation, Mary Lefkowitz, *Not Out of Africa: How Afrocentrism Became an Excuse to Teach Myth as History* (New York: BasicBooks, 1996).

36. SUSAN FALUDI, *Backlash: The Undeclared War against American Women* (New York: Crown, 1991), pp. xviii, xxii, 56, 69, xxi.

37. JOEL KOVEL, *Red Hunting in the Promised Land: Anticommunism and the Making of America* (New York: BasicBooks, 1994), pp. 11–12.

38. PETER H. SMITH, *Talons of the Eagle: Dynamics of U.S.-Latin American Relations* (New York: Oxford University Press, 1996).

39. J. M. Roberts, *The Mythology of the Secret Societies* (New York: Charles Scribner's Sons, 1972), p. 139.

40. William Korey, "The Soviet *Protocols of the Elders of Zion*," in Theodore Freedman, ed., *Anti-Semitism in the Soviet Union: Its Roots and Consequences* (New York: Anti-Defamation League of B'nai B'rith, 1984).

41. Wistrich, Introduction, pp. viii–ix.

42. Nora Levin, *The Jews of the Soviet Union since 1917: Paradox of Survival* (New York: New York University Press, 1988), p. xxiii.

43. EDWARD JAY EPSTEIN, *Inquest: The Warren Commission and the Establishment of Truth* (New York: Viking Press, 1966); MARK LANE, *Rush to Judgment: A Critique of the Warren Commission's Inquiry into the Murders of President John F. Kennedy,*

Officer J. D. Tippitt, and Lee Harvey Oswald (New York: Holt, Rinehart and Winston, 1966).

44. THOMAS C. BUCHANAN, *Who Killed Kennedy?* (New York: G. P. Putnam, 1964); JOACHIM JOESTEN, *Oswald: Assassin or Fall-Guy?* (New York: Marzani and Munsell, 1964); SYLVIA MEAGHER, *Accessories after the Fact: The Warren Commission, the Authorities, and the Report* (Indianapolis: Bobbs-Merrill, 1967); and HAROLD WEISBERG, *Whitewash: The Report on the Warren Report* (Hyattstown, Md.: n.p., 1965).

45. JIM GARRISON, quoted in Gerald Posner, *Case Closed: Lee Harvey Oswald and the Assassination of JFK* (New York: Random House, 1993), p. 443.

46. Steven E. Ambrose, "Writers on the Grassy Knoll: A Reader's Guide," *The New York Times Book Review,* 2 February 1992.

47. Posner, *Case Closed,* p. x.

48. For a definitive repudiation of efforts to link Sirhan to a conspiracy, see Dan E. Moldea, *The Killing of Robert F. Kennedy: An Investigation of Motive, Means and Opportunity* (New York: W. W. Norton, 1995), esp. chap. 30.

49. Unpublished *New York Times*/CBS News poll, 22–25 January 1992; reported in Ted Goertzel, "Belief in Conspiracy Theories," *Political Psychology* 15 (1994): 733.

50. JONATHAN VANKIN, *Conspiracies, Cover-Ups, and Crimes: Political Manipulation and Mind Control in America* (New York: Paragon House, 1991), pp. 205, 191.

51. MICHAEL LIND, *Up from Conservatism: Why the Right Is Wrong for America* (New York: Free Press, 1996), pp. 85, 80–81, 94–95, 86–87.

CHAPTER 9: CONSPIRACISM'S COSTS

1. Norman Cohn, *Warrant for Genocide: The Myth of the Jewish World Conspiracy and the* Protocols of the Elders of Zion (London: Eyre & Spottiswoode, 1967), p. 223.

2. Svetlana Alliluyeva, *Only One Year,* trans. Paul Chavchavadze (New York: Harper & Row, 1969), p. 392.

3. Clarence Page, "Evasive Genocide Blamers," *The Washington Times,* 16 August 1991.

4. JOHN HARRELL, quoted in *The Wall Street Journal,* 24 April 1995.

5. Paul Hollander, *Anti-Americanism: Critiques at Home and Abroad, 1965–1990* (New York: Oxford University Press, 1992).

6. VLADIMIR I. LENIN, *What Is to Be Done? Burning Questions of Our Movement,* trans. George Hanna and Victor J. Jerome (New York: International Publishers, 1969), p. 133.

7. Leonard Schapiro, *The Communist Party of the Soviet Union* (New York: Random House, 1960), p. 61.

8. David Annan, "Nationalist Secret Societies," in Norman MacKenzie, ed., *Secret Societies* (New York: Holt, Rinehart and Winston, 1967), p. 201.

9. Richard Pipes, Introduction to Richard Pipes, ed., *The Unknown Lenin: From the Secret Archive* (New Haven: Yale University Press, 1996), pp. 3–4. For examples of Lenin's conspiracies, see pp. 74, 122, 125, 132, 138, 164.

10. Quoted in Andrew and Gordievsky, *KGB,* p. 48.

11. The Nazis drew on other conspiracist sources as well; the SS, for example, took on the clandestine oaths, rites, hierarchies, and other trappings of the medieval military orders.

12. Quoted in James Webb, *The Occult Establishment*, vol. 2 of *The Age of the Irrational* (La Salle, Ill.: Open Court, 1976), p. 320. Ignatius of Loyola founded the Jesuits.
13. Hermann Rauschning, *Gespräche mit Hitler* (New York: Europa, 1940), pp. 224–25.
14. Alexander Stein, *Adolf Hitler, Schüler der "Weisen von Zion"* (Karlsbad: Graphia, 1936), pp. 34–37, 39–44, provides word-for-word comparisons of *Protocols* text and Hitler speeches for these and many other matters.
15. "Dialogues in Hell" refers to Un Contemporain [pseud. of Maurice Joli], *Dialogue aux enfers entre Machiavel et Montesquieu: ou la politique de Machiavel au XIXe siècle* (Brussels: A. Mertens et Fils, 1864), a satire that forms much of the basis of *The Protocols*.
16. Herman Bernstein, *The Truth about "The Protocols of Zion": A Complete Exposure* (New York: Covici, Friede, 1935), pp. 60–62.
17. *Protocols of the Meetings of the Learned Elders of Zion*, trans. Victor E. Marsden (London: The Britons, 1923), p. 52.
18. Hannah Arendt, *The Origins of Totalitarianism*, 2d ed. (Cleveland: World Publishing, 1958), pp. 362, 360.
19. Norman Cohn, *Warrant for Genocide: The Myth of the Jewish World Conspiracy and the* Protocols of the Elders of Zion (London: Eyre & Spottiswoode, 1967), p. 213. For an outline of the Messianic Age as described in *The Protocols*, see ibid., pp. 70–72.
20. Brandon M. Stickney, *"All-American Monster": The Unauthorized Biography of Timothy McVeigh* (Amherst, N.Y.: Prometheus, 1996), p. 159.
21. *The New York Times*, 13, 18 December 1995.
22. Michael Barkun, quoted in ibid., 26 April 1995.
23. Karl R. Popper, *Conjectures and Refutations: The Growth of Scientific Knowledge* (London: Routledge and Kegan Paul, 1963), p. 342.
24. Walter Laqueur, *Black Hundred: The Rise of the Extreme Right in Russia* (New York: HarperCollins, 1993), p. 103.
25. Michael Billig, *Fascists: A Social Psychological View of the National Front* (London: Academic Press, 1978), p. 326.
26. David Pryce-Jones, *The Closed Circle: An Interpretation of the Arabs* (New York: Harper & Row, 1989), p. 102.
27. Louis Rapoport, *Stalin's War against the Jews: The Doctors' Plot and the Soviet Solution* (New York: Free Press, 1990), pp. 218–19.
28. Robert Wernick, "Don't Look Now—But All Those Plotters Might Be Hiding under Your Bed," *Smithsonian*, March 1994, p. 120.
29. Seymour Martin Lipset and Earl Raab, *The Politics of Unreason: Right-Wing Extremism in America, 1790–1970* (New York: Harper & Row, 1970), p. 95, exaggerate in characterizing anti-Catholicism as "the antisemitism of the Protestant nineteenth century."
30. Quoted in *Anti-Semitism Worldwide, 1995/6*, p. 265. Elsewhere, those "untold numbers" are estimated at three billion.
31. H. D. Schmidt, "The Idea and Slogan of 'Perfidious Albion,'" *Journal of the History of Ideas* 14 (1953): 609.
32. R. J. Rummel, *China's Bloody Century: Genocide and Mass Murder since 1900* (New Brunswick, N.J.: Transaction Publishers, 1991), p. ix.
33. R. J. Rummel, *Death by Government* (New Brunswick, N.J.: Transaction, 1994), p. 4. Even this listing, which goes up to 1987, is far from complete, missing as it

does murderous regimes in Ethiopia and Iraq, as well as more recent ones in Serbia, the Sudan, and Rwanda.

34. Spoken on *The Warren Report*, CBS News, 28 June 1967, pp. 16–17. Quoted in Gerald Posner, *Case Closed: Lee Harvey Oswald and the Assassination of JFK* (New York: Random House, 1993), p. 470.

35. *The New York Times*, 11 August 1991.

36. Charles Paul Freund, "If History Is a Lie," *The Washington Post*, 19 January 1992.

37. Michael Barkun, "Religion, Militias and Oklahoma City: The Mind of Conspiratorialists," *Terrorism and Political Violence*, Spring 1996, pp. 61–62. On the optimistic side, Chip Berlet of Political Research Associates sees the greater attention to militias causing many members to leave these groups. Associated Press, 30 March 1997.

38. Charles Krauthammer, "'JFK': A Lie, But Harmless," *The Washington Post*, 10 January 1992.

39. Kurt Andersen, "The Age of Unreason," *The New Yorker*, 3 February 1997.

40. *L'Express*, 17 January 1992.

41. *The New York Times*, 12 December 1996.

42. For an example, see Akop Nazaretyan, "Don't Forget the Fool," *The Moscow Times*, 19 March 1995.

APPENDIX A: BENIGN ANTISEMITISM

1. Quoted in C. R. Ashbee, *A Palestine Notebook, 1918–1923* (Garden City, N.Y.: Doubleday, Page, 1923), pp. 90–91.

2. Earlier instances along these lines did not include fear of a Jewish world conspiracy, and so are not included here. One example dates from 1807, when Napoleon convened a "Great Sanhedrin" with an eye to giving European Jews a central authority, and thereby winning their favor; in return, he hoped that Jewish businessmen would join his cause and help with the blockade of Great Britain.

3. GYÖZÖ ISTÓCZY, speech to the Hungarian parliament, 25 June 1878. Text in W. MARR, *Vom jüdischen Kriesschauplatz: Eine Streitschrift* (Bern: Rudolph Costenoble, 1879), p. 43. Did ISTÓCZY influence eighteen-year-old Theodor Herzl, then a student in Budapest? Moshe Zimmerman raises this possibility in *Wilhelm Marr: The Patriarch of Anti-Semitism* (New York: Oxford University Press, 1986), p. 87.

4. MARR, *Vom jüdischen Kriesschauplatz*, p. 39.

5. Quoted in David G. Goodman and Masanori Miyazawa, *Jews in the Japanese Mind: The History and Uses of a Cultural Stereotype* (New York: Free Press, 1995), p. 82.

6. Ibid., pp. 82–83.

7. Foreign Office to St. Petersburg, 11 March 1916. Quoted in Elie Kedourie, *Arabic Political Memoirs and Other Studies* (London: Frank Cass, 1974), p. 238.

8. Mark Sykes to George Arthur, 18 March 1916. Text in ibid., pp. 240–41.

9. Quoted in Leonard Stein, *The Balfour Declaration* (New York: Simon & Schuster, 1961), p. 547.

10. Quoted in ibid., p. 348.

11. Moshe Ma'oz, *Syria and Israel: From War to Peace-making* (Oxford: Clarendon Press, 1995), p. 4.

12. Quoted in Neil Caplan, *Futile Diplomacy*, vol. 2, *Arab-Zionist Negotiations and the End of the Mandate* (London: Frank Cass, 1986), p. 49.
13. Quoted in ibid.
14. Israel Television, 25 August 1993.
15. *Ha'aretz*, 16 August 1995.
16. Said in the late 1920s; quoted in Oded Eran and Jerome E. Singer, "Soviet Policy towards the Arab World, 1955–71," *Survey*, Autumn 1971, p. 10, n. 2.
17. KORESHIGE INUZUKA, an "officially recognized antisemite," in a 1939 "Letter to the Leader of the Jews," quoted in Goodman and Miyazawa, *Jews in the Japanese Mind*, pp. 130–31.
18. Marvin Tokayer and Mary Swartz, *The Fugo Plan: The Untold Story of the Japanese and the Jews during World War II* (New York: Paddington Press, 1979), esp. pp. 44–61. (The very tasty but extremely poisonous fugo fish can be consumed safely only if the poisonous parts are expertly removed; likewise, Jews were seen as potentially very useful but fatal if mishandled.)

APPENDIX B: STALIN'S BLIND SPOT

1. Quoted in Christopher Andrew and Oleg Gordievsky, *KGB: The Inside Story of Its Foreign Operations from Lenin to Gorbachev* (New York: HarperCollins, 1990), p. 145.
2. Quoted in Vladimir Petrov, *"June 22, 1941": Soviet Historians and the German Invasion* (Columbia: University of South Carolina Press, 1968), p. 322.
3. Quoted in Andrew and Gordievsky, *KGB*, p. 269.
4. H.P. Willmott, *The Great Crusade: A New Complete History of the Second World War* (New York: Free Press, 1990), p. 144.
5. For a revisionist thesis, that Stalin was actually planning a surprise attack on Germany but Hitler moved first, see Edvard Radzinsky, *Stalin*, trans. H. T. Willetts (New York: Doubleday, 1996), pp. 450–59.
6. Quoted in John Erickson, *Stalin's War with Germany*, vol. 1, *The Road to Stalingrad* (New York: Harper & Row, 1975), pp. 104, 108.
7. Quoted in William L. Shirer, *The Rise and Fall of the Third Reich: A History of Nazi Germany* (New York: Simon & Schuster, 1960), p. 842.
8. "Must be assumed" set off widespread consternation; the "other motives unconnected to Soviet-German relations" may refer to Hitler's confidential letter of a few months earlier in which he explained the eastward movement of German troops in terms of protecting them from British air attacks.
9. Quoted in Dmitri Volkogonov, *Triyumfi i Tragediya: politicheskii portret I. V. Stalina* (Moscow: Novosti, 1989), ed. and trans. as *Stalin: Triumph and Tragedy*, by Harold Shukman (London: Weidenfeld and Nicolson, 1991), p. 396.
10. Quoted in Erickson, *The Road to Stalingrad*, p. 110.
11. Quoted in ibid., p. 111.
12. Quoted in ibid., p. 124.
13. Quoted in Shirer, *Rise and Fall of the Third Reich*, p. 852.
14. Secret speech of February 1956, quoted in Edward Crankshaw, *Khrushchev Remembers*, trans. and ed. Strobe Talbott (Boston: Little, Brown, 1970), p. 610.
15. Erickson, *The Road to Stalingrad*, p. 80.
16. Andrew and Gordievsky, *KGB*, p. 262.
17. Ibid., p. 267.

18. Quoted in Erickson, *The Road to Stalingrad*, p. 109.
19. Secret speech of February 1956, quoted in Crankshaw, *Khrushchev Remembers*, p. 590.
20. Quoted in Robert Leckie, *Delivered from Evil: The Saga of World War II* (New York: Harper & Row, 1987), p. 92.
21. Crankshaw, *Khrushchev Remembers*, p. 128.
22. Quoted in Robert C. Tucker, *Stalin in Power: The Revolution from Above, 1928–1941* (New York: W. W. Norton, 1990), p. 275.
23. Radzinsky, *Stalin*, p. 313.
24. These were not, it bears noting, Stalin's only erroneous conspiracy theories about the Nazis. Earlier, he had conjured up a Nazi connection to his rivals, starting with Trotsky and including many others; then he developed a complex story about their trying to sabotage the Soviet economy. He even saw a German hand in the Red Army.

APPENDIX C: THE INTERNET

1. Kenneth S. Stern, *A Force upon the Plain: The American Militia Movement and the Politics of Hate* (New York: Simon & Schuster, 1996), p. 228.
2. For a point-by-point refutation of the friendly fire theory, see Ronald Lewis at <http://www.infowar.com>. For a piecing together of this odd incident, see Frank J. Prial, "How Salinger Got Tangled in TWA-crash Web," *The Washington Times*, 17 November 1996; and Jonathan Vankin and John Whalen, "How a Quack Becomes a Canard," *The New York Times Magazine*, 17 November 1996.
3. For a survey and analysis of antisemitic activities, see David S. Hoffman, *The Web of Hate: Extremists Exploit the Internet* (New York: Anti-Defamation League, 1996).
4. Robert F. Barsky, *Noam Chomsky: A Life of Dissent* (Cambridge, Mass.: MIT Press, 1997).

2–9; distinct patterns in, 40–42; from 1815 to 1945, 76–105; elements of veracity in, 31; focusing on four groups, 129; genuine scholars caught up in, 34; German term for, 207n.3; in Germany after World War I, 99–102; in history, 207n.4; how they convince, 30–36; identifying, 37–51; in intellectual history, 49–51; on the Internet, 199–201; among Jews, 119–20; as modish, 14; in nineteenth century, 76–92; nineteenth-century books on, 206n.63; in non-Western world, 120–28; occult conspiracy theories, 144; origins of, 53, 213n. 4; from origins to 1815, 52–75; on the periphery since 1945, 106–28; petty conspiracy theories, 21–22; as political pornography, 49; among presidential candidates, 9–14; recurring assumptions of, 42–48; reputable houses publishing, 35; on Right and Left, 77–78, 83, 154–70; in Soviet Union, 95–99, 106–9; susceptibility to more than one, 25; among the suspicious, 9–19; terms and concepts of, 20–30; those in the know endorsing, 32–33; those left out of, 146–53; two traditions of, 129–50; in United States, 89–92, 115–20. See also conspiracism; conspiracy theorists; world conspiracy theories

conspiracy theorists, 23–26; academic titles used by, 33; anti-conspiracy theorists becoming, 35–36; book titles chosen by, 34. See also conspiracy theories

conspiratorial antisemitism, 27–28; as almost ruling the world, 172; anti-secret society theories outlasted by, 141; in black groups, 178; decline after Stalin's death, 107; as disreputable in postwar years, 111, 112; of Hitler, 89, 99; in Japan, 124–25, 165, 180, 187, 190–91; in Jews, 120; in

Middle East, 122–23; in National Socialism, 99, 100, 166; in non-Western world, 122–25; one cohesive Jewish plot seen by, 143–44; operational influence of, 172–73; in Soviet Union, 98, 166; spreading after World War I, 94; violence spawned by, 180

control, benefit indicating, 43
Coogan, Gertrude, 207n.6
Coogan, John, 207n.6
Cooper, Milton William, 206n.60, 230n.27
Cosby, Bill, 3
Coughlin, Father Charles, 50, 65, 76, 92, 100, 149, 226n.42
Council on Foreign Relations (CFR): influence over its members, 47, 212n.51; as invisible government, 116; Robertson on, 10, 11; as secret society, 29
crack cocaine, as government plot against blacks, 3–5, 200
Crusades, the, 52–59; attitudes toward Jews changed by, 53–57; in conspiracism's development, 171; the Templars in, 57–59
Cultural Revolution (China), 109–10, 128, 180
Curtiss, John S., 226n.34
Cutler, Allan and Helen, 56–57
Czechoslovakia, 109, 193

Dallas, 16
Daniel, John, 228n.67
Davis, David Brion, 39, 89, 132, 210n.3
Dawes Plan, 81
de Barruel, Augustin, 69–72; antisemitism in, 74–75, 122, 132, 216n.70; in intellectual history of conspiracism, 49, 50, 206n.63, 215n.57
Decembrists, 64
de Gaulle, Charles, 81
democide, 181–82

Israeli ally, 151

Soviet Union: American conspiracy theories influencing, 118; American fear of, 115–17; antisemitism in, 97–99, 107–8, 166; anti-Zionism of, 98, 107–8, 165–66; as appearing less bad than the Nazis, 164; as bulwark against Jews, 87; collapse of, 110; conspiracy theories in, 95–99, 106–9; coup attempt of 1991 as petty conspiracy, 21; democide in, 181; Doctors' Plot, 28, 98–99, 141, 179; founding conspiracist premise of, 106–7; future of conspiracism in former, 184–85; German attack on, 148, 192–98; German-Soviet Non-Aggression Pact, 98, 103, 192, 196, 197; Gorbachev, 80, 110, 113; Great Purge of 1937–38, 98; imperial plots against alleged, 96–97; and Israel as pursuing common aim, 148; KGB, 37, 107–8, 114, 175; Khrushchev, 24, 43, 107, 195; Molotov, 46, 97, 192; and the Nazis, 102–5, 156; plots and goals as American myth, 48; on Reichstag fire, 154; in Right's conspiracy theories, 7; as sabotage victim, 47; and Saddam Husayn's invasion of Kuwait, 43; United States opposes after World War II, 108–9. *See also* Lenin, Vladimir Ilyich; Stalin, Joseph Vissarionovich; Trotsky, Leon

Spear, Robert K., 222n.36

Spengler, Oswald, 45–46, 137

SS, the, 175, 232n.11

Stalin, Joseph Vissarionovich: as agent of international bankers, 47–48; as believing his own conspiracy theories, 104–5; and class enemies, 133; conspiracy theories about the Nazis, 196–97, 236n.24; death of, 107; on events as not accidental, 44–45; Great Britain demonized by, 181; and

Hitler, 102–5, 162–63, 164–65, 172, 197, 198; on imperialist plots against Soviet Union, 96–97; isolation of, 195–96; Israel supported by, 97–98, 190; mass murder by, xii, 104, 180, 203n.2; on Molotov as agent of imperialism, 97; Nazi attack missed by, 148, 192–98; persecution mania of, 24; preparing attack on Jews, 141; Trotsky as obsession of, 198, 236n.24; on United States as new enemy, 97; Zionism opposed by, 98

Stamp Act of 1765, 89–90

Starck, Johann August, 72, 216n.68

Steed, Henry Wickham, 209n.43, 219n.62

Steinbeck, John, 126

Stern, Kenneth, 142, 199

Stimson, Henry L., 216n.3

Stoecker, Adolf, 151

Stone, Oliver, 9, 16, 18–19, 160, 183

Stormer, John A., 17, 206n.63

Stormfront White Nationalist Resource Page, 200

Student Non-Violent Coordinating Committee, 178

Sublimes Maîtres Parfaits, 63

Sudoplatov, Pavel, 106

Sulh, Riyad as-, 189

Sykes, Mark, 188

Taft, Robert, 37

Taiwan, 151

Tatum, William, 5

television series, 17

Templars, 57–59; banking activities of, 57–58; in Cadet de Gassicourt's chain of secret societies, 29; conspiratorial air of, 58; enduring mystique of, 41–42, 58–59; forgeries regarding, 40; and Freemasons, 31, 62, 69, 134; in French Revolution, 68–69; Hammer-Purgstall on, 35; myth of as eccentric, 145; heresy of, 58,